# VARIATIONS & IMPROVISATIONS

## RECIPES FROM RENAISSANCE RADIO

PRODUCED BY

FRIENDS OF KEDM

90.3FM

MONROE, LOUISIANA

A COOKBOOK

Friends of KEDM is an organization which was formed to support public radio in Northeastern Louisiana and Southeastern Arkansas. The proceeds from this cookbook will be used to establish an endowment fund for KEDM-FM 90.3 in Monroe, Louisiana, a community-supported public radio station featuring both nationally and locally produced programs.

© Copyright 2000
Friends of KEDM Public Radio
Monroe, Louisiana

ISBN 0-9673350-0-0

*Variations & Improvisations*
can be ordered from

Friends of KEDM
225 Stubbs Hall
University of Louisiana ~ Monroe
Monroe, Louisiana 71209

kedm@ulm.edu

$19.95 per book
($3.50 shipping per order)

Printed in the USA by

**WIMMER**
The Wimmer Companies
Memphis
1-800-548-2537

# COOKBOOK COMMITTEE

Too many cooks spoil the broth.
*English Proverb*

The more the merrier.
*Friends of KEDM Cookbook Committee*

*Committee Chair:*     Susan Allain

*Project Director:*     Elisabeth Grant-Gibson

*Marketing Manager:*     Susan Allain

*Business Manager:*     Adrienne Cole

*Artist:*     Anna Rowan Schriefer

*Committee Members*

Amy Norris

Wayne Hopper

Mara Loeb

Angela Short

Lisa Riddle

Lori Tucker

Brenda Cook

Brenda Geiger

Denise Gibson

# SPONSORS

### *Producers*
Mrs. Paula M. Manship
Jackie Yeldell

### *Broadcasters*
Dr. Lauren J. Mickey
Drs. Adrienne Williams and Terry Tugwell
Glenwood Regional Medical Center
CenturyTel
Martin Brothers
Tonore's Wine Cellar & Patrick Gerl

### *Announcers*
Windows a bookshop
Horizons Bank
St. Francis Medical Center
Chef A. Nonni Maus
Anthony, Helen, and Eileanor LaRocco
BellSouth
Kelly Financial Services
Marais Corporation
Morehouse General Hospital
Hibernia Bank

# Contents

## Overture
Be Prepared ... 8
The Cookbook ... 9

## Preludes
Appetizers ... 13
Soups ... 67

## Leitmotifs
Brunch Dishes ... 93

## Main Motifs
Fish & Seafood ... 137
Poultry ... 145
Pork ... 160
Veal ... 167
Beef ... 169
Lamb ... 175

## Accompaniments
Salads ... 181
Side Dishes ... 206
Breads ... 234

## Finales
Desserts ... 251
Candies ... 258
Cookies & Bars ... 262
Cobblers & Desserts ... 271
Pies ... 276
Cakes ... 283

## Flourishes
Libations ... 295
Lagniappe ... 309

## Improvisations ... 331
## Index ... 351

# CONTRIBUTORS

Susan Allain
Deannie Allain
Gabriella Armstrong
Chris Arnold
Reca Bamburg Jones
Mark Barham
Sue Benoit
Charlotte Breard
Marion Callis
Files of Polly Parrish Carpenter
Debbie Carroll
Files of Mina Coats
Files of Idella Cobb
Brenda Cook
Anthony Cortellini
Gretchen Dean
Don Dixon
Julia Dunaway
Barbara & Charles Dunn
Enoch's
Saxon Elliott
Denise Gibson
Marika Gibson
Gayla Goff
Janet Goode
Elisabeth Grant-Gibson
Files of Sara Greene
Arden Greer
Eric Haak
Jerri Harris
Lisa Hawkins
Sue Hayes
Mark Henderson
Marilou Hildenbrand
Wayne Hopper
Doyle & Yvette Jeter
Roxann Johnson
Herb Jones
Vicki Kelly
Annie Kincaid
Rob Lloyd
Kathy Loeb
Mara Loeb
Rosemary Urban Loeb
Fran Luebke
Sandra Lunte
Debbie & Mike Luster
Kelly Martin
Nancy Meinel
Sunny Meriwether
Dale Moses
Amy Norris
Angie O'Pry
Liz Ormes
Betty Pearson
Kay Price
Bill Rambin
René Rambin
Lisa Riddle
Jan Salisbury
Files of Clara H. (Doris) Sartor
Willie Mae Sartor
CJ Sartor
Joe Saunders
Conrad Schott
Anna Rowan Schriefer
Angela Short
William Mark Simmons
Ruth Slemmons
Delton Spillers
Kathy Spreadbury
Marjorie Stricklin
Rebecca Tomlinson
Mary Troy
Lori Tucker
Terry Tugwell
Susan Wheeler
Shirley Whitfield
Lindsey Wilkerson
Sue Zabritski

*Thank you to all who generously offered recipes and support during the creation of this cookbook. You are true "Friends" of KEDM.*

# OVERTURE

> Every noble work is at first impossible.
>
> *Thomas Carlyle*

## Be Prepared

One of the greatest deterrents to creating fabulous meals at home is lack of preparedness. When it seems as if there's nothing in the house to cook, the temptation to eat out or grab junk food becomes overwhelming. Being prepared means keeping your refrigerator, freezer, and pantry stocked with items that can be combined and cooked quickly for those weak "just-walked-in-from-work-and-whose-turn-is-it-to-cook" moments. Regular shopping is a must. You might prefer to make one major trip for pantry and freezer staples each month, supplemented by weekly (or more often) quick trips to restock perishables. If you live very close to a supermarket or greengrocer, you might wish to shop daily for the evening meal, choosing whatever appeals to you for that evening. Remember that shopping is the basis for maintaining a well-stocked kitchen. We recommend that you look over these items and subtract and add your own "must have" ingredients as you work with the recipes.

### Freezer

- 16-ounce bags of vegetables, including leaf spinach, baby lima beans, green peas, corn, whole green beans, Brussels sprouts, mustard greens
- packages of ground round
- pork loin and tenderloin
- boneless chicken breasts
- shrimp
- whole roasted chickens
- frozen stock

### Refrigerator

- cheeses (Parmesan, cheddar, feta)
- brine-cured olives
- capers
- lemons
- limes
- mixed salad greens
- carrots
- bell peppers
- tomatoes
- fresh herbs
- pastas
- sour cream
- whipping cream
- half & half

### Pantry

- olive oil
- balsamic vinegar
- sun-dried tomatoes
- roasted red peppers
- pastas
- baking ingredients
- various kinds of rice (white, brown, wild, risotto)
- canned low-salt chicken broth
- canned beef broth
- canned diced tomatoes
- canned black beans
- canned white cannellini beans
- various nuts (walnuts, almonds, pine nuts, pecans)
- onions
- potatoes
- garlic
- good selection of spices
- wines and liqueurs

## *The Cookbook*

Our Cookbook Committee determined from the outset that we would make something different from all of the other fine cookbooks available in our community. We wanted fabulous recipes, of course, but we also wanted excellent art and good writing so that both reading the book and cooking from the book would be rich experiences. We began with a single unswerving rule: no recipe would contain cream of mushroom soup as an ingredient. From that simple beginning, we have worked to develop dishes that taste fresh and lively, using fresh herbs when possible and an abundance of the beautiful produce in our local markets. As a group, we have explored the flavors of Provence and other sun-soaked Mediterranean countries. We have begun or expanded herb gardens. Our taste buds (and our hearts) have journeyed east, west, north, and south for the best international cuisines. The result is an eclectic mix of foods, often put together in new and surprising ways. We have tasted bits of heaven and bites of things that just didn't turn out quite as we had imagined. We have kept the former and rejected the latter. Most of all, we have feasted. Now we share our feast with you.

One of our most important goals has been to encourage you to explore and journey on your own. We think of each recipe as a jumping-off point, and we delight in the thought of each reader adding, subtracting, adjusting a recipe until it is no longer "ours," but something altogether new. To encourage just such experimentation, we have provided variations for many of the recipes. We have also included an entire section called "Improvisations," where a basic recipe is altered to create several different dishes; then we step back so that you can continue where we have left off. Except in certain very delicate sauces, soufflés, or baked goods (we have tried to avoid delicate handling, but not delicate flavors), measurements are relatively unimportant. If you want more butter, add more butter. If you can't get enough garlic, make yourself happy. Love rosemary but hate thyme? Substitute; double; divide. What matters, what is truly important, is that you please yourself with your own culinary creations. So assemble some ingredients, tie on an apron, and start cooking. If you can squeeze one more person around your table, give us a call. We'd love to taste your *Variations & Improvisations.*

## *The Station*

For many years a small but committed group of people worked to bring public radio to an area comprised of northeast Louisiana, southeast Arkansas, and western Mississippi. A capital campaign was begun to raise the funds to start a station in Monroe, Louisiana. Soon the goal was met and in the spring of 1991, the station became a reality. Now the Arkansas-Louisiana-Mississippi region is home to one of the finest examples of community-supported radio in the country, KEDM (90.3FM). KEDM offers the best of the national programming available from National Public Radio and Public Radio International. But local programming gives KEDM its unique flavor. Locally produced programs such as Kelby Ouchley's "Bayou Diversity," Richard Harrison's "Mostly Big Band Friday Nights," Kenny Bill Stinson's "Blue Monday," Don Dixon's "Pacific Noir" and "Nocturnes," Mike Luster's "Creole Statement" and "Americanarama," and Sunny Meriwether's news and "Lagniappe" interviews all combine to create the character and charm of an unusual station in an unusual place. You can judge the sounds of KEDM for yourself through the miracle of modern technology. The station's website is kedm.ulm.edu, and through Real Audio you can hear all of this great local programming with your own ears. Of course, as soon as you're hooked on our great station, we'll ask you to become a member. That's what "member-supported radio" means—and you'll discover that KEDM boasts members from Marion to Minneapolis, Choudrant to Chicago, Tallulah to Toledo, Bernice to Boston, Pineville to Paris (and yes we do mean France).

## *The Project*

For some time award-winning KEDM Marketing & Development Director Susan Allain has been toying with the idea of a cookbook as a fund-raiser to supplement member support. Eventually she found the right people to toy with, and the project was born. After many months of testing and tasting, the Friends of KEDM Cookbook Committee became the favorite caterers for local arts events and wine tastings. These recipes have been tasted by some of the best cooks and the best eaters around, and people are lining up to purchase our secrets. With that right combination of cooks and tasters, as well as a fine artist who has given generously of her time and talent, the Friends of KEDM cookbook is at last a reality. We hope that you will enjoy *Variations & Improvisations* as much as we have delighted in creating it.

# PRELUDES *Appetizers & Soups*

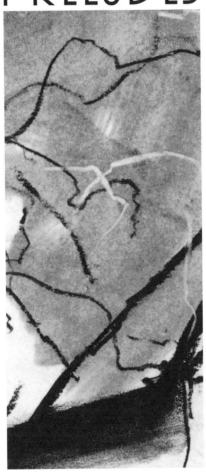

# COCKTAIL PARTY FOR 50

> Hot can be cool and cool can be hot, and each can be both. But hot or cool, man, jazz is jazz.
>
> *Louis Armstrong*

Hosting a cocktail party for 50 people is not nearly as overwhelming as it might sound. The menu below is designed to limit the number of dishes which require last-minute work: most of the recipes can be made hours or days ahead and you could easily eliminate 3 or 4 recipes and still have a stunning table. Make sure that your bar is properly stocked, arrange these foods on large platters, and you will host a smashing success.

## *Bar Recommendations*

Wine: 6 bottles each of red and white
Beer: 12 bottles premium beer (optional)
Liquor: 1 to 2 bottles each, Scotch, vodka, bourbon, gin
Mixers: sweet and dry vermouth, orange juice, spicy tomato juice, soda, tonic, soft drinks, mineral water
Extras: olives, onions, cherries, lemon and lime wedges, ice

## *Food Suggestions*

Rosemary Walnuts
Caviar Squares
Warm Roquefort Spread
Smoked Oyster Tartlets
Lemon-Rosemary Wafers
Pesto Cheesecake
Orange Olives
Green Chile Chicken Tartlets
Spicy Cheese Bites
Stuffed Brie

Blanched Asparagus, Snow Peas, and Red Pepper Strips with Oriental Mayonnaise
Greek Salad Skewers
Baked Crab Dip
Chicken Bites with Spicy Peanut Dressing
Chilled Shrimp with Lime-Cayenne Mayonnaise
Goat Balls
Greek Meatballs

*Red, Hot, and Blue:* **Songs by Cole Porter (various artists)**

# ROSEMARY WALNUTS

*Makes 1 pound*

- Melt the butter in a skillet. Add rosemary and heat for 30 seconds; remove pan from heat. Add walnuts and stir until well-coated.

- Spread the walnuts on a foil-lined cookie sheet and roast at 200° for 30 to 40 minutes. Watch carefully to avoid scorching. Serve warm or at room temperature.

4 tablespoons minced fresh rosemary
4 tablespoons butter
1 pound walnut halves

Good wine is a necessity of life.

*Thomas Jefferson*

 "Hey, There" as performed by Rosemary Clooney

APPETIZERS 13

# LEMON OLIVES

*Makes 4 cups*

| | |
|---|---|
| 1 | (32-ounce) jar large Spanish olives (not pitted) |
| 2 | sprigs fresh oregano |
| 4 | cloves garlic, peeled |
| 1 | large lemon, quartered lengthwise |

- Drain the olives, reserving liquid. In the same jar or in a wide-mouthed bottle, layer the olives with the oregano, garlic, and lemon wedges, spacing evenly. Pour in enough reserved liquid to cover the olives.

- Refrigerate for at least 1 week before serving (will keep for up to 3 weeks). To serve, drain olives and pour into a medium bowl or platter with rim. Garnish with the oregano, garlic, and lemon.

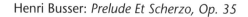
Henri Busser: *Prelude Et Scherzo, Op. 35*

# ORANGE OLIVES

*Makes 6 cups*

- Mix all ingredients in a large bowl. Cover and refrigerate overnight, stirring occasionally. The olives will keep for 4 days.
- Bring to room temperature before serving.

| | |
|---|---|
| 6 | cups olives (use at least 3 to 4 different types, choosing from Greek olives, almond or garlic stuffed Spanish olives, Niçoise olives, or others) |
| ¼ | cup olive oil |
| ¼ | cup lemon juice |
| ¼ | cup orange juice |
| 2 | tablespoons shredded orange zest |
| 1 | tablespoon fennel seeds, lightly toasted in a dry skillet |
| ½ | teaspoon crushed red pepper flakes |

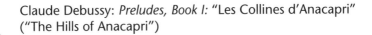

Claude Debussy: *Preludes, Book I:* "Les Collines d'Anacapri" ("The Hills of Anacapri")

# MARINATED MUSHROOMS

*Makes 1 quart*

- ⅔ cup olive oil
- ⅓ cup lemon juice
- 2 tablespoons chopped fresh mint
- 1½ tablespoons Greek seasoning
- ½ teaspoon black pepper
- ½ teaspoon red pepper
- ½ teaspoon white pepper
- 3 cloves garlic, crushed
- 1 pound fresh button mushrooms

- In a 2-cup measure, whisk together oil, lemon juice, mint, Greek seasoning, and peppers. Let stand 15 minutes.

- Wipe or rinse off any dirt from mushrooms. Remove stems and place mushroom caps in a 1-quart jar, adding flattened garlic cloves at bottom, middle, and top. Whisk marinade again and pour over mushrooms.

- Cover jar tightly and transfer to refrigerator. Invert jar every few hours. Mushrooms must marinate for at least 24 hours.

A large income is the best recipe for happiness I ever heard of.

*Jane Austen*

 Claude Debussy: *Preludes, Book II:* "Les Fees sont d'exquises danseuses" ("The fairies are dancers of delight")

## *Makes 48* SPICY CHEDDAR SNAPS

- Cream butter in mixer until light. Sift together flour, red pepper, and salt; stir into butter. Add cheese, seeds, and nuts; mix until thoroughly combined.

- Roll mixture into nickel-sized balls and place on ungreased cookie sheet. Bake at 350° for 17 minutes or until lightly browned and crispy. Cool on rack.

| | |
|---|---|
| 1 | cup butter, room temperature |
| 2 | cups flour |
| 1¼ | teaspoons cayenne pepper |
| ½ | teaspoon salt |
| ½ | pound sharp cheddar cheese, finely shredded |
| 1 | tablespoon caraway seeds |
| 1 | cup finely chopped pecans |

 Claude Debussy: *Preludes, Book II:* "General Lavine"

# BLEU BALLS

*Makes 24*

3 ounces bleu cheese
1 ounce Monterey Jack cheese
½ cup butter, room temperature
1 clove garlic, pressed
  Salt, black pepper, Cajun seasoning
1⅓ cups flour

- Chop cheeses in food processor or shred by hand. Add butter, garlic, and seasonings. Add flour and process or mix by hand until mixture begins to hold together in a ball.

- Roll dough into 1-inch balls or use pastry gun to form straws. Line a baking pan with foil and arrange the balls or straws with about 1 inch between them. Bake at 275° for 20 to 30 minutes or until crisp.

The appetite grows by eating.

*Francois Rabelais*

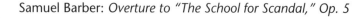
Samuel Barber: *Overture to "The School for Scandal,"* Op. 5

# LEMON-ROSEMARY WAFERS

*Makes 2 to 3 dozen*

- Cream butter and sugar until light. Add egg and vanilla; beat well. Beat in rosemary and lemon zest. Mix in flour. Shape dough into a slender log about 1½-inches in diameter. Cover with plastic wrap and refrigerate for at least 2 hours or overnight.

- Remove plastic wrap and slice log into ¼-inch thick rounds. Transfer to ungreased baking sheets. Bake at 350° until set and just beginning to turn golden on the edges. Transfer cookies to rack and cool.

½ cup butter
½ cup sugar
1 egg white, beaten
½ teaspoon vanilla
2 tablespoons minced fresh rosemary
2 tablespoons shredded lemon zest
1 cup flour

*These cookies are fabulous with red wine.*

... with inimitable fragrance and soft fire
... wine is bottled poetry.

*Robert Louis Stevenson*

Johann Sebastian Bach: *Air on the G String*

APPETIZERS 19

# GREEN FIRE

*Makes 1¼ cups*

12  jalapeño peppers
20-25  cloves garlic, peeled
        Water

- Put jalapeños in baking dish under broiler. Broil on high, shaking pan occasionally, until peppers are charred.

- Place whole peppers (including stems and seeds) into a blender container with all of the garlic. Puree with a tablespoon of water, adding more water if necessary, until mixture has a thick sauce consistency. (Warning: Don't breathe in the pepper fumes. They hurt.)

*The extreme heat and the tasty garlic flavor can add a kick to stews, casseroles, and soups. Spread this on a block of cream cheese to reduce the heat impact. Those who are brave actually eat this on a tortilla chip. Try adding 1 tablespoon of the pepper mixture to ½ cup of mayonnaise for a great hamburger or grilled chicken sandwich dressing.*

There is no feeling, except the extremes of fear and grief, that does not find relief in music.

*George Eliot*

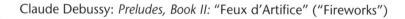
Claude Debussy: *Preludes, Book II:* "Feux d'Artifice" ("Fireworks")

# GARDEN SALSA

*Makes 3 cups*

- Cut tomatoes crosswise in half and squeeze to release seeds. Char peppers under broiler or on grill; remove seeds. Dice tomatoes and peppers.

- Combine all ingredients in a medium bowl. Allow to stand at room temperature for 1 hour. Drain off excess liquid. Toss mixture and serve immediately with chips or over baked chicken or swordfish, or refrigerate and use within 2 days.

| | |
|---|---|
| 8-10 | Roma tomatoes |
| 4 | jalapeño peppers |
| 2-3 | cloves garlic, minced |
| ½ | cup frozen whole kernel corn, thawed |
| ½ | cup finely chopped fresh cilantro |
| ¼ | cup diced red onion |
| ¼ | cup diced Vidalia or Texas 1015 sweet yellow onion |
| 4 | green onions, chopped (including tops) |
| 1 | avocado, peeled and diced |
| ½ | cup peeled and diced jícama |
| ¼ | cup sliced ripe olives (optional) |
| ¼ | cup vegetable oil |
| 1 | teaspoon sugar |
| | Salt |

 Franz Liszt: *Rhapsodie Espagnole*

# TZATZIKI

*Makes 3 cups*

| | |
|---|---|
| 2 | cups plain yogurt |
| 2 | tablespoons olive oil |
| 3-5 | cloves garlic, minced (do not use processed garlic from jar) |
| 2 | cups finely chopped or shredded cucumber |

- Line a strainer with a double layer of cheesecloth or large coffee filter. Place strainer over a bowl, pour in yogurt, and place in refrigerator. Allow to drip overnight or for at least one hour. Once you have strained the yogurt and released the excess liquid, the consistency should thicken and be similar to that of yogurt cheese or kefir cheese. If you don't have time to allow the yogurt to thicken, use half yogurt and half sour cream.

- Add olive oil to yogurt and stir vigorously until all the oil is incorporated. Stir in the chopped garlic.

- Drain cucumbers on several layers of paper towel for a few minutes. Blot dry. Add to yogurt mixture and stir well. Let stand in refrigerator for at least an hour for flavors to develop. Will keep for about 3 days.

*Serve with peasant bread, pitas, or crackers. Makes a delicious sauce for shrimp, meatballs, fried fish, or a pita sandwich.*

 Yanni: *Live at the Acropolis:* "Santorini"

# HUMMUS

*Makes 2 cups*

- In blender or processor, puree chickpeas, ¼ cup reserved liquid, garlic, salt, and lemon juice. Add tahini; blend until smooth and creamy, adding more reserved liquid if necessary. Taste mixture and add more salt or lemon juice if desired.

- Refrigerator overnight, tightly covered, to develop flavors. To serve, mound in shallow bowl and sprinkle with parsley. Use as a dip with pitas, flatbread, cucumber slices, cherry tomatoes, or crackers.

**Variations:** Roasted Garlic Hummus is easy to make. Roast 1 head of garlic by trimming top of bulb and drizzling with olive oil. Wrap in foil and bake at 375° for about 1 hour. Squeeze cloves out; add to blender with chickpeas. For Roasted Red Pepper Hummus, add 1 cup chopped, drained, roasted red pepper (from jar) to chickpeas in blender.

| | |
|---|---|
| 1 | (16-ounce) can chickpeas, drained, liquid reserved |
| 2 | cloves garlic, coarsely chopped |
| ½ | teaspoon salt |
| ¼ | cup lemon juice |
| ½ | cup tahini |
| 2 | tablespoons minced fresh parsley |

 Claude Debussy: *Preludes, Book I:* "Voiles" (either "Sails" or "Veils")

APPETIZERS 23

# CLASSIC TAPENADE

*Makes ⅔ cup*

- 4 cloves garlic, peeled
- 3 anchovy fillets, rinsed
- 1 teaspoon lemon juice
- Coarse salt and freshly ground black pepper
- 1 teaspoon Herbes de Provence
- 1½ cups pitted Kalamata or other brine-cured olives
- ½ cup capers, rinsed and drained
- 3 tablespoons olive oil

- In food processor or blender, puree garlic and anchovies. Add lemon juice, salt, pepper, and Herbes de Provence; blend thoroughly. Add olives and capers and puree.

- Add the oil slowly, 1 tablespoon at a time, until the mixture forms a soft paste. Serve with peasant bread or spread on bruschetta.

*This spread makes a delicious pizza or veggie sandwich topping and can be spread on grilled fresh tuna.*

Wine cheers the sad, revives the old, and inspires the youth.

*Byron*

 Johann Sebastian Bach: *Cantata #29:* "Sinfonia"

# AVOCADO TAPENADE
*Makes 3 cups*

- Peel the garlic and press or mince. Mash the anchovies with a fork. Mix garlic and anchovies with the ripe olives in medium bowl.

- Peel the avocados; reserve pits. Mash pulp and combine with other ingredients.

- Chill for an hour, inserting avocado pits into the mixture or sprinkling the top with lemon juice to keep avocado from browning.

*Serve as a topping for croutons or crackers. This tapenade is also delicious served over grilled chicken or fish. For an usual first course, layer with shrimp or crab in a tall ice cream sundae glass.*

3 large cloves garlic
1 (2-ounce) can anchovies, drained
2 cups finely chopped ripe olives
2 large ripe avocados
  Lemon juice

Edouard Lalo: *Symphonie Espagnole, Op. 21*

# PEANUT-CILANTRO PESTO

*Makes 1 cup*

- ¾ cup roasted peanuts
- 2 cloves garlic
- 1 tablespoon chili oil (or 1 tablespoon peanut oil and a pinch of red pepper flakes)
- 1 tablespoon molasses
- 1 tablespoon soy sauce
- 1 tablespoon olive oil
- 1 teaspoon grated fresh ginger
- 2 tablespoons lime juice
- 1 cup chopped fresh cilantro
- 1 cup chopped fresh parsley

- Place all ingredients in food processor or blender. Process until a paste forms.

- Serve immediately at room temperature or refrigerate for up to 2 days.

*This pesto is delicious as a spread for Paprika Triangles (see page 28). For Peanut-Cilantro Chicken, coat boneless, skinless chicken breasts with mixture. Seal each breast in plastic and refrigerate overnight. Remove plastic wrap and grill, broil, or sauté chicken until cooked through.*

 "Salt Peanuts" as performed by Dizzy Gillespie

# ROASTED RED PEPPER AND ALMOND PESTO

*Makes 2½ cups*

- Put all ingredients except almonds into food processor or blender. Pulse or whirl until peppers and cilantro are finely chopped. Scrape down the sides of container and process until smooth.

- Add the almonds and pulse until the mixture is well combined and almond pieces are no larger than a peppercorn. Serve in bowl with Paprika Triangles (see page 28) or crackers. Can be refrigerated up to 2 days.

| | |
|---|---|
| 1 | (12-ounce) jar roasted red peppers, drained |
| ½ | cup chopped fresh cilantro |
| 1 | tablespoon tomato paste |
| 1 | tablespoon sherry vinegar or white wine vinegar |
| 2 | teaspoons lemon juice |
| 1½ | teaspoons minced garlic |
| 1¼ | teaspoons kosher salt |
| ½ | teaspoon paprika |
| ½ | teaspoon chili powder |
| ¼ | teaspoon cayenne pepper |
| 1 | cup coarsely chopped blanched almonds |

> A bottle of wine begs to be shared; I have never met a miserly wine lover.
>
> *Clifton Fadiman*

 Abraham Goldfadden: *Raisins and Almonds*

APPETIZERS 27

# PAPRIKA TRIANGLES

*Makes 64*

½ teaspoon paprika
½ teaspoon ground fennel seed
½ teaspoon garlic powder
¼ teaspoon cinnamon
¼ teaspoon salt
4 pita bread rounds
¼ cup vegetable oil

- Combine paprika, fennel seed, garlic powder, cinnamon, and salt in a small bowl or custard cup. Insert a small sharp knife into the side of a pita; cut gently around until the pita has split into two circles.

- Brush the rough sides of the pita rounds with the oil. Sprinkle the spices evenly over the top. Stack the pita rounds and cut into 8 wedges.

- Place the wedges in a single layer on ungreased baking sheets with the spice side up. Bake at 350° for 9 minutes or until crisp and golden.

*Serve with Roasted Red Pepper and Almond Pesto (see page 27), Hummus (see page 23), or Eggplant Dip (see page 29).*

 Claude Debussy: *Preludes, Book II:* "Feuilles mortes" ("Dead leaves")

# EGGPLANT DIP

*Makes 2½ cups*

- Grill whole eggplants until blackened and very soft. To cook in oven, prick whole eggplants several times and place on foil-lined baking pan. Broil until blackened, turning once or twice. Bake at 400° for 15 minutes or until very soft.

- Cut the eggplants in half lengthwise and scoop pulp into a colander lined with paper towels. Allow to drain for about 20 minutes, pressing the pulp with more paper towels.

- Transfer eggplant pulp to a medium bowl and mash with a fork or potato masher. Add olive oil, feta, garlic, and parsley; mash everything together. Using a fork, stir in mayonnaise and check consistency. The mixture should be quite creamy. Add more mayonnaise as needed. Season to taste.

**Variations:** *For a chunkier dip, chop eggplant pulp (don't mash) and omit the feta cheese and mayonnaise. Add 1 cup of finely diced tomatoes. Mix everything lightly with a fork.*

| | |
|---|---|
| 2 | medium eggplants |
| 2 | tablespoons olive oil |
| 2-4 | ounces feta cheese, crumbled |
| 1 | clove garlic, minced |
| 2 | tablespoons chopped fresh parsley |
| ¼ | cup mayonnaise (or more) |
| | Salt and black pepper |

Michael Franks: *Eggplant:* "The Art of Tea"

# FRESH SPINACH DIP

*Makes 3 cups*

| | |
|---|---|
| 1 | tablespoon olive oil |
| 2 | teaspoons finely chopped garlic |
| 8 | cups fresh spinach leaves, packed |
| ½ | cup chopped green onions |
| 1 | cup sour cream |
| 1 | teaspoon lime or lemon juice |
| | Salt, black pepper, Cajun seasoning |

- Heat oil in large nonstick skillet. Add garlic and sauté until lightly golden. Add spinach and sauté until wilted and tender, about 3 minutes. Cool.

- Puree spinach and green onions in food processor or blender. Transfer to bowl. Mix in sour cream and lime or lemon juice. Season to taste. Good with toasted pita chips, crackers, or raw vegetables.

Claude Debussy: *Preludes, Book II:* "Bruyeres" ("Heathland")

# FIESTA DIP

*Makes 4 cups*

- Mix all ingredients in a large bowl. Refrigerate overnight to develop flavors. This dip will keep for 3 days.

  *Corn and peppers can be replaced by 2 (11-ounce) cans of Mexican corn, drained. Because this is a thick and firm dip, use a sturdy chip such as Fritos Scoops. The dip is also delicious served on top of an omelette.*

| | |
|---|---|
| 1 | (16-ounce) bag frozen yellow corn, thawed |
| ¼ | cup finely diced red bell pepper |
| ¼ | cup finely diced green bell pepper |
| 1 | cup sour cream, regular or low-fat |
| 1 | cup mayonnaise, regular or low-fat |
| 3 | green onions, chopped |
| 1 | (4 to 5-ounce) can chopped green chiles |
| 2 | small jalapeños, minced |
| 1 | cup grated cheddar cheese, regular or low-fat |

Claude Debussy: *Preludes, Book II:* "La Puerta del Vino"

# MUSHROOM-OLIVE SPREAD

*Makes 3 cups*

| | |
|---|---|
| 1 | cup finely chopped mushrooms |
| 1 | teaspoon butter |
| ⅔ | cup chopped ripe olives |
| ½ | cup finely chopped green olives (without pimientos) |
| 16 | ounces cream cheese, room temperature |
| | Cajun seasoning |

- Sauté mushrooms with butter in small skillet or saucepan. Allow any juices to evaporate. Allow to cool.

- Stir mushrooms, olives, and cream cheese together; mix thoroughly. Season to taste with Cajun seasoning.

- Spread on crustless white bread for finger sandwiches or serve with crusty French bread or crackers.

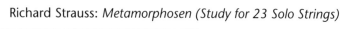

Richard Strauss: *Metamorphosen (Study for 23 Solo Strings)*

# HERBED CHEESE

*Makes 2½ cups*

- Mix softened cream cheese with remaining ingredients. Refrigerate overnight to develop flavors.

  *Serve in crock or molded on platter surrounded by crackers.*

  **Variations:** *Make delicious Cocktail Sandwiches by spreading cocktail slices of dark pumpernickel or rye bread with cheese mixture and topping with smoked chicken and avocado. For Creamy Mushroom-Herb Pasta, add some cheese mixture and white wine to sautéed mushrooms; toss with pasta.*

| | |
|---|---|
| 16 | ounces cream cheese, regular or low-fat |
| ¼ | cup mayonnaise |
| 2 | teaspoons Dijon mustard |
| 2 | tablespoons chopped fresh chives |
| 2 | tablespoons chopped fresh dill |
| | Garlic to taste |

 Claude Debussy: *Preludes, Book II:* "Canope"

# CHIHUAHUA CHEESE SPREAD

*Makes 3 cups*

| | | |
|---|---|---|
| 3-4 | cups shredded cheddar cheese | • Combine all ingredients in a food processor. Pulse until spreadable. |
| 1 | (4-ounce) can chopped green chiles | *Serve dip in a hollowed-out bread bowl.* |
| ½ | cup chopped ripe olives | |
| 1 | large clove garlic, chopped | |
| ¼ | teaspoon cumin | |
| 2 | tablespoons mayonnaise | |
| ¼ | teaspoon hot sauce | |
| ½ | teaspoon cayenne pepper | |

 Manuel Ponce: "Estrellita" ("My Little Soul")

# WARM BLEU CHEESE SPREAD WITH PECANS

*Makes 4 cups*

- Toast pecans in skillet over medium heat with 2 tablespoons butter, stirring constantly. Remove from heat and cool.

- Blend cheeses together until smooth. Stir in pecans. Spoon mixture into a greased 1½-quart baking dish.

- Melt remaining 1 tablespoon butter. Combine breadcrumbs, parsley, and butter; sprinkle crumb mixture over cheese. Bake at 350° for 20 minutes or until nicely browned. Serve warm with simple crackers or apple slices.

| | |
|---|---|
| 1 | cup chopped pecans |
| 3 | tablespoons butter |
| 16 | ounces cream cheese |
| 8 | ounces bleu cheese |
| 1 | cup soft breadcrumbs |
| ¼ | cup chopped fresh parsley |

---

Claude Debussy: *Preludes, Book I:* "Le vent dans le plaine" ("The wind on the plain")

# WILD DUCK PÂTÉ

*Serves 16 to 20*

| | |
|---|---|
| 2 | duck breasts, boned and cut into long strips about the thickness of a pencil |
| 1 | large slice ham, cut into long strips |
| | Fajita or similar seasoning |
| ½ | cup brandy |
| 2 | tablespoons olive oil |
| 1 | large onion, coarsely chopped |
| 3 | large cloves garlic, chopped |
| 2 | cups coarsely chopped duck breast meat (Mallard or Gadwall) |
| 2 | cups coarsely chopped pork and pork fat |
| 2 | cups ground turkey (about 1 pound) |
| 3 | eggs |
| 2 | tablespoons salt |
| 1 | tablespoon black pepper |
| 2 | teaspoons cayenne pepper |
| ½ | teaspoon cinnamon |
| 1 | tablespoon fresh thyme leaves |
| ¼ | teaspoon allspice |
| ½ | cup blanched almonds |
| ¼ | cup shelled pistachios or toasted pine nuts |
| 2 | bay leaves |

- Put duck and ham strips in glass bowl. Sprinkle with fajita seasoning and pour brandy on top. Refrigerate overnight, turning occasionally.

- Heat olive oil in nonstick skillet. Sauté onion until soft; add garlic. Cook until translucent but not brown. Cool.

- Put onion mixture, chopped and ground meats, eggs, 3 tablespoons brandy from the bowl of marinating strips, salt, black pepper, red pepper, cinnamon, thyme, and allspice into the bowl of a food processor and pulse until well chopped, or put the mixture through a meat grinder.

- Oil a pâté mold or two standard loaf pans. Spread a layer of chopped meat mixture evenly on the bottom of the pan (about ¾-inch deep). Arrange rows of marinated meat strips and nuts lengthwise on top. Add another layer of the chopped meat mixture, then more marinated strips and nuts, ending with a layer of chopped meat mixture.

- Lay bay leaves on top and cover pan(s) with foil. Puncture the top. Put pan(s) into a large roasting pan and add 1 inch of hot water to the bottom of pan. Bake at 350° for 2 hours. Remove and place a 5-pound weight on top (a brick or two will work). Cool.

- Refrigerate for 24 to 48 hours. Unmold pâté and cut into ½-inch slices. Serve with crusty baguette or homemade bread.

"Cold Duck Time" as performed by Jack McDuff

# BAKED CRAB DIP

*Serves 12*

- Pick over crab, removing any cartilage or shell. In a 1-quart casserole or square glass baking dish, combine the crab, cream cheese, lemon juice, mayonnaise, seasoned salt, pepper, and ⅓ cup of almonds. Sprinkle remaining ⅓ cup almonds on top.

- Bake at 300° for 30 minutes. Serve hot with crackers.

| | |
|---|---|
| 1 | cup crabmeat |
| 8 | ounces cream cheese |
| 1 | tablespoon lemon juice |
| ½ | cup mayonnaise |
| ½ | teaspoon seasoned salt |
| ¼ | teaspoon black pepper |
| ⅔ | cup slivered almonds |

*King crab legs from the supermarket seafood market are a good source of very sweet and tasty crabmeat for this recipe.*

**Variations:** *Add chopped green onions, fresh parsley, fresh dill, or celery.*

Michael Jones: *Seascapes:* "Seascapes"

# CRAWFISH SAGANAKI

*Serves 20*

- ½ cup olive oil
- 1 large onion, finely chopped
- 1 medium green bell pepper, finely chopped
- 2-5 large cloves garlic, minced
- 2 large tomatoes, peeled, seeded, finely chopped
- ½ cup finely chopped fresh parsley
- 1 teaspoon red pepper flakes (optional)
- 2 pounds peeled Louisiana crawfish tails
- 2 tablespoons lemon juice
- Salt and black pepper
- 1 cup crumbled feta cheese
- 2 baguettes, sliced ½-inch thick

- Heat olive oil in a large, deep skillet or Dutch oven. Add onion and green pepper; sauté over medium-low heat until very soft, about 15 minutes. Add garlic and sauté 1 minute longer. Add the chopped tomatoes and sauté for 5 minutes, stirring frequently. Mix in parsley and red pepper flakes, if desired.

- Put crawfish tails along with their juices into tomato mixture. Stir well and sauté on medium-high for about 5 minutes, stirring frequently, until crawfish tails are fully cooked. Add lemon juice and season to taste. Just before serving, add feta cheese and stir well.

- Transfer to chafing dish or heated ceramic casserole. Surround with sliced baguettes; spoon hot crawfish mixture onto bread rounds.

🍷 *Try a Mataro with this, one that's earthy with lots of mushroom and spice flavors.*

 Enrique Granados: *Danzas Espanolas #2 in C Minor, Op. 37*

# CLASSIC BRUSCHETTA

*Makes 24*

- Mix 1 tablespoon oil, tomatoes, garlic, basil, and vinegar. Season with salt and pepper. Allow flavors to blend for at least two hours (room temperature) or overnight (refrigerate).

- Place bread slices on foil-lined baking sheet. Brush tops with 1 tablespoon olive oil and bake at 400° for 5 minutes. Turn slices over and brush with another 1 tablespoon olive oil; bake for an additional 5 minutes or until golden. (The toasted rounds can be cooled and stored in an airtight bag overnight.)

- Just before serving, use slotted spoon to scoop 1 generous tablespoon of tomato mixture onto each toast.

3 tablespoons olive oil
1½ cups fresh tomatoes, diced
3-4 cloves garlic, chopped
½ cup packed fresh basil, sliced
1 teaspoon balsamic vinegar
Salt and black pepper
1 baguette, sliced into 24 rounds (⅓-inch thick)

**Variations:** *Tomato-Feta Bruschetta: Omit garlic and basil. Mix tomatoes with fresh oregano, slivered red onion, and crumbled feta. Top with a pitted Greek olive.*

 Johann Sebastian Bach: *Brandenburg Concerto #3 in G*

# PESTO ROUNDS

*Makes 24 rounds*

| | |
|---|---|
| 1 | baguette |
| 1/3 | cup Classic Pesto, see page 326 |
| 1/4 | cup finely chopped oil-packed sun-dried tomatoes |
| 1/2 | cup shredded mozzarella cheese |

- Slice baguette into 1/3-inch thick rounds. Top each round with 2 teaspoons of Classic Pesto. Sprinkle with 1/2 teaspoon chopped sun-dried tomatoes and 1 tablespoon mozzarella. Place on a cookie sheet and bake at 400° for 3 to 5 minutes or until cheese is melted and beginning to brown. Serve warm.

 Henry Purcell: "Rondo"

# ARTICHOKE BRUSCHETTA

*Serves 4*

- Heat 1½ tablespoons olive oil in a small skillet or medium saucepan. Add the artichoke bottoms and sauté for 2 minutes. Add the garlic and salt and pepper to taste. Sauté for an additional 2 minutes. Add 2 tablespoons water and simmer for 5 minutes or until liquid is absorbed.

- Using a potato masher or fork, mash the artichoke mixture to a coarse paste. Add the olives, tomato, parsley, and capers to the pan; turn heat to lowest temperature. (The artichoke mixture can be made 1 day ahead and reheated.)

- Just before serving, grill or toast the bread. Drizzle with additional olive oil, top with artichoke mixture, and garnish with additional chopped parsley.

| | |
|---|---|
| 1½ | tablespoons olive oil |
| 1 | (14-ounce) can artichoke bottoms |
| 2 | cloves garlic, pressed |
| | Salt and black pepper |
| 2 | tablespoons water |
| 6 | Kalamata or other brine-cured olives, pitted and chopped |
| 1 | small tomato, seeded and chopped |
| 2 | tablespoons chopped fresh parsley |
| 1 | tablespoon capers |
| 4 | thick slices French or Italian bread |
| | Additional olive oil |
| | Additional chopped fresh parsley |

**Variations:** *Caponata Bruschetta:* Omit artichoke bottoms and substitute 1 cup peeled, diced eggplant.
*Caesar Bruschetta:* Omit olives. Mix in ¼ cup freshly grated Parmesan and ¼ cup mayonnaise. Run bruschetta under broiler until golden.

 Johann Sebastian Bach: *Brandenburg Concerto #5 in D*

APPETIZERS 41

# CROUTONS WITH APPLE, PECAN BUTTER, AND BRIE

*Makes 20*

| | |
|---|---|
| 1 | baguette |
| 1 | (8-ounce) round of Brie |
| 1 | small Granny Smith apple |
| ½ | cup pecan butter |
| 2 | tablespoons olive oil |

- Place bread slices on foil-lined baking sheet. Brush tops with 1 tablespoon oil. Bake at 400° for about 5 minutes. Turn slices and brush with remaining 1 tablespoon oil. Bake 5 more minutes or until golden.

- Slice Brie as if it were a small pie into 20 thin pieces. Peel and core the apple and slice into 20 thin wedges.

- Spread each crouton with 1 generous teaspoon pecan butter. Top with a slice of apple, followed by a slice of cheese. Run under the broiler until the Brie melts. Serve warm.

*If prepared Pecan Butter is not available, make your own with 1 cup of pecans and 1 teaspoon (or more) of vegetable oil in a small food processor. Grind to fine paste, adding more oil as necessary.*

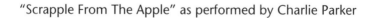

"Scrapple From The Apple" as performed by Charlie Parker

# THREE-CHEESE SPINACH BREAD

*Makes 32 pieces*

- Melt butter in nonstick skillet. Sauté the onions until transparent. Add cream cheese and stir until cheese is melted. Add spinach, pepper, and herbs. Cook over medium heat until the spinach is thawed and ingredients are blended.

- Split bread lengthwise and place on foil-lined baking sheet. Spoon half of spinach mixture evenly onto cut side of each half. Sprinkle mozzarella and Parmesan over both halves. Place baking sheet under broiler until cheese melts and bubbles. Using a sharp knife, slice each half into 16 pieces. Serve hot.

| | |
|---|---|
| ¼ | cup (½ stick) butter |
| 1 | cup chopped onions |
| 8 | ounces cream cheese |
| 1 | (16-ounce) bag frozen chopped spinach |
| ¼ | teaspoon white pepper |
| 2 | tablespoons chopped fresh herbs, including basil, oregano, and thyme |
| 2 | cups shredded mozzarella cheese |
| ½ | cup freshly grated Parmesan cheese |
| 1 | large loaf French bread |

**Variations:** Use hot pepper cheese on top instead of mozzarella and Parmesan.

Claude Debussy: *Preludes, Book II:* "Les tierces alternees"

APPETIZERS 43

# CAVIAR SQUARES

*Makes 48 pieces*

48 pieces cocktail pumpernickel bread (or cut 12 full-size pieces of bread into 4 squares)
1½ cups sour cream
4 ounces black caviar
Shredded zest from 2 lemons

- Spread each square of bread with 1½ teaspoons sour cream. Place ½ teaspoon caviar in the center.

- Sprinkle a few shreds of lemon zest on each square. Serve immediately or within 1 hour (hold in refrigerator).

*For a holiday look, make Red Squares using red caviar. These taste truly celestial when served with frigid vodka.*

*If you don't want vodka, pour a sparkling Blanc de Blanc with a good balance of acid to fruit.*

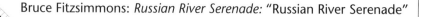
Bruce Fitzsimmons: *Russian River Serenade:* "Russian River Serenade"

# CAVIARTICHOKES

*Serves 6*

- Mix sour cream, onions, chopped basil, and 1 teaspoon lemon zest in small bowl. Season to taste with salt and pepper.

- Fill artichoke bottoms with sour cream mixture. Top with 1 teaspoon caviar. Garnish with remaining 2 teaspoons lemon zest and basil leaves.

| | |
|---|---|
| ⅓ | cup sour cream |
| 3 | tablespoons chopped green onions (green part only) |
| 3 | tablespoons chopped fresh basil |
| 3 | teaspoons shredded lemon zest |
| | Salt and black pepper |
| 6 | artichoke bottoms (from 14-ounce can), drained and patted dry |
| 2 | ounces black caviar |
| 6 | small basil leaves |

 Reinhold Gliere: *The Red Poppy:* "Russian Sailor's Dance"

# GOAT BALLS

*Makes 24*

| | |
|---|---|
| 1 | cup pecans |
| 2 | tablespoons walnut oil |
| 3 | ounces cream cheese, room temperature |
| 6 | ounces goat cheese, room temperature |
| 24 | seedless green grapes |

- Over low heat, sauté pecans in walnut oil until lightly toasted. Drain on paper towels; chop finely.

- Mix cheeses with a fork until thoroughly blended. Take 1 tablespoon cheese and flatten slightly. Press grape into center. Press cheese around grape; roll between palms until round and smooth. Continue with remaining grapes and cheese.

- Roll each ball in pecans until completely covered. Refrigerate for 30 minutes to firm cheese (these can be made 8 hours ahead and refrigerated). Allow to stand 15 minutes before serving.

🍷 *Pour a crisp and clean Chablis to marry these creamy cheese and fruit flavors.*

Kate Price: *Deep Heart's Cove:* "Sonatina Montenegro"

# TOMATOES STUFFED WITH GOAT CHEESE AND CHIVES

*Makes 18*

- Cut the tomatoes in half lengthwise and scoop out seeds and some pulp. Drain the halves and pat dry.

- Mix goat cheese, chives, oil, and pepper in a bowl. Mash and blend until creamy.

- Spoon the cheese mixture into the tomato halves. Serve chilled.

9 large plum tomatoes
8 ounces creamy goat cheese
½ cup chopped fresh chives
¼ cup olive oil
Black pepper

 Frederic Chopin: *Prelude in C, Op. 28, #1*

# GREEK SALAD SKEWERS  *Makes 24*

| | |
|---|---|
| 2 | seedless cucumbers |
| 24 | large (or 48 small) cherry tomatoes |
| 16 | ounces feta cheese |
| 48 | pitted Greek olives |
| 24 | bamboo skewers |
| ¼ | cup olive oil |
| | Slivered red onion |
| | Dried oregano |
| | Salt and black pepper |

- Peel cucumbers. Slice in half lengthwise, then slice crosswise into ½-inch pieces. (If cucumber is very large, quarter lengthwise, then cut into ½-inch pieces.) Cut the large cherry tomatoes in half or leave small cherry tomatoes whole. Cut feta cheese into ½-inch cubes. (If the feta is too dry, it will crumble. Get a fairly creamy feta.)

- To assemble, thread 1 cherry tomato (or half) onto the skewer. Add a cube of cheese, then a piece of cucumber, then an olive. Repeat once more. Place skewers on a large platter or tray (can be refrigerated for several hours at this point). When ready to serve, drizzle with olive oil; sprinkle with slivered onion, crushed oregano, salt, and pepper. Serve chilled or at room temperature.

 Samuel Barber: *Medea's Dance of Vengeance, Op. 23a*

# ROASTED RED PEPPERS WITH FRESH MOZZARELLA

*Makes 8*

- Place peppers cut side down on foil-lined baking sheet. Broil until blistered and beginning to blacken. Turn cut side up and broil until just tender.

- Slice mozzarella into 8 pieces. Place a slice of cheese in the cavity of each pepper half.

- Broil until the cheese melts. Drizzle with olive oil and sprinkle with basil.

*Two halves make a good first course serving.*

| | |
|---|---|
| 4 | small red bell peppers, halved lengthwise and seeded (retain stem for a rustic look) |
| 8 | ounces fresh mozzarella |
| 1 | tablespoon olive oil |
| 2 | tablespoons chopped fresh basil |

Dimitri Shostakovich: *Festive Overture*

# GREEK MEATBALLS

*Makes 24 2-inch balls or 48 1-inch balls*

| | |
|---|---|
| 2 | pounds ground sirloin |
| 1 | small onion, grated |
| 1 | cup packed parsley leaves, minced |
| 2 | slices stale white bread, crusts trimmed |
| 1/3 | cup milk |
| 2 | large eggs |
| 1/4 | cup olive oil |
| 1 | tablespoon salt |
| 1 | teaspoon black pepper |
| 1 | teaspoon dried oregano |
| | Flour for dredging |
| | Olive oil for frying |

- Place ground sirloin, onion, and parsley in large mixing bowl. Soak the bread in milk in a shallow bowl for a few minutes. Squeeze excess liquid out. Rub bread between your hands over bowl until it disintegrates. Add eggs, oil, salt, pepper, and oregano. Use your hands to mix lightly but thoroughly.

- Cover the bottom of a rimmed baking sheet with 1/4-inch of flour. Shape the meat mixture into 2-inch balls (for dinner servings) or 1-inch balls (cocktail size); place on baking pan. When all of the mixture has been rolled, dredge the meatballs in flour and allow to sit in the refrigerator for 20 minutes.

- In large skillet (or use two), heat 1/2-inch of olive oil over high temperature. Coat meatballs with additional flour, shake off excess, and place in hot oil. Don't crowd the pan. Cook on high for about 3 minutes; lower heat to medium and cook about 5 minutes more (longer for larger meatballs). Turn with spoon or tongs. Raise heat to high again for 3 minutes. Return to medium and cook meatballs until very brown and crusty and cooked through.

- Serve the meatballs plain or with a drizzle of olive oil and fresh chopped parsley. They are delicious alongside pasta or stuffed in pita with tomatoes and topped with Tzatziki (see page 22).

 Claude Debussy: *A L'Apres-Midi d'un Faune*

# FROMAGE PROVENÇAL

*Serves 16 to 20*

- Mince garlic in food processor. Add cream cheese, butter, salt, and parsley. Pulse until thoroughly blended.

- Line a medium-size shallow bowl with plastic, leaving a long overhang. Put cheese mixture in bowl, cover top with the excess plastic wrap, and press down evenly. Refrigerate for 20 minutes or up to 2 days.

- Peel plastic from top of cheese. Invert bowl onto platter and remove plastic completely. Cover cheese with cracked pepper. Serve with crackers.

16 ounces cream cheese
½ cup butter
4 medium cloves garlic
½ teaspoon salt
¼ cup fresh parsley
Cracked pepper (don't use pepper from pepper mill)

Darius Milhaud: *Suite Provençale, Op. 152*

# CHICKEN-DOVE ROLL WITH CILANTRO-CUMIN SAUCE AND ROASTED PEPPERS

*Serves 8 to 10*

**Chicken-Dove Roll**

- ½ cup pecans
- Olive oil
- 10 whole cloves garlic, unpeeled
- 3 jalapeño peppers
- 1 red pepper
- 1 yellow pepper
- 4 dove breasts
- 1 whole fryer, boned with skin intact
- Seasoning mix such as fajita, Cajun, or Greek
- 1 ounce thinly sliced smoked ham
- 1 ounce thinly sliced smoked turkey
- Bacon slices to completely cover roll
- Green jalapeño jelly
- Cilantro-Cumin Sauce

- Sauté pecans in olive oil until toasted and set aside. Boil garlic cloves for 20 minutes; drain and peel.

- Blacken all the peppers under the broiler or on a grill. Place in paper bag for 5 minutes to steam. Peel jalapeños; seed them and cut into strips. Peel red and yellow peppers and seed from stem end. Slice into rings.

- Steam dove breasts in the microwave until just cooked. Bone the breasts and set aside.

- Place the boned chicken skin side down on a work surface. Sprinkle with your choice of spicy seasoning. Cover the chicken with waxed paper and pound to spread the meat out evenly, shaping into a rectangle. Remove waxed paper and place sliced ham on top of the chicken.

Ottorino Respighi: *The Birds* (Especially II "The Dove" and III "The Hen")

52 PRELUDES

# CHICKEN-DOVE ROLL *continued*

- Add a layer of sliced turkey. Spread pecans over the top. Add the garlic cloves and jalapeño strips in rows. Line up the dove breasts on one long side. Roll up tightly; tie roll crosswise with kitchen string at 1-inch intervals. Cover the roll completely with strips of bacon.

- Bake at 325° for 45 minutes. Cool to room temperature and chill in refrigerator overnight. To serve, slice roll crosswise into ½-inch slices. Put 2 slices on each plate. Add a red pepper ring filled with green jalapeño jelly and a yellow pepper ring filled with Cilantro-Cumin Sauce.

- Whisk sour cream, mayonnaise, whipping cream, and lemon juice until smooth. Stir in cilantro and seasonings. Cover and refrigerate until needed.

### Cilantro-Cumin Sauce

| | |
|---|---|
| 1 | cup sour cream |
| ¼ | cup mayonnaise |
| ⅓ | cup whipping cream |
| 2 | teaspoons lemon juice |
| 1 | bunch fresh cilantro, finely chopped |
| ¼ | teaspoon ground cumin |
| | Salt |

# SMOKY CHEESE PÂTÉ

*Makes 3 cups*

16  ounces smoked Gouda or cheddar cheese, shredded
2  (4-ounce) jars Old English cheese, room temperature
1  large onion, grated
5  cloves garlic, pressed
1  tablespoon Worcestershire sauce
   Salt, black pepper, chili powder, hot sauce
   Mayonnaise

- Combine all cheeses, onion, garlic, and Worcestershire sauce in food processor. Add salt, pepper, chili powder, and hot sauce to taste. Pulse until smooth.

- Scrape down sides of work bowl. Add 2 tablespoons of mayonnaise and process briefly, adding more mayonnaise to reach a very smooth consistency.

- Line a 3 to 4-cup bowl with plastic wrap, leaving plenty of overhang. Pack the pâté into the bowl; smooth top. Cover top with plastic wrap and chill for 4 hours or overnight. Peel back plastic wrap from top, invert bowl onto platter, and peel remaining plastic wrap off. Surround with crackers.

---

Frederic Chopin: *Prelude in A Minor, Op. 28, #2*

# BASIL-CHEESE STRATA

*Serves 16 to 20*

- Mix the two cheeses together until thoroughly blended. Place half the cheese mixture in bottom of a serving bowl (clear glass makes a nice presentation). Top with half the basil leaves; drizzle half the oil over. Sprinkle with salt and pepper. Repeat the layering once more.

6 ounces soft goat cheese
6 ounces mascarpone cheese
30 basil leaves, washed and patted dry
4 tablespoons olive oil
Salt and black pepper

*Serve as a spread with toasted baguette slices or use to top broiled tomatoes.*

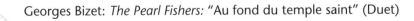

Georges Bizet: *The Pearl Fishers:* "Au fond du temple saint" (Duet)

# TRI-COLOR TORTA  *Serves 20 to 24*

1½ ounces sun-dried tomatoes in oil, drained
Olive oil
16 ounces Neufchâtel cheese (light cream cheese)
2 cloves garlic
4 ounces shredded Parmesan cheese
1¾ ounces pine nuts
1 cup firmly packed fresh basil leaves

- Spray a 24-ounce ring mold with nonstick spray. Cover the bottom of the mold with chopped sun-dried tomatoes (scissors make cutting easy); drizzle in some olive oil.

- Put 8 ounces of Neufchâtel cheese, garlic, and Parmesan in a food processor and pulse until smooth. Pack firmly into the mold on top of the tomatoes, smoothing into an even layer.

- Put the remaining 8 ounces of Neufchâtel, the pine nuts, and the basil into the processor (no need to clean the bowl) and process until smooth. Pack into the top of the mold, pressing firmly. Cover and freeze for at least 1 hour.

- An hour or so before serving, remove from freezer and unmold onto serving platter. Cover and let come to room temperature before serving. Fill the center of the ring with fresh basil and surround torta with crackers or crusty bread.

 Ottorino Respighi: *I pini del gianicola (The Pines of Rome)*

# GOAT CHEESE PESTO PLATTER

*Serves 12*

- Puree garlic in processor or blender. Add herbs and process until finely chopped. Add cheese and pulse or whirl until smooth. Slowly add oil with machine running.

- Spread cheese mixture on a decorative platter, smoothing it flat. This layer should be no more than ¼-inch thick. Refrigerate until firm.

- Spread pesto evenly over cheese mixture. Top with sun-dried tomatoes. Garnish with Kalamata olives and serve with a knife for spreading on slices of peasant bread.

 *A light and fruity Italian red with lots of cherry flavors will work well with this highly-flavored appetizer.*

2 cloves garlic
2 tablespoons fresh parsley
1 tablespoon fresh basil
1 tablespoon fresh rosemary
1 tablespoon fresh thyme
8 ounces soft goat cheese
2 tablespoons olive oil
½ cup Classic Pesto, see page 326
½ cup sun-dried tomatoes, softened in warm water, drained and chopped
   Kalamata olives
   Sliced peasant bread

It is better to have bread left over than to run short of wine.

*Spanish Proverb*

Frederic Chopin: *Prelude in G, Op. 28, #3*

# MEDITERRANEAN STUFFED BREAD

*Serves 16 to 20*

| | |
|---|---|
| 1 | round loaf of peasant bread |
| 8 | ounces feta cheese, crumbled |
| 12 | ounces Neufchâtel cheese (light cream cheese) |
| 1 | cup regular or low-fat sour cream |
| 3 | green onions, chopped |
| 1½ | cups dry-pack sun-dried tomatoes, soaked in warm water, drained, and sliced |
| 1 | cup coarsely chopped walnuts |
| 1 | tablespoon chopped fresh rosemary |

- Cut the top off the bread and hollow out the center, leaving a 1-inch shell. Cut removed bread into 1-inch x 2-inch chunks. Toast bread chunks and set aside.

- Mix together the remaining ingredients. Spoon the mixture into the bread shell, mounding slightly on top. Bake at 350° for 45 to 60 minutes. Serve with toasted bread chunks, crackers, Paprika Triangles (see page 28), or raw vegetables.

Claude Debussy: *Preludes, Book I:* "Ce qu'a vu le vent d'ouest" ("What the West Wind Saw")

# PIZZA WITH BLEU CHEESE AND MUSHROOMS

*Makes 1 12-inch pizza*

- Sauté mushrooms in oil over high heat until tender and golden. Season with salt and pepper.
- Place pizza crust on large baking sheet. Sprinkle bleu cheese and thyme over crust. Top with mushrooms. Bake at 450° until cheese melts, about 15 minutes. Allow to cool for 5 minutes before slicing into wedges.

8 ounces fresh shiitake mushrooms, stemmed and thinly sliced
1½ tablespoons olive oil
 Salt and black pepper
1 (12-inch) baked pizza crust or focaccia
8 ounces crumbled bleu cheese
1 tablespoon fresh thyme leaves or 1 teaspoon dried

 Jim Chappell: *Nightsongs & Lullabys:* "Friends with the Moon"

# RADIO SHRIMP

*Serves 16*

- 16 ounces cream cheese
- 2 (12-ounce) bottles cocktail sauce
- 1 pound cooked shrimp, shelled and chopped
- 8 ounces mozzarella cheese, shredded
- 6 green onions
- 1 green bell pepper
- 3 tomatoes
- Paprika

- Soften cream cheese and shape into a flat circle on a large platter. Pour cocktail sauce on top of cream cheese. Sprinkle shrimp over sauce and top with mozzarella.

- Chop the onions, pepper, and tomatoes, and mix lightly. Sprinkle over the platter. Decorate with paprika. Serve with crispy toast points or crackers.

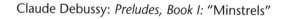

Claude Debussy: *Preludes, Book I:* "Minstrels"

# STUFFED BRIE

*Serves 18 to 20*

- Refrigerate Brie until chilled and firm (or freeze 30 minutes). Cut wheel in half horizontally so that you have 2 thin wheels.

- In small bowl, combine butter and garlic. Add walnuts, basil, and olives, if desired; mix well.

- Spread the mixture evenly over the cut side of one wheel of Brie. Top with the other half, cut side down. Lightly press together. Wrap in plastic wrap and refrigerate. (May be refrigerated for up to 2 days.)

- To serve, bring the Brie to room temperature. Serve with plain crackers.

| | |
|---|---|
| 1 | 14-ounce wheel of Brie or 2 8-ounce wheels |
| ½ | cup unsalted butter |
| 1 | large garlic clove, pressed |
| ⅓ | cup finely chopped walnuts |
| 2 | tablespoons chopped fresh basil |
| ¼ | cup finely chopped ripe olives (optional) |

*A large wedge of Brie, approximately 16 ounces, can be stuffed in the same manner. To stuff a 1 kilo wheel (2.2 pounds), double the ingredients for the butter mixture. Try substituting other nuts (pine nuts, almonds, pecans) and vary the herbs and flavorings.*

Rentard Taki: "Kojo non Tsuki" ("Moon over the Ruined Castle")

APPETIZERS

# BRIE PINWHEEL

*Serves 20 to 24*

| | |
|---|---|
| 1 | 1-kilogram (2.2-pound) wheel of ripe Brie |
| 1 | cup currants, dried cherries, or dried cranberries |
| 1 | cup walnuts, pecans, slivered almonds, or cashew pieces |
| 1 | cup chopped fresh dill |
| ½ | cup poppy seeds or toasted sesame seeds |
| ½ | cup toasted cumin seeds |

- Carefully cut the bottom rind off the Brie. Score the top of the Brie with a knife, making 10 pie-shaped wedges. Place cheese on work surface.

- Press each of the ingredients onto 2 opposing wedges, pressing firmly into the top of the Brie. Place complementary flavors next to each other. For example, pecans would work very well next to dried cherries, and the cherries are good beside poppy seeds. You should end up with alternating colors and textures.

- Wrap the wheel of Brie tightly in plastic wrap and refrigerate for no more than 4 hours. Let stand at room temperature for 30 minutes before serving.

*Measurements of toppings are approximate. The pinwheel can also be made in a mini-version with an 8-ounce wheel of Brie (use only 3 toppings spread over 6 wedges) or in a larger version with a 2-kilogram (5-pound) wheel.*

---

Siguard von Koch: "Af lotusdoft och manens sken" ("Of lotus scent and moonlight")

# BLEU CHEESECAKE WITH ROSEMARY WALNUTS

*Serves 20*

- Preheat oven to 325°. Butter the bottom and sides of a 10-inch springform pan.

- Combine rosemary and walnuts in small bowl of food processor. Pulse into crumbs. Put nut mixture into prepared pan; shake to coat bottom and sides.

- In large bowl, combine ricotta and cream cheeses. Beat with electric mixer until creamy. Beat in bleu cheese (1 cup for mild flavor or 2 cups for more assertive flavor). Add eggs 1 at a time, beating after each addition. Pour into prepared pan. Place in oven and bake until center is just firm, about 1 to 1¼ hours. Remove from oven and place pan on rack. Cool 15 minutes.

- While cheesecake is warm, drop mascarpone cheese by tablespoons onto the top. Wait 5 minutes. Gently spread the cheese into a thin layer. Cool completely. Cover with plastic wrap and refrigerate overnight.

- To serve, run a sharp knife around the inside rim of pan; release sides. Place cake on large round or oval serving platter. Decorate cake with Rosemary Walnuts; scatter remaining walnuts around base of cheesecake. Surround with crackers and garnish with fresh rosemary.

|  |  |
|---|---|
|  | Butter for greasing pan |
| 2 | tablespoons fresh rosemary |
| ⅓ | cup walnut pieces |
| 1 | cup ricotta cheese |
| 16 | ounces cream cheese |
| 1-2 | cups crumbled blue cheese |
| 3 | eggs |
| 1 | cup mascarpone cheese |
| 2 | cups Rosemary Walnuts, see page 13 |

🍷 *Pour a big, bold Cabernet with this savory first course.*

APPETIZERS

# MEXICAN CHEESECAKE

*Serves 16 to 20*

**Cheesecake**

- 1½ cups crushed tortilla chips
- 4 tablespoons unsalted butter, melted
- 16 ounces cream cheese, room temperature
- 8 ounces shredded Monterey Jack cheese
- 3 large eggs
- 1 cup sour cream, divided
- 1 (4.5-ounce) can diced green chiles
- 1 cup picante sauce

Guacamole
Salsa Diablo

- Preheat oven to 350°. Combine crushed chips and butter; press onto bottom of greased 9-inch springform pan. Bake 10 minutes.

- In processor or electric mixer, combine cream cheese and Monterey Jack cheese. Add eggs and ½ cup sour cream, pulsing or mixing to combine. Add green chiles and picante sauce; mix well.

- Pour cheese mixture into crust and spread evenly. Place pan on baking sheet and bake 40 minutes. Spread remaining ½ cup sour cream over top of hot cheesecake. Cool to room temperature and chill.

- To assemble, run sharp knife around inside rim of springform pan and release cheesecake. Transfer to serving plate. Mound Guacamole on center top of cheesecake. Drizzle with some Salsa, pouring remainder of Salsa around base of cheesecake. Serve with tortilla chips.

 Manuel Ponce: Tres canciones populares Mexicanas

## MEXICAN CHEESECAKE *continued*

- Mash avocados with fork in medium bowl. Add onion, cilantro, jalapeño, lime or lemon juice, and hot pepper sauce. Salt to taste. Put avocado pits in bowl with mixture to help prevent browning; refrigerate Guacamole until needed. Discard pits before using.

- Combine all salsa ingredients in a glass bowl. Stir well. Cover and chill thoroughly.

### Guacamole

| | |
|---|---|
| 2 | avocados, pitted and peeled, pits reserved |
| 2 | tablespoons minced or grated onion |
| 1 | teaspoon chopped fresh cilantro |
| 1 | teaspoon minced fresh jalapeño |
| | Juice of ½ lime or lemon |
| | Dash hot pepper sauce |
| | Salt |

### Salsa Diablo

| | |
|---|---|
| 3 | fresh tomatoes, peeled, seeded, and diced |
| ½ | large red onion, finely chopped |
| 1 | large clove garlic, minced |
| 2 | large serrano peppers, seeded and minced |
| ½ | bunch fresh cilantro, minced |
| ¼ | cup fresh lime juice |
| ½ | teaspoon ground cumin |
| | Salt and freshly ground black pepper |

APPETIZERS

# PESTO CHEESECAKE

*Serves 20*

|   |   |
|---|---|
| | Butter for greasing pan |
| ¼ | cup Italian seasoned breadcrumbs |
| 2 | tablespoons freshly grated Romano cheese |
| 16 | ounces cream cheese, room temperature |
| 1 | cup ricotta cheese |
| ½ | cup freshly grated Parmesan cheese |
| 3 | large eggs |
| ½ | cup Classic Pesto, see page 326 |
| ¼ | cup pine nuts |

- Preheat oven to 325°. Butter the bottom and sides of a 10-inch diameter springform pan.

- Mix crumbs and 2 tablespoons grated Parmesan; coat pan with mixture.

- In large bowl of an electric mixer, beat cream cheese, ricotta, and Parmesan until light. Add eggs 1 at a time, beating well after each addition. Pour half of the mixture into a medium bowl; add pesto to the bowl and mix thoroughly.

- Pour pesto mixture into the springform pan and smooth the top. Spoon the remaining cheese mixture over the top; smooth gently, taking care not to mix layers. Sprinkle pine nuts on top.

- Bake until the center is just firm, about 45 minutes. Transfer pan to rack and cool completely. Wrap pan with plastic wrap; refrigerate overnight.

- To serve, run a small knife around the inside edge of the pan. Release the sides and place the cheesecake on a platter. Top with fresh basil sprigs; surround the cheesecake with buttery crackers.

*The cheesecake can also be cut into 20 thin wedges and served as a first course.*

Claude Debussy: *The Children's Corner:* #6: Golliwog's Cakewalk

# GAZPACHO CON GUSTO

*Serves 4*

- Put garlic and herbs into a large serving bowl. Gradually beat in the oil, then the lemon juice, and then the seasonings. Mixture must be thick and well-blended or it will separate later.

- Stir in the broth and blend well. Add onion, bell pepper, and tomatoes. Chill all day or overnight.

- Serve in chilled bowls topped with diced cucumber.

    **Variations:** Add additional tender garden vegetables such as zucchini, yellow squash, or radishes.

| | |
|---|---|
| 2 | cloves garlic, pressed or minced |
| | Fresh herbs (parsley, chives, dill, mint, basil, marjoram, or oregano), snipped finely |
| 1/3 | cup olive oil |
| | Juice of 1 lemon |
| | Salt, freshly ground pepper, paprika |
| 4 | cups chicken stock, defatted |
| 1 | red onion, sliced into paper-thin rings |
| 1 | bell pepper, chopped |
| 2-3 | tomatoes, peeled and chopped |
| 1 | cup peeled, diced cucumber |

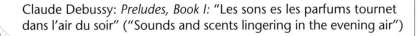

Claude Debussy: *Preludes, Book I:* "Les sons es les parfums tournet dans l'air du soir" ("Sounds and scents lingering in the evening air")

# GARDEN GAZPACHO

*Serves 4*

| | |
|---|---|
| 4 | large red tomatoes, quartered |
| 2 | medium cucumbers, peeled |
| 1 | green bell pepper, cored and quartered |
| 1-3 | cloves garlic (to taste) |
| | Juice of 1 lemon or lime |
| | Salt and black pepper |

- Put tomato, cucumber, bell pepper, garlic, and lemon juice into a blender or processor. Puree.

- Season to taste. Chill thoroughly. Serve in bowls with spoons or in mugs or glasses for drinking.

*Pour soup into bowls. Top each with a dollop of sour cream or with an icy scoop of lemon sorbet or frozen guacamole. Another way to maintain the chilly temperature is to garnish bowls with Lemon Cubes or Lime Cubes: cut thin slices of lemon or lime into four quarters. Place quarter slices into the spaces in an ice cube tray. Add water and freeze.*

 Percy Aldridge Grainger: *Country Gardens*

# CHILLED CUCUMBER SOUP

*Serves 6*

- Put 1 can chicken broth, green onions, and garlic into a blender or processor. Puree. Cut 1 cucumber into chunks; add to mixture and pulse until cucumber is coarsely chopped.

- Pour mixture into a large bowl. Add the yogurt and whisk to blend.

- Put 1 can chicken broth, lemon juice, and oil into blender or processor. Cut remaining cucumber into chunks and add. Again, pulse until cucumber is coarsely chopped.

- Add to yogurt mixture and blend with whisk. Season with salt and pepper. Chill thoroughly.

- Serve in bowls topped with chopped chives and tomatoes, if desired.

4 cups chicken stock or canned low-salt broth, chilled, visible fat removed
1 bunch green onions
2 cloves garlic
2 cucumbers, unpeeled (unless cucumbers have heavy wax coating)
3 cups plain yogurt
Juice of 1 lemon
1 tablespoon olive oil
Salt and freshly ground pepper
Chopped chives
Chopped ripe tomatoes (optional)

A cucumber should be well sliced, and dressed with pepper and vinegar, and then thrown out, as good for nothing.

*Samuel Johnson*

 Claude Debussy: *Preludes, Book II:* "Ondine"

# SPRING PEA SOUP

*Serves 4*

| | |
|---|---|
| 1 | (16-ounce) bag frozen green peas |
| 1 | cup half & half |
| ⅓ | cup whipping cream |
| ¼ | cup finely chopped herbs (choose from parsley, chives, tarragon, or chervil) Additional whipping cream |

- Bring 4 cups water to boil in a medium saucepan. Add frozen peas and return to boil; cook for 1 minute. Drain and rinse with cold water.

- Put peas in blender or processor with half & half. Puree until smooth.

- Pour pea mixture into bowl. Stir in whipping cream. Chill.

- Divide soup evenly among 4 bowls. Top each with 1 tablespoon of chopped herbs. Put 2 to 3 tablespoons whipping cream into a squeeze bottle. Squeeze a spiral or zigzag design with whipping cream on surface of soup.

*This soup can also be served warm; simply reheat before serving.*

Claude Debussy: *Preludes, Book I:* "La cathedrale engloutie" ("The submerged cathedral")

# OUZO SOUP

*Serves 6*

- Heat oil in a 4-quart Dutch oven. Add onions and fennel; cover and cook over medium-low heat for about 25 minutes or until vegetables are soft but not brown.

- Uncover and add water. Bring to boil; reduce heat and simmer uncovered until vegetables are very tender, about 25 minutes.

- Work in batches to puree soup in blender. Pour into bowl; season to taste. Stir in ouzo. Chill for at least three hours (can be made 1 day ahead).

- Serve as a refreshing first course, garnished with fennel fronds.

3 tablespoons olive oil
2 cups chopped onions
6 cups chopped, trimmed fennel bulb (about 3 large bulbs)
5 cups water
Salt and black pepper
3 tablespoons ouzo or other anise-flavored liqueur

Aram Khachaturian: *Gayaneh:* "Sabre Dance"

# BUTTERNUT AND DOUBLE GINGER SOUP

*Serves 4*

- 2½ pounds butternut squash
- 1 tablespoon vegetable oil
- 1 small onion, thinly sliced
- 2 teaspoons brown sugar
- 1 teaspoon minced fresh ginger
- 1 large garlic clove, finely chopped
- 1 teaspoon cinnamon
- 2½-3 cups chicken stock or low-salt broth
- Salt and black pepper
- ½ cup sour cream or lightly whipped cream (optional)
- ¼ cup chopped crystallized ginger

- Preheat oven to 375°. Spray a baking sheet with nonstick cooking spray. Halve and seed squash. Place cut side down on prepared baking sheet. Bake until very soft, about 30 to 50 minutes. Scrape pulp into bowl and reserve.

- Heat oil in heavy saucepan over medium low heat. Add onion, brown sugar, fresh ginger, garlic, and cinnamon. Cover and cook until onion is tender, stirring frequently, about 15 minutes. Add squash and 2½ cups stock. Bring to boil; simmer 10 minutes.

- Puree soup in batches in a blender or processor until silky smooth. Return to pot and season with salt and pepper. Bring to simmer, adding more broth if soup is too thick.

- Divide among 4 bowls. Top each serving with 2 tablespoons sour cream or whipping cream (optional) and 1 tablespoon crystallized ginger.

*Try serving this soup chilled.*

A first-rate soup is more creative than a second-rate painting.

*Abraham Maslow*

Nicolai Rimsky-Korsakov: *Le coq d'or Suite*

# THAI SHRIMP BROTH

*Serves 6*

- Peel and devein shrimp, reserving shells. Transfer shrimp to small bowl; chill.

- Combine shrimp shells, broth, carrot, lemongrass, ginger, and garlic in large saucepan. Bring to boil. Simmer uncovered 20 minutes, stirring occasionally.

- Strain broth into large bowl, pressing on solids with back of spoon; discard solids. Return broth to saucepan.

- Bring to simmer; add shrimp, herbs, chile, and lime juice. Remove from heat, cover, and let stand until shrimp are opaque, stirring once, about 2 minutes.

- Serve in bowls garnished with lime slices.

| | |
|---|---|
| ½ | pound uncooked medium shrimp in shell |
| 4 | (14½-ounce) cans low-salt chicken broth |
| ⅔ | cup finely chopped carrot |
| ¼ | cup thinly sliced lemongrass |
| 2 | tablespoons finely chopped ginger |
| 1½ | tablespoons minced garlic |
| 1 | tablespoon finely chopped fresh basil (preferably Thai) |
| 1 | tablespoon finely chopped fresh mint |
| 1 | tablespoon finely chopped fresh cilantro |
| 1 | small serrano chile, stemmed and thinly sliced into circles |
| 1 | teaspoon fresh lime juice |
| 4 | thin lime slices |

Claude Debussy: *Estampes:* I. Pagodes

# SHRIMP EGGDROP SOUP

*Serves 6*

| | |
|---|---|
| 2 | cans low-salt chicken broth |
| 1 | cup sliced button mushrooms |
| 2 | cloves garlic, sliced |
| 1 | teaspoon soy sauce |
| ¼ | pound medium shrimp, peeled and deveined |
| ⅛ | teaspoon white pepper |
| 1 | egg, lightly beaten |
| 1 | teaspoon sesame oil |
| 2 | green onions, chopped |

- Combine chicken broth, mushrooms, garlic, and soy sauce in medium saucepan. Bring to a boil. Cover and reduce heat; simmer for 30 minutes.

- Add shrimp and pepper. Cook for 3 minutes. Remove from heat.

- Combine egg and oil, stirring well. Slowly pour mixture into soup, stirring constantly, until the egg forms strands. Divide among 6 bowls and sprinkle with green onions.

 "Good Bait" as performed by John Coltrane

# BASIL-EGGPLANT SOUP

*Serves 6*

- Grill or broil the eggplant until charred and tender. Cut in half lengthwise, scoop out pulp, and discard skin.

- Sauté the onion, garlic, and oregano in 3 tablespoons of olive oil in a large saucepan until onion is tender. Add the eggplant, tomatoes, and stock. Season with salt, pepper, and cayenne.

- Simmer, partly covered, for 35 minutes. Puree soup in batches in blender and return to saucepan.

- In small processor or blender, puree the basil with remaining 2 tablespoons olive oil. Blend in the goat cheese.

- Reheat soup. Ladle into bowls and top each with a dollop of basil-cheese mixture.

| | |
|---|---|
| 1 | medium eggplant |
| 1 | small onion, minced |
| 1 | large clove garlic, crushed |
| ½ | tablespoon minced fresh oregano |
| 5 | tablespoons olive oil |
| 3-4 | large ripe Italian plum tomatoes, peeled, seeded, and chopped |
| 1½ | cups chicken stock or low-salt broth |
| | Salt and black pepper |
| | Pinch of cayenne pepper |
| 1 | cup (packed) fresh basil |
| 2 | ounces goat cheese |

---

Frederic Chopin: *Prelude in E Minor, Op. 28, #4*

SOUPS

# SPICY BROCCOLI SOUP

*Serves 6 to 8*

| | |
|---|---|
| 2 | bunches broccoli |
| 6 | medium red potatoes, peeled and quartered |
| 1 | medium onion, peeled and quartered |
| 2 | green onions, sliced |
| 3 | (14½-ounce) cans low-salt chicken broth or vegetable broth |
| ½ | cup half & half |
| ½ | cup milk |
| 1 | cup shredded mixed cheeses (mozzarella, provolone, Parmesan) |
| 1 | cup shredded hot pepper cheese |
| | Salt, black pepper, Creole seasoning |

- Place broccoli, potatoes, and onions in 4-quart saucepan or Dutch oven. Cover with broth.

- Bring to a boil over medium heat. Cover and simmer for 20 minutes or until vegetables are soft. Allow to cool.

- Puree soup in batches in processor or blender. Return to pan.

- Over medium heat, reheat soup. Whisk in half & half and milk. When the mixture is thoroughly hot, add cheeses. Stir well and remove from heat.

- Season with salt, pepper, and Creole seasoning.

 Maurice Ravel: *Miroirs:* "Une barque sur l'ocean"

# ROASTED RED PEPPER AND WHITE WINE SOUP

*Serves 6*

- Place peppers on a foil-lined baking sheet. Broil 5 inches from the heat for about 5 minutes on each side or until peppers look blistered. Immediately put peppers into a paper bag; close bag and let peppers stand for 10 minutes. Remove blistered skin, stem, and seeds from peppers. Set aside.

- Melt 1 tablespoon of butter in a Dutch oven over medium heat. Add garlic and onions and sauté for about 2 minutes. Add the chicken broth, wine, bay leaf, salt, and pepper. Bring to a boil; reduce heat and simmer for 30 minutes. Strain the soup, reserving all liquids.

- Put all remaining solids and roasted peppers into blender or processor. Add ½ cup of reserved liquid and puree until smooth. Set puree aside.

- Melt remaining 2 tablespoons butter in same Dutch oven. Blend in flour, stirring constantly. Cook over medium heat for 1 minute.

- Gradually add reserved broth and cook over medium heat, stirring frequently, until thickened and bubbly. Add red pepper puree and cream. Heat through.

| | |
|---|---|
| 8 | large red bell peppers |
| 6 | cloves garlic, minced |
| 1 | small onion, chopped |
| 3 | tablespoons butter |
| 2 | (14½-ounce) cans low-salt chicken broth |
| 2 | cups dry white wine |
| 1 | bay leaf |
| ½ | teaspoon salt |
| ¼ | teaspoon black pepper |
| 2 | tablespoons flour |
| 1½ | cups whipping cream |

*Try a light Sauvignon Blanc.*

Benjamin Britten: *Four Sea Interludes:* I. Dawn

# WILD MUSHROOM BISQUE

*Serves 12*

¼  cup olive oil
1  large onion, diced
2  pounds mushrooms (a mixture of button, shiitake, cremini, or other types)
1  teaspoon sugar
   Salt and white pepper
3  cups Chardonnay
6  cups water
3  tablespoons cornstarch
3  tablespoons cold water
4  tablespoons minced fresh herbs (choose from tarragon, thyme, chives, parsley, chervil)
2  cups whipping cream

- Heat olive oil in a 4-quart Dutch oven. Sauté onions until softened and nearly transparent.

- Stem mushrooms if necessary and slice. Add mushrooms, sugar, salt, and pepper to onions. Sauté over medium-high heat for about 4 minutes or until mushrooms soften and release their liquid.

- Add the Chardonnay and simmer until most of the liquid has evaporated. Add the 6 cups of water and simmer for 20 minutes. Adjust seasonings.

- Dissolve cornstarch in 3 tablespoons of cold water; add to simmering soup along with the fresh herbs. Simmer 5 minutes. Add cream and heat through. Garnish with sprigs or sprinkles of fresh herbs.

Claude Debussy: *Preludes, Book I:* "La danse de Puck" ("Puck's dance")

# CREAM OF CHARD SOUP

*Serves 4*

- Wash chard thoroughly. Remove and discard the tough center rib (or reserve for another use). Stack chard leaves on cutting board and slice thinly.

- In large saucepan, melt butter with oil. Add onions; sauté on medium-high until just starting to brown, stirring frequently. Add chard. Cover pan and cook on low heat for 2 to 3 minutes, stirring once or twice, until chard wilts.

- Transfer mixture to blender or processor. Puree with ¼ cup half & half. Return to pan.

- Add whipping cream, 1 cup half & half, and nutmeg. Season to taste. Simmer over medium heat for 2 minutes or until heated through and slightly thickened.

**Variations:** *In place of chard, try substituting spinach, romaine lettuce, or even a bag of mixed spring greens. For a totally different experience, substitute 4 cups cooked, drained yellow squash for Summer Squash Soup.*

| | |
|---|---|
| 1 | large bunch chard, white or red |
| 1 | tablespoon butter |
| 1 | teaspoon olive oil |
| 1 | small onion, chopped |
| 1¼ | cups half & half |
| 1 | cup whipping cream |
| | Pinch of nutmeg |
| | Salt and black pepper |

---

Ludwig Van Beethoven: *Calm Sea and Prosperous Voyage, Op. 112*

# BAKED POTATO SOUP *Serves 6*

| | |
|---|---|
| 3 | cups peeled and diced potatoes |
| ½ | cup chopped onion |
| ¼ | cup chopped celery |
| 4 | cups low-salt chicken broth |
| 2 | cups milk |
| 3 | tablespoons butter |
| 1⅓ | cups sour cream |
| 2 | tablespoons flour |
| | Salt and black pepper |
| ½ | cup shredded cheddar cheese |
| 6 | strips bacon, cooked until crisp and crumbled |
| 2 | tablespoons chopped fresh chives |
| | Additional sour cream |

- Put potatoes, onion, celery, and broth into a 4-quart Dutch oven. Bring to a boil and cook until the potatoes are tender. Add milk and butter; stir well.

- Mix sour cream and flour together until smooth. Add this mixture to the soup and mix well. Cook for 10 minutes over low heat, stirring occasionally.

- Ladle soup into bowls. Pass cheese, bacon, chives, and additional sour cream for topping soup.

**Variations:** *For a more traditional potato soup, mix the flour with 1 cup of half & half and omit the sour cream and other toppings. Mix in fresh herbs such as chives, thyme, or sage. Sprinkle with fresh parsley.*

 Benjamin Britten: *Four Sea Interludes:* II. Sunday Morning

# CAULIFLOWER-CHEDDAR CHOWDER

*Serves* 6

- Wash cauliflower and break into florets. Put cauliflower in a saucepan and cover with water. Bring to a boil and cook until very tender. Drain the cauliflower and mash it with a potato masher or fork.

- Melt butter in a large saucepan. Add green onions, then flour. Stir well and cook for 2 minutes. Add milk and half & half. Cook over medium heat until thickened, stirring constantly.

- Stir in the cauliflower and the broth. Heat through. Add the cheeses and remove from heat, stirring until the cheeses have melted. Season with salt and pepper.

| | |
|---|---|
| 1 | head cauliflower |
| 2 | tablespoons butter |
| 3 | tablespoons sliced green onions |
| 2 | tablespoons flour |
| 1½ | cups milk |
| 1½ | cups half & half |
| 1 | (14½-ounce) can low-salt chicken broth |
| ¾ | cup diced cheddar cheese |
| ¾ | cup diced Swiss cheese |
| | Salt and black pepper |

 Benjamin Britten: *Four Sea Interludes:* III. Moonlight

# SHERRIED CRAB SOUP

*Serves 4*

| | |
|---|---|
| ½ | pound fresh lump crabmeat |
| 2 | tablespoons butter |
| 2 | tablespoons flour |
| 3 | cups whole milk or skimmed evaporated milk |
| ½ | cup half & half |
| ⅛ | teaspoon white pepper |
| ¼ | cup dry sherry |

- Pick over crab, removing any cartilage. (King crab legs from the supermarket seafood counter are an excellent source of crabmeat for this recipe.) Set aside.

- Melt butter in heavy medium saucepan over low heat. Blend in flour. Cook for 1 minute, stirring constantly. Add milk and cook over low heat, stirring constantly, until a white sauce forms and mixture is thickened and bubbly.

- Stir in half & half, crabmeat, and pepper; cook over low until heated through, about 10 minutes (do not boil). Stir in sherry and cook 1 minute.

**Variations:** For a tasty Crab au Gratin, double butter and flour to 4 tablespoons each. Make white sauce as directed, adding half & half with the milk (mixture will be very thick). Divide crabmeat among four 15-ounce au gratin dishes or other ceramic dishes. Pour white sauce over crabmeat; top each dish with ⅓ cup shredded Swiss cheese. Broil until cheese is browned and bubbly.

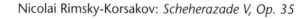
Nicolai Rimsky-Korsakov: *Scheherazade V, Op. 35*

# FRESH CORN AND CHICKEN SOUP

*Serves 6*

- Using sharp knife, slice corn kernels from cobs. Scrape the dull side of knife blade down the cob to release the milk. Discard cobs and set corn aside.

- Melt butter in large saucepan. Add celery and red pepper; sauté for 2 minutes. Add okra and garlic and sauté 1 minute longer. Add broth and bring to simmer over medium heat. Cook 20 minutes or until vegetables are tender.

- Gradually add corn and milk, stirring constantly. Simmer for 5 minutes. Season with salt and pepper.

- Stir in chicken; bring to simmer. Season with salt and pepper.

| | |
|---|---|
| 4 | ears of fresh corn |
| 1 | tablespoon butter |
| ½ | cup diced celery |
| ½ | cup diced red bell pepper |
| ½ | cup sliced okra |
| 1 | clove garlic, minced |
| 2 | (14½-ounce) cans low-salt chicken broth |
| 1 | cup diced cooked chicken |
| 2 | cups hot milk |
| | Salt and black pepper |

Leroy Anderson: *Chicken Reel*

# CALYPSO SOUP

*Serves 6*

| | |
|---|---|
| 1 | pound bulk pork sausage |
| 1 | large onion, chopped |
| 4 | medium sweet potatoes, peeled and cut into 1½-inch pieces |
| 4 | cups chicken stock or low-salt chicken broth |
| 2 | cups water |
| 2 | teaspoons cinnamon |
| ½ | teaspoon ground cloves |
| 1 | teaspoon ground coriander |
| 1 | teaspoon turmeric |
| ½ | teaspoon cardamom |
| 1 | teaspoon cumin |
| ¼ | teaspoon red pepper flakes |
| ¾ | cup canned or shelled roasted peanuts (optional) |

- Brown sausage and onion in a Dutch oven. Use paper towel to blot away as much fat as possible. Add sweet potatoes and all spices; sauté 2 minutes more.

- Add stock and water. Bring to boil. Reduce heat to simmer; cover and cook until sweet potatoes are just tender.

- Ladle into bowls. Add peanuts just before serving or pass the bowl and allow diners to serve themselves.

*The cinnamon, cloves, coriander, turmeric, cardamom, and cumin can be replaced by 2 tablespoons curry powder.*

*This highly-flavored soup calls for a big Zinfandel, bold and heavy with flavors of berry and spice, or a medium-bodied Syrah. If you feel that you can dine without wine, try an Asian beer.*

 Jean Michel Jesre: *Calypso I:* "En Enterdant Cousteau"

# WHITE CORN SOUP WITH SAUTÉED SCALLOPS

*Serves 6*

- Bring broth to boil in a large saucepan. Add 5 cups of corn and return to boil. Reduce heat and simmer for 2 minutes or until corn is barely tender. Transfer mixture to blender. Add ¼ cup half & half; puree until smooth and light. Return soup to saucepan and stir in remaining half & half.

- In a skillet, melt the butter and fry the remaining 1 cup of corn over high heat. Use a splatter screen to prevent corn from popping out of pan. When corn is well browned, transfer with slotted spoon to bowl lined with paper towel. Add scallops to the same skillet; sauté over high heat, searing on both sides and cooking an additional 3 to 5 minutes until just cooked through. Lightly salt and pepper the scallops.

- Bring soup to a simmer. The texture should be very light and fluffy and quite thick. If it seems thin, add a few tablespoons of whipping cream. Ladle soup into wide,shallow bowls. Place 2 scallops in the center of each bowl. Sprinkle the fried corn around the scallops and grind black pepper over the top.

**Variations:** *Avoid extra carbohydrates by making this Summer Squash Soup; simply replace corn with boiled or steamed squash.*

🍷 *A bold and buttery California Chardonnay with plenty of pear spice and honey will work beautifully with this first course.*

| | |
|---|---|
| 1 | (14½-ounce) can low-salt chicken broth |
| 6 | cups white corn kernels, fresh or frozen |
| 1 | cup half & half |
| 3 | tablespoons butter |
| 12 | large sea scallops |
| | Salt and black pepper |
| | Freshly ground black pepper |

*Wine. . .is a necessary tonic, a luxury, and a fitting tribute to good food.*

*Colette*

SOUPS 85

# CHICKEN AND SAUSAGE GUMBO

*Serves 8 to 10*

| | |
|---|---|
| 1 | pound andouille or other spicy smoked sausages |
| 1 | (3- to 4-pound) whole fryer |
| 3 | stalks celery, chopped |
| ½ | bunch parsley, stemmed and chopped |
| 1 | medium green bell pepper, chopped |
| 1 | large yellow onion, chopped |
| | Chicken base (found in jar in soup section) |
| | Salt and freshly ground black pepper |
| 1 | cup peanut oil or vegetable oil |
| 1 | cup flour |
| | Cayenne pepper |
| | Hot cooked rice |
| | Filé powder |

- Cut sausages in half lengthwise, then slice crosswise into ½-inch thick half circles. Brown the sausage in a skillet; drain and set aside.

- Place chicken in a stockpot with 6 quarts of water. Add half the celery, parsley, pepper, and onion, the chicken base (adds to richness of stock; add a little, a lot, or omit completely), and salt and freshly ground black pepper. Bring to a boil; reduce heat to simmer, cover partly, and cook until chicken is very tender, skimming once or twice. Remove chicken from pot. When cool enough to handle, remove skin and bones from chicken, leaving fairly large chunks of meat. Chill chicken stock and remove fat from top.

- Make a roux with equal parts of oil and flour blended in a large skillet until smooth. Cook over medium-low heat, stirring constantly during the first 10 minutes and then frequently after that, until the mixture reaches a rich chocolate color. When it looks like peanut butter, it's about half done. Do not turn the heat up higher to speed the process; the flour will burn and the result will be a bitter, burnt flavor instead of a deep nutty flavor. A good roux requires patience and commitment. With luck it will be ready in about 20 to 30 minutes, but it could take an hour or longer. Watch very carefully at the end to avoid scorching.

# CHICKEN AND SAUSAGE GUMBO *continued*

- Remove roux from heat and add remaining vegetables. Stir for 1 minute. Bring stock to boil and add vegetable-roux mixture. Simmer about 30 minutes.

- Add the sausage and simmer about 20 minutes. Add the boned chicken and simmer 5 to 10 minutes more. Season with cayenne pepper to taste, and then add a bit more cayenne.

- To serve, place a mound of rice in the bottom of each bowl. Ladle gumbo on top. Pass filé powder for sprinkling on top.

**Variations:** For a Duck Gumbo, omit the chicken and sausage; substitute 2½ pounds of cooked duck meat (prepared like the chicken in this recipe) added in the last 15 minutes of cooking. For a Seafood Gumbo, omit chicken and sausage; add 2 pounds of peeled and deveined medium shrimp, 1 pint of oysters, and 4 soft shell crabs, halved (optional).

The first man gets the oyster; the second man gets the shell.

*Andrew Carnegie*

Beethoven: Overture to "The Creatures of Prometheus," Op. 43

# HEARTY TORTELLINI SOUP

*Serves 8*

2 (28-ounce) cans diced tomatoes with liquid
3 (14½-ounce) cans beef broth
2 tablespoons chopped fresh basil
1 tablespoon chopped fresh rosemary
1 teaspoon fresh thyme leaves
½ teaspoon freshly ground black pepper
1 medium zucchini, halved lengthwise and sliced crosswise into ¼-inch half circles
¾ pound green beans, trimmed and cut into thirds
¾ pound sweet Italian sausage, casings removed, crumbled, browned, and drained
1 (9-ounce) package fresh tortellini with cheese
Freshly grated Parmesan cheese

- Combine tomatoes with their liquid, broth, basil, rosemary, thyme, and pepper in stockpot. Bring to boil.

- Reduce heat and add zucchini, green beans, and sausage. Simmer for 10 minutes. Add tortellini and cook until tender, about 5 to 7 minutes.

- Ladle into shallow soup bowls and top with Parmesan cheese. Garnish with a sprig of one of the herbs used in the soup.

 Benjamin Britten: *Four Sea Interludes:* IV. Storm

# TORTELLINI SOUP WITH BABY SPINACH

*Serves 4*

- In small skillet or saucepan, sauté garlic in oil over medium heat until golden. Remove to cutting board and slice.

- In large saucepan, bring broth to boil. Add garlic and tortellini. Cook until tortellini is nearly done.

- Add spinach and thyme to the soup. Stir gently until spinach is wilted.

- Ladle into bowls and sprinkle with Parmesan cheese.

6 small cloves garlic, peeled
2 teaspoons olive oil
3 (14½-ounce) cans low-salt chicken broth
1 teaspoon fresh thyme or ¼ teaspoon dried
1 (9-ounce) package fresh tortellini (stuffed with cheese or Italian sausage)
1 (10-ounce) package baby spinach leaves
½ cup freshly grated Parmesan cheese

Claude Debussy: "La Mer"

# OXTAIL SOUP

*Serves 8*

| | |
|---|---|
| 2 | pounds oxtails |
| | Salt and black pepper |
| 2 | large carrots, peeled |
| 2 | large leeks |
| 1 | tablespoon butter |
| 1 | tablespoon olive oil |
| | Pinch of sugar |
| | Fresh thyme |
| | Beef base (optional) |
| | Freshly ground black pepper |

- Put oxtails in a shallow roasting pan and season liberally with salt and pepper. Roast at 425° until they are well-browned, turning pieces as necessary.

- While the oxtails are browning, cut carrots and leeks into ¼-inch dice. Melt butter with oil in stockpot. Add vegetables and a pinch of sugar; cook over low heat until they caramelize to a rich brown.

- Transfer the browned oxtails to the stockpot, scraping up any browned bits. Cover the oxtails and vegetables with water. Add thyme, beef base (optional), and freshly ground pepper to taste. Bring to a boil; reduce heat, cover, and simmer.

- Test seasonings, adding more as needed to make the stock tasty without disguising the meat flavor. When the oxtails are tender, remove from pot and let cool. Chill stock.

- Skim excess fat from top of chilled stock. Remove meat from bones and return meat to stockpot. Reheat before serving.

Wine makes every meal an occasion, every table more elegant, every day more civilized.

*Andre Simon*

Alberto Ginastera: *Danzas Argentinas, Op. 2:* "Danza Del Viejo Boyero" ("Dance of the Old Ox Driver")

# LEITMOTIFS *Brunch Dishes*

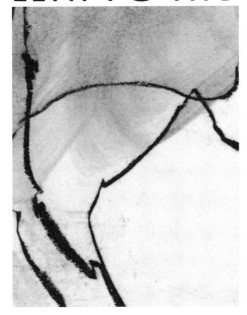

# BRUNCH BUFFET FOR 12 TO 20

A cheerful look makes a dish a feast.

*George Herbert*

Royal Frozen Mimosas or Peach Spritzers

Morning Glory Muffins

Bread of the Islands

Lemon-Poppyseed Scones

Warm Pear and Cherry Conserve with Triple Ginger

Frittata

Southwestern Spoonbread

Ham Cakes with Mango Salsa

Oven-Grilled Veggies (asparagus, red bell pepper)

Spinach, Cheese, and Tomato Pie

 Ottorino Respighi: *Feste Romane (Roman Festival)*

# SAVORY GRITS

*Serves 2 to 4*

- Bring water to boil in medium saucepan. Stir in grits and salt. Cover and simmer until thick, 5 to 10 minutes, stirring occasionally.

- Add butter and stir until melted. Add eggs and stir vigorously until they are incorporated into the mixture (grits will fluff up). Cover and cook for 2 minutes, stirring twice. Add cheese and cook until cheese melts, about 1 minute longer.

| | |
|---|---|
| 2 | cups water |
| ⅓ | cup quick cooking grits (not instant) |
| ½ | teaspoon salt |
| 1 | tablespoon butter |
| 2 | eggs |
| 2 | ounces cheese (Swiss, cheddar, or American), diced or shredded |

*The grits can be served in 1 large bowl or in individual ramekins or custard cups. If you use cheddar cheese, try serving Garden Salsa (see page 21) or Salsa Diablo (see page 65) alongside. This can serve as a brunch main dish or as a side dish.*

 "A Little Taste" as performed by Cannonball Adderly

BRUNCH DISHES 93

# HOMINY SOUFFLÉ

*Serves 6 to 8*

| | |
|---|---|
| 2¼ | cups milk |
| ½ | cup quick cooking grits (not instant) |
| 1 | teaspoon salt |
| ½ | cup butter |
| 4 | egg yolks |
| ¼ | cup grated Parmesan cheese |
| 6 | egg whites |
| ½ | teaspoon cream of tartar |

- Heat milk in medium saucepan. When it begins to boil, add grits and salt, pouring grits slowly and stirring constantly. Lower heat; cover and cook, stirring frequently, for about 15 minutes or until thick. Add butter and stir until melted. Add egg yolks and cheese; stir well. Cool for at least 10 minutes.

- Beat egg whites with cream of tartar until stiff but not dry. Beat ¼ of egg whites into grits mixture. Fold in remaining egg whites.

- Pour into a greased 2-quart casserole and bake at 350° for 30 to 40 minutes or until set and golden on top.

 Edvard Grieg: *Holberg Suite*

# BANANA OMELETTE

*Serves 2*

- Beat together eggs, sour cream, and water.

- Melt butter in a medium omelette pan or 10-inch skillet. Pour egg mixture into the pan, swirling to distribute evenly to edges. Slice banana onto top of eggs. Add plenty of salt and freshly ground black pepper.

- Cover and cook over medium-low heat until set. Fold omelette in half and serve.

4 eggs, preferably brown
2 tablespoons sour cream, regular or low-fat
Splash of water
1 small banana
1 tablespoon butter
Salt and freshly ground black pepper

> Truly there would be reason to go mad were it not for music.
>
> *Tchaikovsky*

 Georges Bizet: *Carmen:* "Toreador Song"

# BRIE OMELETTE

*Serves 1 to 2*

| | |
|---|---|
| 1 | tablespoon butter |
| 3 | eggs |
| 1 | teaspoon fresh thyme |
| 1 | teaspoon minced chives |
| ¼ | teaspoon cracked black pepper |
| ½ | cup of cubed Brie, rind removed |

- Melt butter in omelette pan. Beat eggs until creamy. When butter foam subsides, pour eggs into pan. Lift edges to allow liquid to run underneath.

- When omelette is ⅔ cooked, sprinkle half with thyme, chives, and pepper; sprinkle the other half with Brie cubes. Cover and allow to cook until the eggs are just set and the cheese is melting. Fold omelette in half and serve, garnishing with additional whole or chopped herbs.

 Georges Bizet: *Carmen:* "Habanera"

# FRITTATA

*Serves 4 to 6*

- Cover the bottom of a large cast iron or other heavy ovenproof skillet with olive oil. Add the potatoes, onion, bell pepper, and garlic. Sauté over medium heat until the potatoes are brown on all sides, adding more oil if necessary to avoid sticking.

- Add mushrooms and ripe olives. Sauté until mushrooms release their liquid and the liquid begins to evaporate, about 3 minutes. Sprinkle the cheeses evenly on top of the vegetables; pour the egg mixture over all.

- Bake at 350° until eggs are set and top of frittata puffs up. Remove from oven and let stand for 5 minutes before cutting into slices.

|      | Olive oil |
|------|-----------|
| 3-4  | medium russet potatoes, peeled and diced |
| 1    | medium onion, chopped |
| ½    | bell pepper, chopped |
| 2    | cloves garlic, pressed or minced |
| 4    | ounces fresh mushrooms, sliced |
| 3    | ounces ripe olives, sliced |
| 8    | eggs, lightly beaten |
| ½    | cup shredded cheddar cheese |
| ½    | cup shredded Monterey Jack cheese |
| ¼    | cup Parmesan cheese |

**Variations:** *This wonderful recipe lends itself to an infinite number of variations. Cheeses such as Swiss cheese, feta cheese, goat cheese, even cream cheese can be substituted for those listed here. Try your favorite vegetable and meat combinations. Some good choices are bacon, onion, and zucchini (perhaps with some chopped tomato); mushroom and fresh spinach or chard; zucchini and yellow squash with chopped tomatoes and lots of fresh herbs; bacon, corn, black olive, and avocado; grilled or roasted onion and red pepper (always grill extra veggies—you'll find a dozen ways to use them).*

Johann Sebastian Bach: *Magnificat in D*

BRUNCH DISHES

# ARTICHOKE SOUFFLÉ        *Serves 8*

|   |   |
|---|---|
|   | Butter |
|   | Dry breadcrumbs |
| 2 | (10-ounce) packages frozen artichokes |
|   | Salt and black pepper |
| 4 | tablespoons butter |
| ½ | flour |
| 2 | cups milk |
| 2 | cups Gruyère or Swiss cheese, shredded |
| 2 | whole eggs |
| 2 | egg yolks |
| 2 | egg whites |

- Butter a 2-quart soufflé dish and coat lightly with dry breadcrumbs. Set aside.

- Cook artichokes in boiling water until just tender. Drain and sauté in a small amount of butter; season with salt and pepper. Set aside.

- Melt 4 tablespoons butter in a medium saucepan. Stir in flour and cook for 2 minutes over medium heat. Slowly add milk, stirring or whisking constantly, until sauce begins to thicken and bubble.

- Remove sauce from heat and quickly stir in cheese. Add whole eggs and egg yolks one at a time, stirring vigorously after each addition. Stir in artichokes and allow mixture to cool slightly. Beat the egg whites until stiff; carefully fold into the mixture in two additions.

- Transfer the soufflé mixture into the prepared dish. Bake at 350° for 1 hour or until knife tip inserted in center comes out clean. The soufflé can be unmolded. Don't worry if it falls; simply slice and serve.

 Michael Franks: *Dragonfly Summer:* "Practice Makes Perfect"

# FRESH ASPARAGUS AND EGG CASSEROLE

*Serves 4 to 6*

- Snap the tough ends off the asparagus. Blanch spears in boiling water for 1 minute. Set aside.

- Melt butter in small skillet or saucepan. Add both onions and cook until tender. Stir in flour and cook, stirring frequently, for 2 minutes. Gradually add milk and cook until smooth and thick, stirring constantly. Season with salt and pepper to taste.

- In a greased 6-inch by 10-inch glass baking dish, layer the asparagus and the sliced eggs. Pour the cream sauce over all. Top with cheese and buttered crumbs. Bake at 350° for 20 minutes or until top is lightly browned and casserole is heated through. Garnish with fresh herbs or green onions, asparagus tips, or sliced toasted almonds.

| | |
|---|---|
| 1 | pound fresh asparagus |
| 3 | tablespoons butter |
| 1 | tablespoon grated onion |
| 3 | tablespoons chopped green onions |
| 2 | tablespoons flour |
| 1 | cup milk |
| | Salt and black pepper |
| 3 | hard-boiled eggs, sliced |
| ½ | cup shredded sharp cheese |
| ½ | cup buttered breadcrumbs |

 "Butter and Egg Man" as performed by Louis Armstrong

BRUNCH DISHES

# SPINACH, CHEESE, AND TOMATO PIE

*Serves 6*

**Parmesan Pie Crust**
1¼ cups flour
¼ cup grated Parmesan cheese
¼ teaspoon salt
¼ cup butter
2 tablespoons ice water

- Stir flour, cheese, and salt together. Cut in butter with pastry blender or two forks until mixture resembles coarse crumbs.

- Sprinkle water over flour mixture. Toss with fork until pastry holds together, adding up to 2 more tablespoons ice water if necessary.

- Shape dough into a ball and flatten slightly. Wrap and refrigerate for at least 30 minutes.

- Roll pastry out on lightly floured surface, making an 11-inch round. Transfer to a 9-inch pie plate. Fold edge of pastry under to form stand-up edge. Prick bottom and sides of pastry several times with a fork.

- Line pie shell with aluminum foil. Fill with pastry weights or dried beans. Bake at 425° for 5 minutes or until set. Allow to cool in pie plate on wire rack. Remove weights and foil.

Johannes Brahms: *Concerto in A minor for Violin, Cello & Orchestra, Op. 102*

# SPINACH, CHEESE, AND TOMATO PIE *continued*

- Combine cottage cheese, milk, egg, flour, and mint in blender or processor. Whirl or pulse until smooth.

- Heat oil in a large skillet over medium heat. Add onion and sauté 2 minutes. Add garlic and sauté for 1 additional minute. Add tomatoes, salt, and pepper; sauté for 2 minutes. Add spinach; cook for 3 to 5 minutes or until spinach is tender and liquid evaporates.

- Transfer cottage cheese mixture to pastry shell. Top with spinach mixture. Sprinkle Parmesan cheese on top. Bake at 375° for 30 minutes. Let stand at least 20 minutes before serving warm or at room temperature. Cut into 6 wedges.

*Filling*

| | |
|---|---|
| 1 | cup cottage cheese, regular or low-fat |
| ¼ | cup milk, regular or low-fat |
| 1 | egg |
| 2 | tablespoons flour |
| ⅛ | teaspoon dried mint, crumbled |
| 1 | tablespoon vegetable oil |
| ¾ | cup chopped green onions |
| 1 | large clove garlic, minced |
| 8 | ounces plum tomatoes, seeded and finely chopped |
| ⅛ | teaspoon salt |
| ⅛ | teaspoon black pepper |
| 12 | ounces fresh spinach, chopped |
| 1 | teaspoon grated Parmesan cheese |

# TOMATO-CHEESE TART  *Serves 6*

| | |
|---|---|
| 1 | Parmesan Pie Crust, see page 100 |
| 2 | tablespoons Dijon mustard |
| 3 | tomatoes, sliced |
| 2 | cups shredded Swiss or Gruyère cheese |
| 2 | tablespoons Herbes de Provence |
|   | Salt and black pepper |
| 2 | tablespoons olive oil |
| 1 | tablespoon Parmesan cheese |
| 1 | tablespoon mozzarella cheese |

- Roll Parmesan pastry out to an 11-inch round. Transfer to a 10-inch tart pan with removable bottom.

- Spread mustard on bottom of pie crust. Top with slices of tomato. Cover tomatoes with Swiss or Gruyère cheese. Add herbs, salt, and pepper. Drizzle with olive oil and top with garnishing cheeses.

- Bake at 400° for 40 to 45 minutes or until well browned. Cut into wedges to serve.

 Heitor Berlioz: *Symphonie Fantastique, Op. 14:* I. Reveries - Passions

# RATATOUILLE PIZZA

*Serves 3 to 4*

- Spread crust with olive oil and pesto sauce. Cover with Ratatouille. Top with cheeses and olives.

- Bake on pizza stone heated to 400° or on pizza pan in center of 400° oven for 10 to 15 minutes.

| | |
|---|---|
| 1 | 10-inch pizza crust, freshly made or store bought |
| 1 | tablespoon olive oil |
| 3 | tablespoons Classic Pesto, see page 326 |
| 2 | cups Garden Fresh Ratatouille, see page 219 |
| 1 | cup feta cheese, crumbled |
| ½-1 | cup freshly grated Parmesan cheese |
| 10 | Niçoise or other brine-cured olives, pitted and slivered |

Without question, the greatest invention in the history of mankind is beer. Oh, I grant you that the wheel was also a fine invention, but the wheel does not go nearly as well with pizza.

*Dave Barr*

Antonio Vivaldi: *Concerto in C for Diverse Instruments*

# GRILLED VEGGIE FOCACCIA SANDWICH

*Serves 2 to 4*

| | |
|---|---|
| 1 | 12-inch focaccia or pizza crust |
| | Olive oil |
| 1 | cup shredded provolone cheese |
| ¼ | cup grated Parmesan cheese |
| 2½ | cups Oven-Grilled Veggies, see page 206 |
| 2 | tablespoons chopped basil |
| 2 | teaspoons balsamic vinegar |

- Place focaccia on baking sheet. Spritz or brush with olive oil. Spread cheeses evenly over crust and bake at 425° until cheese is melted and crust is crisp but not hard and crunchy. Remove from oven and let rest 10 minutes.

- Cut crust in half down center. Arrange Veggies on 1 half. Sprinkle with basil and vinegar. Top with remaining half and press down. Cut the half circle into 4 wedges. Serve 1 to 2 wedges per person.

*These make great picnic fare, delicious either warm or room temperature. Wrap each sandwich wedge in foil and put wrapped sandwiches into 250° oven. Just before leaving the house, remove foil-wrapped sandwiches and place in a basket or insulated bag.*

Nicolai Rimsky-Korsakov: *Scheherazade, Op. 35:* "Le recit du Prince Kalender"

# ROAST BEEF AND BRIE SANDWICH

*Serves 2*

- Cut baguette crosswise in half. Cut each half horizontally into a top and bottom.

- On bottom halves, arranged the sliced Brie. Top with roast beef slices.

- Divide the mayonnaise between the two top halves and spread to edges. Place top half on roast beef. Cut each sandwich on the diagonal into two pieces.

| | |
|---|---|
| 1 | crusty baguette or 2 sandwich rolls |
| 4 | ounces rare roast beef, thinly sliced |
| 2 | ounces Brie cheese, thinly sliced |
| 1/3 | cup Rosemary-Horseradish Mayonnaise, see page 341 |

> Lots of people think a song without singing is not a song. Tell that to Beethoven and he'll kick your ass.
>
> *Eddie Van Halen*

 Aaron Copland: *Rodeo:* Four Dance Episodes

# ONION TART

*Serves 6*

|     |                                          |
|-----|------------------------------------------|
|     | Parmesan Pie Crust, see page 100         |
| 3½  | cups thinly sliced onions                |
| 3   | tablespoons butter                       |
| ½   | cup milk                                 |
| 1½  | cups sour cream                          |
| 1   | teaspoon salt                            |
| 3   | tablespoons flour                        |
| 2   | eggs, well beaten                        |
| 3   | slices bacon, cooked and crumbled        |

- Roll out Parmesan Pie Crust to 11-inch round. Transfer to 10-inch tart pan with removable bottom.

- Sauté onions in butter in a large skillet until lightly browned. Spoon into tart crust. Add milk and 1¼ cups sour cream.

- Mix flour with remaining sour cream and salt. Mix in eggs and bacon. Pour over the onion mixture in the crust.

- Bake pie at 325° until set in center, about 22 minutes.

**Variations:** Sprinkle 1½ cups shredded Jarlsberg or Emmental cheese over top before baking.

Life is like an onion; you peel it off one layer at a time, and sometimes you weep.

*Carl Sandburg*

 Wolfgang Amadeus Mozart: *The Magic Flute:* "The Queen of the Night's Aria" ("Ach, ich Funls")

# CURRIED CHICKEN AND DRIED CHERRY SALAD

*Serves 4*

- Mix the spices into the mayonnaise in a medium bowl. Stir in the cherries and allow to stand for 5 minutes. Mix in the chicken and chill.

*1 tablespoon of curry powder can replace the spices. Spices can be doubled for a bolder flavor, and mayonnaise can be doubled for a creamier dish.*

*Serve over lettuce for a meal. For an appetizer, serve in a shallow bowl with toast points or toasted baguette slices.*

| | |
|---|---|
| ½ | cup mayonnaise |
| ½ | teaspoon turmeric |
| ½ | teaspoon ground cumin |
| ½ | teaspoon ground coriander |
| ½ | teaspoon ground clove |
| 3 | ounces (about ⅔ cup) dried cherries |
| 2 | cups diced, cooked chicken breast (premium canned chicken will work) |

Orlando Gibbons: "Dainty Fine Bird"

# TOMATOES AND FRESH MOZZARELLA WITH CAPONATA AND PEPERONATA

*Serves 6 to 8*

- 2 tablespoons chopped fresh basil
- 1-2 tablespoons olive oil
- 6 yellow Roma tomatoes
- 6 red Roma tomatoes
- 1 pound fresh mozzarella
- Caponata
- Peperonata

- Mix basil and oil and let stand until platter is assembled.

- Slice the tomatoes and the cheese into 1/3-inch slices. Arrange alternating slices of the two colors of tomatoes and the cheese around the edge of a large round platter.

- Place the Caponata and Peperonata side by side in the center of the platter.

- Drizzle the olive oil and basil mixture over the tomatoes and cheese. Sprinkle entire platter with additional chopped basil if desired. Serve at room temperature with crusty bread or toasted baguette slices.

### Caponata
- 1 large eggplant
- 4 tablespoons olive oil
- 6-10 large cloves garlic
- 1/4 cup thinly sliced celery
- 2 tomatoes, chopped
- 2 tablespoons fresh oregano
- 2 teaspoons dried oregano (substitute 1 tablespoon dried for both oreganos)
- 1 tablespoon capers
- 1/4 cup pitted Greek olives, halved

- Cut eggplant into 1-inch cubes. Immerse in heavily salted water for 20 minutes. Drain and rinse.

- Heat 2 tablespoons olive oil in nonstick skillet. Halve garlic cloves and add to skillet. Reduce heat to medium-low and cook garlic until just golden (don't scorch). Remove to small dish.

- Add celery to skillet and sauté at medium heat for 2 minutes. Add eggplant and 1 additional tablespoon oil. Sauté for 1 minute. Add tomatoes, garlic, and oregano. Cover and cook over medium

# TOMATOES AND FRESH MOZZARELLA *continued*

- heat until eggplant is very tender, about 15 minutes. If necessary, add water 1 tablespoon at a time to keep mixture from sticking. When eggplant is very tender, remove lid and allow juice to be absorbed.

- Add remaining 1 tablespoon oil to mixture. Season with salt and pepper. Allow to cool to room temperature.

- Heat oil in a nonstick skillet. Halve, seed, and slice peppers. Add onion slices and peppers to pan. Sauté at medium-high heat for about 2 minutes; do not brown. Reduce heat to low and cook slowly until peppers are tender, about 30 to 40 minutes.

- Sprinkle with fresh thyme. Add vinegar and season with salt and pepper. Allow to cool to room temperature.

1/3 cup pitted green olives, halved
2 tablespoons chopped fresh parsley
Salt and black pepper

*Peperonata*

2 tablespoons olive oil
1 large yellow bell pepper
1 large red bell pepper
1 large orange bell pepper (can be replaced by additional red or yellow pepper)
1 medium onion, halved lengthwise and thinly sliced across
1 tablespoon fresh thyme or lemon thyme
1 tablespoon balsamic vinegar
Salt and black pepper

# MADRAS RICE AND CHICKEN SALAD

*Serves 6 to 10*

4 cups chicken stock
1 cup wild rice
1 cup brown rice
4 boneless, skinless chicken breast halves, cooked and cubed
1 cup chopped toasted pecans
3 green onions, sliced
½ cup golden raisins
½ cup chopped celery
2 teaspoons shredded orange zest
    Madras Vinaigrette
2 tablespoons minced fresh chives or parsley

*Madras Vinaigrette*
¼ cup rice vinegar
¼ cup fresh orange juice
2 tablespoons Dijon mustard
2 tablespoons mango chutney
1 teaspoon salt
¼ teaspoon white pepper
¼-½ cup canola oil

- Bring chicken stock to boil in a large saucepan. Stir in wild rice. Reduce heat; cover and simmer 10 minutes. Add brown rice; cover and simmer an additional 30 to 35 minutes or until liquid is absorbed. Remove from heat and cool to room temperature.

- Combine rice, chicken, pecans, green onions, raisins, celery, and orange zest in a large bowl. Pour vinaigrette over rice mixture. Toss gently until thoroughly combined. Refrigerate at least 4 hours or overnight for flavors to blend.

- To serve, bring to room temperature and sprinkle with chives or parsley.

- Whisk vinegar, orange juice, mustard, chutney, salt, and pepper in a small bowl until combined. Add oil slowly, whisking constantly, until slightly thickened and thoroughly combined.

 Robert Schumann: *Quintet in E-Flat for Piano & Strings, Op. 44*

# PASTA WITH BURNT BUTTER AND CHEESE

*Serves 2 to 4*

- Cook pasta according to package directions. Remove from heat when just tender and drain.

- While pasta is cooking, melt butter in a small saucepan over medium heat. Continue cooking butter until it turns very dark brown and releases a nutty fragrance (do not burn).

- Transfer pasta to large bowl. Sprinkle liberally with salt and pepper and the Parmesan cheese; toss thoroughly. Pour hot butter over the pasta and toss until well coated. Serve immediately.

10 ounces fresh or dry pasta
3 tablespoons butter
¼ cup grated Parmesan cheese
Salt and freshly ground black pepper

No man is lonely eating spaghetti; it requires so much attention.

*Christopher Morley*

"Oodles of Noodles" as performed by Jimmy Dorsey

# THAI PEANUT CHICKEN AND NOODLE SALAD

*Serves 4 to 6*

| | |
|---|---|
| 10 | ounces snow peas, trimmed |
| 2 | large red bell peppers |
| 18-20 | ounces fresh linguine |
| 1 | cup thinly sliced green onions |
| 3 | cups sliced roasted chicken breast |
| | Spicy Peanut Dressing |

- Bring a large pot of water to boil over high heat. Add snow peas and blanch for 30 seconds. Remove with a slotted spoon to a bowl of ice water to stop cooking process. Pat dry and slice diagonally into ½-inch pieces. Stem and seed red bell peppers and slice into thin strips.

- Return pot of water to boil. Add linguine and cook until barely tender, about 2 minutes. Rinse under cold water and drain well.

- Toss snow peas, bell peppers, green onions, and linguine with half of the dressing and transfer to large serving bowl or platter. Arrange chicken on top. Drizzle remaining dressing over top of chicken and noodles. Serve, tossing once more at table.

 "Peanut Vendor" as performed by Stan Kenton

# THAI PEANUT CHICKEN AND NOODLE SALAD *continued*

- Mix peanut oil, soy sauce, brown sugar, sesame oil, and garlic in a medium bowl.

- Use a zester to shred the zest from the limes and the orange. Juice the fruit. Add juice and zest to dressing mixture. Remove the stems from the chiles and slice into thin rounds. Add to dressing. Blend in peanut butter.

- Allow dressing to stand for at least 30 minutes before using. The dressing will keep in the refrigerator for 3 days but will get much hotter as it stands.

**Variations:** *Omit peanut butter for a wonderful Asian Sesame-Soy Vinaigrette.*

*This dressing makes a fabulous dip for vegetables or for chicken or shrimp skewers.*

*These hot and spicy flavors call for a medium-sweet German wine such as a Riesling. With a dish of this sort, you can always give up on wine and pour a chilled Asian beer.*

### Spicy Peanut Dressing

| | |
|---|---|
| 4 | tablespoons peanut oil |
| 4 | tablespoons soy sauce |
| 2 | tablespoons (packed) dark brown sugar |
| 1½ | tablespoons toasted sesame oil |
| 1-2 | tablespoons minced garlic |
| 2 | limes |
| 1 | small orange |
| 2 | small serrano chiles |
| ½ | cup chunky peanut butter |

BRUNCH DISHES

# PASTA GREMOLATA

*Serves 2*

- 3 tablespoons olive oil
- ⅓ cup minced parsley
- 1 tablespoon shredded lemon zest
- 2 large cloves of garlic, minced
- 10 ounces fresh or dry pasta
- Salt and freshly ground black pepper

- Mix oil, parsley, lemon zest, and garlic in a small bowl. Allow to stand for at least ½ hour.

- Cook pasta until just tender; toss with oil mixture until well coated. Season to taste with salt and freshly ground pepper.

We may live without friends; we may live without books; but civilized man cannot live without cooks.

*Bulwer Lytton*

Johannes Brahms: *Sonata #1 in G for Violin & Piano, Op. 78*

# PASTA WITH GARLIC AND HOT PEPPERS

*Serves 2*

- Mix pressed garlic into oil and allow to stand for at least 30 minutes.
- Cook pasta according to package directions until just tender. Drain.
- Heat the garlic-oil mixture in a large skillet. Sauté the minced peppers in the oil for 1 minute. Add pasta to skillet and toss until thoroughly coated with oil. Season with salt and pepper. Serve immediately.

| | |
|---|---|
| 2 | tablespoons olive oil |
| 3 | garlic cloves, pressed |
| 10 | ounces fresh or dry pasta |
| 1 | tablespoon minced hot red pepper (cayenne, red serrano, red jalapeño) |
| | Salt and black pepper |

Claude Debussy: *Preludes, Book I:* "La fille aux cheveus de lin" ("The girl with the flaxen hair")

# GREEK PASTA

*Serves 8*

| | |
|---|---|
| 16 | ounces pasta (rotini or small shells) |
| 1 | tablespoon olive oil |
| 1 | bunch green onions, sliced |
| 2 | cloves garlic, pressed or minced |
| 8 | ounces mushrooms, sliced |
| 2 | pounds fresh spinach, sliced, or 1 pound frozen spinach, thawed and squeezed |
| 1 | cup half & half or 1½ cups evaporated skimmed milk |
| 2 | tablespoons chopped fresh dill |
| ½ | teaspoon salt |
| | Freshly ground black pepper |
| | Dash hot pepper sauce |
| 1 | cup peeled, seeded, and chopped tomatoes |
| ½ | cup crumbled feta cheese |

- Cook pasta according to package directions. Drain and keep warm.

- Heat the olive oil in a skillet. Sauté the onions, garlic, and mushrooms until soft. Add spinach, half & half (or evaporated milk), dill, salt, pepper, and hot pepper sauce; simmer until heated through, about 2 minutes. Stir in tomato and cook 1 minute more.

- Spoon mixture over hot pasta. Add feta cheese and toss well. Serve immediately.

 Erik Satie: "Ouverture A Danser"

# TORTELLINI WITH GREENS AND WALNUTS

*Serves 4*

- Cook tortellini according to package directions. Drain pasta; rinse saucepan.

- Using the same saucepan, heat olive oil and sauté the walnuts until lightly browned (don't scorch). Add hot pasta to pan along with greens. Toss gently. Add salt, pepper, and half the cheese; toss again.

- Transfer to a large serving platter and sprinkle the remaining cheese on top.

*This is a good "emergency" dish. If you don't have any fresh spinach or chard, open a bag of mixed salad greens and pick out some pieces of sturdy greens. Slice them for the pasta dish, and toss the remaining salad with an oil and vinegar dressing for a fast and fabulous meal.*

**Variations:** *Pine nuts make a good substitute for walnuts, or try chopped hazelnuts. Bleu cheese creates a whole new character for this dish. Finely sliced or chopped mustard or turnip greens add spunk—just add them with the walnuts.*

9 ounces fresh tortellini or ravioli stuffed with meat or cheese
2 tablespoons olive oil
⅓ cup broken walnuts
1 cup thinly sliced sturdy greens (spinach, chard, radicchio, endive, lettuce)
¼ cup Pecorino Romano or Parmesan cheese, freshly grated
Salt and freshly ground black pepper

A painter paints pictures on canvas, but musicians paint their pictures on silence.

*Leopold Stokowski*

Wolfgang Amadeus Mozart: *The Marriage of Figaro:* "Overture"

BRUNCH DISHES 117

# LINGUINE WITH BACON AND PEAS

*Serves 2*

- 8 ounces linguine
- 2 tablespoons butter
- 4 strips bacon
- 1 small onion, coarsely chopped
- 1 cup frozen green peas, thawed
- ¼ cup freshly grated Parmesan cheese
- Freshly ground black pepper

- Cook linguine according to package directions. Drain and rinse with cold water.

- Melt butter in a large skillet. Add bacon strips and cook until crisp. Remove strips and crumble.

- In the same pan with butter and bacon drippings, sauté the onion until just barely cooked but still slightly crunchy, about 3 minutes over medium heat. Add the peas and sauté for 2 minutes.

- Add the drained pasta. Stir well, cover, and cook until pasta is heated through, about 4 minutes, stirring occasionally.

- Transfer pasta to a large bowl or platter. Top with bacon and cheese and toss well. Serve immediately.

**Variations:** *Substitute 1 cup diced zucchini for the peas and add 1 cup of chopped fresh tomatoes with the pasta.*

 Gioacchino Reggini: *The Barber of Seville:* "Overture"

# PASTA WITH BACON, FRIED PECANS, AND CORN

*Serves 2*

- Cook penne according to package direction. Drain and rinse with cold water.

- Cook the bacon in a skillet until crisp. Remove strips and crumble. Sauté pecans in bacon drippings until just toasted (don't scorch). Remove pecans and reserve with bacon.

- Add corn to the same skillet. Sauté for 2 minutes or until golden. Add drained pasta and butter. Season with pepper. Toss until heated through. Transfer pasta to bowl or platter. Add bacon and pecans and toss well. Serve immediately.

10 ounces penne pasta
4 slices bacon
¼ cup broken pecans
1 cup frozen corn, thawed
1 tablespoon butter
Freshly ground black pepper

**Variations:** Add ¼ cup diced red bell pepper along with corn for a color and flavor kick.

Carl Nielsen: "Masquerade Overture"

# PASTA WITH PESTO CHICKEN AND RED PEPPERS

*Serves 4*

| | |
|---|---|
| 4 | boneless, skinless chicken breast halves (about 1½ pounds) |
| 1 | cup Classic Pesto, see page 326 |
| 1 | large red bell pepper |
| | Salt and black pepper |
| 1 | pound fresh pasta (fettuccine or linguine) |
| 1 | tablespoon olive oil |
| 2 | tablespoons butter |
| ½ | cup Parmesan cheese |

- Put chicken and ½ cup Classic Pesto into plastic zipper bag. Refrigerate for 1 hour, turning occasionally.

- While chicken is marinating, blacken the pepper over a gas burner or grill or in the broiler. Place pepper in paper bag for 5 minutes. Peel and seed the pepper; cut into matchstick strips.

- Coat heavy skillet with nonstick cooking spray. Place skillet over medium heat. Add chicken breasts and cook until light brown and done throughout, turning once. Transfer to cutting surface; tent and let rest 5 minutes. Slice diagonally. Place in bowl and season with salt and pepper; toss with remaining pesto.

- Cook pasta; drain and rinse with cold water. Return to saucepan with oil and butter; season with salt and pepper. Heat, covered, over medium-low, tossing frequently. Add pepper strips and toss.

- Mound pasta and peppers on large platter. Place chicken in center of pasta. Sprinkle cheese over entire dish. Garnish with basil if desired.

 George Gershwin: *Lady be Good:* "Little Jazzbird"

# CHICKEN-ARTICHOKE FETTUCCINE

*Serves 6 to 8*

- Cut chicken breasts into bite-size pieces. Heat oil in a skillet. Add garlic, onions, and chicken. Cook over medium-high heat until chicken is browned. Lower heat and add artichokes and black olives. Allow to stay warm on burner.

- In a large saucepan, melt the butter. Sprinkle in flour and cook for 2 minutes, stirring constantly. Add half & half, cheese, salt, and pepper. Cook over medium-low heat until cheese has melted and sauce has thickened.

- When sauce is thick, drain the chicken mixture, blotting excess oil, and stir into the sauce. Serve over hot fettuccine or toast points.

| | |
|---|---|
| 4-6 | boneless, skinless chicken breasts |
| 2 | tablespoons olive oil |
| 2 | cloves garlic, minced |
| ⅓ | cup chopped onions |
| 1 | (16-ounce) can artichokes, quartered |
| 1 | cup pitted ripe olives, halved lengthwise |
| ½ | cup butter |
| 1 | tablespoon flour |
| 1 | cup half & half, regular or low-fat |
| ½ | cup freshly grated Parmesan cheese |
| | Salt and black pepper |
| | Flour |

 Giacchino Rossini: *La Gazza Ladra:* "Overture"

# PASTA WITH HAM, BLEU CHEESE, AND WALNUTS

*Serves 6*

- 4 ounces Roquefort (or other bleu cheese), crumbled
- 4 ounces thinly sliced ham, preferably smoked, cut into small pieces
- 1 cup broken walnuts, toasted
- ½ cup chopped fresh parsley
- ½ cup chopped fresh rosemary
- 3 cloves garlic, minced
- 1½ teaspoons freshly ground black pepper
- ¾ cup olive oil
- ¼ cup dry white wine
- 1 pound linguine
- Freshly grated Parmesan cheese (optional)

- In a large bowl, combine cheese, ham, walnuts, parsley, rosemary, garlic, pepper, olive oil, and wine. Mix well and allow to stand at least 1 hour at room temperature to blend flavors.

- Cook pasta according to pasta directions until just barely done. Drain and toss the steaming hot pasta with the sauce. Top with Parmesan cheese if desired. Serve immediately.

Trying to understand modern art is like trying to follow the plot in a bowl of alphabet soup.

*Anonymous*

---

 Giuseppi Verdi: *Un Ballo In Maschera:* "Overture"

# HAM CAKES

*Serves 4 to 6*

- Combine ham and breadcrumbs; set aside.

- Melt 1 tablespoon butter in small skillet. Add onion and celery; sauté until soft. Toss onion and celery with ham.

- Beat together eggs, mustard, Worcestershire sauce, and pepper. Add egg mixture to ham and combine thoroughly.

- Using ¼ to ⅓ cup at a time, form mixture into thick patties or ovals. Refrigerate for at least 1 hour.

- Heat oil and remaining butter in a skillet. Cook cakes over medium high heat until dark golden, turning once, about 4 minutes per side. Top with Mango Salsa and serve immediately.

- Mix mango and lime juice in a medium bowl. Allow to stand at room temperature.

- Remove stems and seeds from jalapeños. Mince and add to mango along with red onion. Add salt and pepper to taste. Stir in cilantro.

- Cover salsa and refrigerate for at least 2 hours to allow flavors to develop. The salsa will keep for 2 days and is also delicious with tortilla chips.

2 cups finely chopped or ground ham
1 cup fresh breadcrumbs
2 tablespoons butter
½ cup finely chopped onion
½ cup finely chopped celery
2 eggs
2 teaspoons prepared yellow mustard
1 teaspoon Worcestershire sauce
¼ teaspoon pepper
2 tablespoons olive oil
Mango Salsa

*Mango Salsa*

2 cups diced peeled mango
2 tablespoons lime juice
2 jalapeño peppers
¼ cup finely chopped red onion
Salt and black pepper
½ cup chopped fresh cilantro (packed)

 Luckey Roberts: "Pork and Beans Rag"

# MARINATED SHRIMP SALAD

*Serves 6*

| | |
|---|---|
| ½ | cup white wine vinegar |
| ⅓ | cup olive oil |
| 6 | green onions, chopped |
| 3 | tablespoons chopped fresh parsley |
| 1 | clove garlic, pressed |
| 1½ | tablespoons minced fresh basil |
| 1 | tablespoon chopped fresh dill |
| 1 | teaspoon freshly ground black pepper |
| 1½ | pounds medium shrimp, cooked and cleaned |
| ½ | red onion, thinly sliced |

- In blender or food processor, whirl or pulse vinegar, oil, green onions, parsley, garlic, basil, dill, and pepper until smooth.

- In medium bowl, combine shrimp and red onion. Pour marinade over shrimp mixture. Stir until well coated. Cover and refrigerate 8 hours or overnight.

*Serve chilled salad on a bed of lettuce or stuffed into ripe tomato halves or avocado halves. Add 2 cups of cooked, drained pasta for a delicious pasta salad.*

**Variations:** *Endless variations on the marinade can be created by adding or substituting ingredients. Some excellent additions include capers, fresh lemon zest, lemon juice, dry vermouth, rosemary, oregano, hot pepper sauce, hearts of palm, Greek olives, and horseradish.*

 "Chim-Chim-Cheree" as performed by Seldom Scene

# GRILLED TUNA QUESADILLAS

*Serves 6*

- Grill or broil tuna steaks to desired degree of doneness. Be careful not to overcook because they will get additional cooking inside the quesadillas. Allow to stand for 5 minutes, then slice thinly.

- Melt butter in large skillet until it sizzles. Add tortillas 2 at a time and cook until crisp and brown on one side. Spread 2 tablespoons Olive Pesto on half of unbrowned side of each tortilla. Layer sliced tuna and 2 tablespoons crumbled feta cheese on top of pesto. Fold empty half of tortilla to cover filling. Flip tortillas so that the cheese side is down and cook until cheese melts. Cut each tortilla into three wedges and serve with Smooth Salsa.

- Puree all ingredients in blender or processor until thick and smooth.

*This recipe is extremely easy to improvise on. Substitute grilled, sliced lamb loin chops for the tuna; you'll get a totally different taste sensation. Chicken or shrimp would be delicious in these as well. Or consider changing the pesto type or the cheese. For an unforgettable combination, use Rosemary-Horseradish Mayonnaise (see page 341), rare roast beef or steak, and Brie cheese.*

| | |
|---|---|
| 2 | tuna steaks |
| 2 | tablespoons butter |
| 6 | flour tortillas |
| ¾ | cup Olive Pesto, see variation page 326 |
| ¾ | cup crumbled feta cheese |
| | Smooth Salsa |

**Smooth Salsa**

| | |
|---|---|
| 2 | pounds fresh tomatoes, coarsely chopped |
| 1 | red onion, quartered |
| 3 | cloves garlic |
| 1 | jalapeño, stem and seeds removed |
| 3 | tablespoons cilantro |
| 1 | tablespoon fresh lime juice |
| | Salt, black pepper, cumin to taste |

 Maurice Ravel: *Alborda Del Gracioso (Morning Song of the Jester)*

# SALMON BAKED ALASKA

*Serves 10 to 12*

- 1 large or two small salmon fillets (about 4 to 5 pounds)
- 1 tablespoon Cajun or Creole seasoning
- ⅔ cup mayonnaise, regular or low-fat
- ⅔ cup shredded sharp cheddar cheese

- Place salmon on foil-lined cookie sheet. Sprinkle evenly with seasoning.

- Mix mayonnaise and cheese. Spread mixture over fish.

- Bake at 350° for 25 to 30 minutes, being careful not to overcook. Check by inserting a fork into the fillet; the center should be opaque.

*Try a medium-bodied Chardonnay with a light spiciness.*

Wine is the only natural beverage that feeds not only the body, but the soul and spirit. . .

*Robert Mondavi*

 Paul Speer: *True North:* "True North"

# Serves 4 SASSY SHRIMP RISOTTO

- Boil shrimp using any spicy shrimp boil powder or liquid. Drain and allow to cool. Peel and devein shrimp; set aside. Place shells in a saucepan and cover with 2 cups water; boil briskly for 20 minutes. Strain broth and discard shells; keep broth warm on the stove.

- Melt butter with oil in a large skillet over low heat. Add the onions and sauté until tender, about 5 minutes. Add white wine and cook until almost evaporated. Add rice and stir until well coated. Add broth slowly, 1 cup at a time, stirring occasionally until liquid is absorbed.

- In a separate skillet, sauté the mushrooms, peas, and garlic with 1 tablespoon of chicken stock until mushrooms have softened. Keep warm.

- Continue adding broth to rice 1 cup at a time, supplementing with chicken broth when shrimp broth runs out, until the risotto is very creamy (about 7 cups of liquid will be needed). Just before adding last cup of liquid, stir the mushroom mixture into the risotto and blend well. Add shrimp, cumin, and saffron. Stir in final cup of liquid. When all liquid is absorbed, add Parmesan cheese. Blend well. Serve immediately.

| | |
|---|---|
| 1 | pound medium shrimp in shells |
| 2 | tablespoons butter |
| 2 | tablespoons olive oil |
| ½ | cup chopped onion |
| ¼ | cup dry white wine |
| 1½ | cups Arborio rice |
| | Shrimp broth supplemented with chicken broth |
| 8 | ounces fresh mushrooms, sliced |
| 8 | ounces frozen green peas |
| 1 | teaspoon minced garlic |
| | Chicken stock or canned low-salt broth, about 5 cups |
| ¼ | teaspoon cumin |
| ¼ | teaspoon saffron |
| ½ | cup freshly grated Parmesan cheese |

Isaac Albeniz: *Espana, Op. 165:* "Tango"

# SALSA QUICHE

*Serves 6*

3 slices bacon, diced
1 cup diced red onion
¾ cup diced bell pepper
1 teaspoon chili powder
1 (9-inch) deep-dish pie crust
1 cup shredded pepper Jack cheese
1 cup shredded cheddar cheese
1 cup milk
2 eggs
⅓ cup flour
Salsa Diablo, see page 65
Sour cream
Sliced green onions
Sliced ripe olives
Chopped tomatoes

- Cook bacon in medium skillet until crisp. Remove with slotted spoon to paper towels. Drain off drippings, leaving enough to coat skillet. Add onion and bell pepper; cook over medium-high heat 5 minutes or until softened, stirring occasionally. Stir in chili powder, then turn off heat and allow skillet to stand for a few minutes, stirring once or twice.

- Press pie crust into a 9-inch pie pan. Sprinkle ½ cup pepper Jack cheese over bottom of pie shell; add onion mixture. Beat milk, eggs, and flour in a large bowl until well blended. Stir in remaining 1½ cups cheese and mix thoroughly. Pour into pie shell and smooth top.

- Place pie on a cookie sheet and bake at 375° for 45 to 55 minutes or until knife inserted in center comes out clean. Cover loosely with foil if crust browns too quickly. Let stand for 5 to 10 minutes before slicing into wedges (the pie will fall slightly as it cools).

- Top each wedge with Salsa Diablo and sour cream. Sprinkle with green onions, chopped black olives, and tomatoes.

 Heitor Villa-Lobos: "Bachianas Brasileiras #5"

# GREEN CHILE PIE

*Makes 6 servings*

- Combine eggs, butter, flour, and baking powder in bowl of electric mixer. Beat well at medium speed. Stir in remaining ingredients. Pour into well-greased 9-inch pie plate.

- Bake at 400° for 10 minutes. Reduce heat to 350° and bake an additional 20 minutes or until knife inserted in center comes out clean. Cut into wedges to serve.

| | |
|---|---|
| 5 | eggs, beaten |
| 2 | tablespoons butter, melted |
| ½ | cup flour |
| ½ | teaspoon baking powder |
| 8 | ounces cream-style cottage cheese |
| 2 | cups shredded Monterey Jack cheese |
| 4 | ounces canned chopped green chiles, drained |

Heitor Villa-Lobos: "Bachianas Brasileiras #1"

# TAMALE VEGGIE PIE  *Serves 4 to 6*

- 1 large onion, finely chopped
- ½ bell pepper, finely chopped
- 2 tablespoons olive oil
- 1½ cups canned diced tomatoes (use tomatoes with green chiles for extra heat)
- 1 cup yellow cornmeal
- 2 cups milk
- 3 eggs, slightly beaten
- 1½ cups whole-kernel corn
- 1 teaspoon salt
- ½ teaspoon black pepper
- 1 tablespoon chili powder
- 2 cups pitted black olives
- ½ cup shredded cheddar cheese

- Sauté onion and pepper in olive oil until soft. Add tomatoes and simmer 20 minutes.

- In medium saucepan, mix cornmeal and milk; cook over medium heat, stirring often, to a soft mush consistency. Beat eggs in a large bowl. Add mush, corn, salt, pepper, and chili powder; stir well. Add tomato mixture and olives; mix thoroughly.

- Pour mixture into a greased 2-quart casserole and top with cheese. Bake at 350° for about 1 hour or until firm.

"Hot Tamale Man" as performed by Arthur Collins

# BLACK BEAN TOSTADAS

*Serves 8 to 10*

- Rinse the beans well. Put in Dutch oven with enough water to cover and cook for about 1½ hours or until beans are nearly done.

- Heat the oil in a skillet or large saucepan. Sauté the onions, garlic, cumin, coriander, and jalapeño over medium-low heat until onions are soft.

- When beans are done, drain them and mash them coarsely. Add the onion mixture to the beans. Squeeze the oranges into the bean mixture and add the chopped tomatoes. Cook over low heat for 10 to 15 minutes, stirring frequently to prevent sticking.

- Preheat oven to 350°. Place tortillas on a cookie sheet, making sure they are open flat, and bake until they are lightly browned (they burn quickly). Spread bean mixture over tortillas and serve with assorted toppings.

| | |
|---|---|
| 1 | pound dried black beans |
| 1 | tablespoon olive oil |
| 3 | medium onions, chopped |
| 3 | cloves garlic, minced |
| 2 | teaspoons ground cumin |
| 2 | teaspoons ground coriander |
| 1-3 | jalapeño peppers |
| 2 | oranges |
| 2 | tomatoes, chopped |
| | Corn tortillas |
| | Garden Salsa, see page 21 |
| | Guacamole |
| | Shredded cheese |
| | Sliced black olives |
| | Sliced lettuce |
| | Chopped tomatoes |
| | Sour cream |

 Claude Debussy: *Estampes:* "La Soiree Dans Grenade"

# HUEVOS JOSE

*Serves 4*

| | |
|---|---|
| ¼ | cup finely chopped onion |
| ¼ | cup finely chopped bell pepper |
| 1 | garlic clove, minced |
| 6 | fresh mushrooms, sliced |
| 6 | large black olives, sliced |
| 6 | eggs, lightly beaten |
| 8 | flour tortillas |
| | Shredded cheddar and Monterey Jack cheeses |
| | Sour cream |
| | Salsa Diablo, see page 65 |

- Coat a sauté pan or skillet with nonstick spray. Sauté the onion, pepper, and garlic over low heat until soft. Add mushrooms and sauté a few minutes more. Add beaten eggs and black olives; cook over low heat, scrambling with a fork or large spoon, until eggs are set.

- Place tortillas on paper plate. Cover with a damp paper towel and microwave until warm. Spoon egg mixture onto warmed tortillas and garnish with cheese, sour cream, and Salsa Diablo. Serve rolled up.

 Isaac Albeniz: *Suite Espanola, Op. 47:* "Asturias"

# HUEVOS RANCHEROS

*Serves 6*

- Fry tortillas one at a time in ¼ cup hot oil for 3 to 5 seconds or each side or just until softened. Add additional oil if necessary. Drain the tortillas on paper towels. Place the tortillas on the bottom and ½-inch up the sides of a 12 x 8 x 2-inch baking dish. Set aside.

- Sauté the onion, green pepper, and garlic in olive oil until softened. Stir in flour and cook for 1 additional minute. Drain the tomatoes, reserving ¼ cup juice. Add tomatoes, juice, and seasonings to onion mixture. Cook over medium heat for 5 minutes.

- Pour tomato mixture over corn tortillas. Make 6 indentations in the mixture and break an egg into each. Cover and bake at 350° for 25 minutes. Uncover and sprinkle with cheese and olives. Bake an additional 5 minutes. Serve hot.

*Try serving this with a dollop of Lime-Cilantro Sour Cream (see page 321).*

| | |
|---|---|
| 6 | corn tortillas |
| | Vegetable oil |
| 1 | cup chopped onion |
| 1 | cup chopped bell pepper |
| 2 | cloves garlic, minced |
| 3 | tablespoons olive oil |
| 1 | tablespoon flour |
| 2 | (16-ounce) cans diced tomatoes |
| ½ | teaspoon dried oregano |
| ½ | teaspoon ground cumin |
| ½ | teaspoon chili powder |
| ¼ | teaspoon salt |
| ⅛ | teaspoon black pepper |
| 6 | eggs |
| ½ | cup shredded sharp cheddar cheese |
| ¼ | cup sliced ripe olives |

---

Isaac Albeniz: *Suite Espanola, Op. 47:* "Sevilla"

BRUNCH DISHES

# LOWER EAST SIDE PEPPER & EGG SANDWICH

*Makes 4 sandwiches*

| | |
|---|---|
| 4 | tablespoons olive oil |
| 1 | large green bell pepper, sliced in 3 x ½-inch strips |
| 4 | eggs |
| | Salt, black pepper, and garlic powder to taste |
| 4 | fresh Italian rolls, toasted |
| | Mayonnaise to taste |

- Heat olive oil in an omelet pan.

- Add bell pepper strips to olive oil and sauté until peppers are soft, burning slightly if you wish.

- Whip eggs with salt, black pepper, and garlic powder. Pour egg mixture into olive oil and bell pepper mixture. Add more olive oil if needed.

- Cook until eggs are just firm, stirring frequently. Remove from heat.

- Spread toasted rolls with mayonnaise. Divide egg mixture among the four rolls.

**Variations:** *Mushrooms, lox, capers, cheese, hot peppers, or alfalfa sprouts may be added if you wish.*

"Autumn in New York" as performed by Sarah Vaughan

# MAIN MOTIFS
Fish & Seafood, Poultry, Pork, Veal, Beef, Lamb

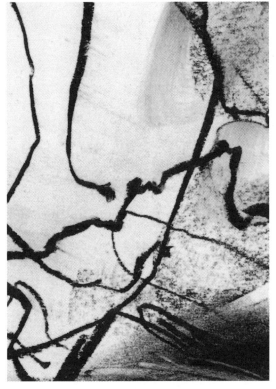

# A MENU FOR SPRING

> For a man seldom thinks with more earnestness
> of anything than he does of his dinner.
>
> *Samuel Johnson*

### *Appetizer*
Caviar Squares

### *Soup*
Spring Pea Soup

### *Main Plate*
Salmon Baked Alaska
Oven-Grilled Asparagus
Carrots with Leeks

### *Dessert*
Pavlova

 Aaron Copland: *Appalachian Spring*

# SWORDFISH WITH TOMATO-PARSLEY SAUCE

*Serves 4*

- Sauté onion in olive oil in a skillet or large saucepan until translucent; add garlic and sauté 1 additional minute. Add tomatoes and juice, parsley, sugar, and salt and pepper to taste. Cover and cook for about 15 minutes or until parsley has wilted and onion is very soft.

- Place fish fillets on foil-lined baking sheet. Top with sauce. Bake at 350° for 20 minutes or until fish is opaque.

**Variations:** *This same sauce can be poured over extra large, cooked lima beans. Bake dish for 20 minutes.*

¼ cup olive oil
1 onion, finely chopped
1 large clove garlic, minced
2 (16-ounce) cans diced tomatoes with juice
2 cups chopped fresh parsley
1 teaspoon sugar
Salt and black pepper
4 (8-ounce) swordfish fillets

If food is the body of good living, wine is its soul.

*Clifton Fadiman*

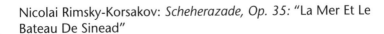

Nicolai Rimsky-Korsakov: *Scheherazade, Op. 35:* "La Mer Et Le Bateau De Sinead"

# SOLE WITH BROWN BUTTER SAUCE

*Serves 4*

| | |
|---|---|
| 1 | lemon |
| ¼ | cup flour |
| ½ | teaspoon paprika |
| ½ | teaspoon salt |
| ¼ | teaspoon black pepper |
| 4 | (10-ounce) sole fillets |
| 3 | tablespoons butter |
| 1 | tablespoon drained capers |
| 1 | tablespoon chopped fresh parsley |

- Remove and reserve zest from lemon. Juice lemon and reserve 1 tablespoon juice (save remainder for another use).

- Mix flour, paprika, salt, and pepper in a shallow plate. Coat fish with mixture. Melt 2 tablespoons butter in large skillet; add fish and sauté until golden brown and just cooked (about 2 minutes per side). Remove fish to platter or plates; tent with foil to keep warm.

- Add remaining butter to pan and stir until well-browned, scraping up any browned bits, about 2 minutes. Add lemon juice, capers, and parsley. Stir and spoon over fish. Garnish with shredded lemon zest.

*Whole small trout can be substituted for Trout with Lemon and Brown Butter. Add a few minutes to the cooking time.*

🍷 *This sole is lovely with a French Pouilly-Fuisse.*

Only those who lack imagination cannot find a reason to drink good wine.

*Anonymous*

 Claude Debussy: *Image, Set II:* "Poissons D'or"

# CATFISH PARMESAN

*Serves 4*

- Combine breadcrumbs, Parmesan cheese, and seasonings. Dip fillets in milk and roll in crumb mixture.

- Spray baking pan with nonstick coating. Arrange fish in pan. Drizzle oil over fillets. Bake at 450° about 8 to 10 minutes or until fish flakes easily with a fork.

| | |
|---|---|
| ½ | cup dry breadcrumbs |
| ¼ | cup Parmesan cheese |
| 2 | tablespoons chopped parsley |
| ½ | teaspoon paprika |
| 1 | teaspoon minced fresh oregano |
| 1 | teaspoon minced fresh basil |
| ¼ | teaspoon black pepper |
| 1 | pound skinless catfish fillets |
| ⅓ | cup milk |
| 2 | tablespoons vegetable oil |

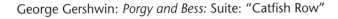

George Gershwin: *Porgy and Bess:* Suite: "Catfish Row"

# SHRIMP LOUISIANA     *Serves 8 to 16*

| | |
|---|---|
| 1 | cup olive oil |
| ¾ | cup clarified butter |
| ¼ | cup brown sugar |
| 2 | tablespoons Worcestershire sauce |
| 3 | bay leaves |
| 1 | lemon, grated zest and juice |
| 2 | tablespoons chopped fresh oregano or 1 tablespoon dried |
| 2 | tablespoons fresh thyme leaves or 1 tablespoon dried |
| 2 | tablespoons chopped fresh rosemary or 1 tablespoon dried |
| 4-6 | garlic cloves, minced or pressed |
| 1 | tablespoon salt |
| 1 | tablespoon black pepper |
| 1-2 | teaspoons cayenne pepper |
| 1 | teaspoon red pepper flakes |
| 1 | teaspoon hot pepper sauce |
| 3 | tablespoons chopped ginger |
| 4-5 | pounds of medium shrimp with shells on |

- Mix all ingredients except the shrimp and let stand for a few hours or overnight.

- Put shrimp in a large glass baking dish. Pour the marinade mix over the shrimp. Toss until the shrimp are well coated. Let stand for 1 hour at room temperature, stirring a few times.

- Bake shrimp at 425° for about 20 minutes, stirring once, until shrimp turn bright pink. Warn guests that they will be peeling and sopping. Serve in baking dish with sauce; offer plenty of crusty bread.

*To clarify butter, melt in a saucepan and keep over heat, skimming the foam until no more rises to the top. Pour butter out carefully, using only the clear yellow part and discarding the milk solids in the bottom.*

There's nothing better than being a cook every night.

*Paul Prudhomme*

"Do You Know What It Means to Miss New Orleans" as performed by Louis Armstrong

# DEVILED SHRIMP

*Serves 6 to 8*

- Peel and devein shrimp.

- Make a roux by heating the oil in a skillet and adding the flour. Cook slowly until at least the color of peanut butter, but preferably the color of chocolate (the darker the roux, the richer the flavor, but don't scorch it or the flour will taste bitter). Add the onion and bell pepper and sauté for about 2 minutes. Add the parsley and water. Simmer together until thickened, stirring occasionally, about 15 to 20 minutes.

- When the liquid is thick and smooth, add the shrimp. Simmer for 2 to 3 minutes. Add the horseradish, mustard, salt, and cayenne pepper. Cook an additional 5 minutes. Serve over hot white rice or on toast points.

| | |
|---|---|
| 2 | pounds medium shrimp |
| ½ | cup oil |
| ½ | cup flour |
| 1 | onion, chopped |
| 1 | bell pepper, chopped |
| ½ | cup chopped fresh parsley |
| 1 | quart water |
| 3 | tablespoons prepared horseradish |
| 3 | tablespoons mustard |
| | Salt |
| | Cayenne pepper |
| | Additional chopped fresh parsley |

 Jacques Offenbach: *Orpheus in the Underworld:* "Hell's Gallop"

# CAJUN SHRIMP BALLS — *Serves 6*

**Shrimp Balls**

- 1 pound cleaned shrimp, coarsely chopped
- 1 large onion, coarsely chopped
- 4 garlic cloves, halved
- 1 cup fresh breadcrumbs
- 2 eggs
- 1 teaspoon Worcestershire sauce
- ¼ cup chopped fresh parsley
- Salt and black pepper
- Cayenne pepper
- Flour
- Oil for frying
- Tomato Gravy

- Process shrimp, onion, and garlic in a food processor or blender until finely chopped (this can also be done by hand). Transfer to a mixing bowl.

- Add breadcrumbs, eggs, Worcestershire sauce, and parsley; mix well. Add salt, pepper, and cayenne pepper to taste. Put mixing bowl in refrigerator and allow to chill for 30 minutes while you prepare the Tomato Gravy.

- Pinch off some of shrimp mixture and shape into a slightly flattened ball the size of a walnut. Dredge in flour. Fry the balls in batches in a skillet with ¼-inch of oil. Remove with a slotted spoon and drain on paper towels. Serve with Tomato Gravy.

*Variations:* For an excellent hors d'oeuvre, turn these into Asian Shrimp Balls by adding ¼ cup finely chopped water chestnuts and ¼ cup chopped green onions. Replace the Worcestershire sauce with 1 tablespoon soy sauce. Fry as directed and serve alone or with teriyaki dipping sauce.

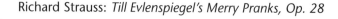

Richard Strauss: *Till Evlenspiegel's Merry Pranks, Op. 28*

## CAJUN SHRIMP BALLS *continued*

- Make a roux by heating oil in a large skillet and adding the flour. Cook, stirring often, until the color is a nutty brown. Watch carefully to avoid scorching. Add onions and bell pepper and sauté about 2 minutes. Add water, tomato paste, bay leaves, basil, salt, and pepper. Cook until thickened to a gravy consistency.

**Variations:** For an easy Crawfish Étouffée, add 1 pound cleaned crawfish tails (usually packaged with the fat of the crawfish—don't rinse or you will lose half the flavor) before you add water; sauté for 2 minutes, then make gravy as directed. Serve over hot rice or linguine.

### Tomato Gravy

| | |
|---|---|
| ½ | cup oil |
| ½ | cup flour |
| 1 | onion, chopped |
| 1 | bell pepper, chopped |
| 1 | quart water |
| 1 | (6-ounce) can tomato paste |
| 2 | bay leaves |
| 1 | tablespoon chopped fresh basil |
| | Salt and black pepper |

# CRAWFISH STUFFED CAJUN PEPPERS

*Serves 6 to 10*

| | |
|---|---|
| 6 | medium or 4 large red bell peppers |
| 2 | pounds peeled crawfish tails or 2 pounds cleaned shrimp |
| ¼ | cup oil |
| 1 | large bell pepper, chopped |
| ¾ | cup chopped onion |
| ¾ | cup chopped celery |
| 3-6 | cloves garlic, finely chopped |
| ½ | cup sliced green onions |
| ¼ | cup chopped fresh parsley |
| 1-3 | teaspoons cayenne pepper |
| | Salt and black pepper |
| 2 | eggs |
| 1 | cup fresh breadcrumbs |
| ¼ | cup melted butter (optional) |

- Char whole peppers under broiler until thoroughly blackened. Transfer to paper bag, seal, and allow to stand for 10 minutes. Peel peppers and halve lengthwise, removing seeds and stems. Set aside.

- Sauté crawfish in oil in large skillet over medium-high heat for 5 minutes. Add chopped bell pepper, onion, celery, and garlic; cook an additional 10 minutes, adding a few drops of water if necessary to prevent sticking. Add green onions, parsley, cayenne, salt, and pepper. Stir well. Remove from burner and allow to cool.

- When cool, add eggs and stir well. Add breadcrumbs and mix thoroughly. Loosely stuff mixture into roasted red pepper halves (breadcrumbs will swell, so don't pack it in). Place filled halves on foil-lined baking sheet. Drizzle each with melted butter if desired. Bake at 350° for 15 to 20 minutes or until lightly browned (can be broiled for quicker browning).

 Joaquin Rodrigo: *Fantasia Para Un Gentilhombre*

# SOY SAUCE CHICKEN

*Serves 6*

- Put chicken in a Dutch oven and cover with water. Add enough soy sauce to the water to make it take on the approximate color of the soy sauce. Bring to a boil; cook uncovered until nearly all the water is gone. Add vinegar and let cook again until almost all liquid is gone. Remove chicken with a fork or slotted spoon.

- Sauté mushrooms in butter in a skillet. Put cooked rice into the chicken pot and stir it around to coat with the remaining juices. Add mushrooms and water chestnuts; toss thoroughly. Mound rice in the center of a platter. Top with chicken. Sprinkle with green onions.

1 whole chicken, cut into pieces, or 6 boneless, skinless chicken breasts
Water to cover chicken
Soy sauce
1 cup white vinegar
8 ounces fresh mushrooms, sliced
2 tablespoons butter
2 cups cooked rice
1 (8-ounce) can sliced water chestnuts
4 green onions, sliced

Cyril Scott: "Paradise Birds"

# SKILLET CHICKEN PROVENÇAL

*Serves 6 to 8*

- 3 teaspoons olive oil, divided
- 2 large lemons
- ½ teaspoon salt
- ¼ teaspoon black pepper
- 4 garlic cloves, minced
- 6 boneless, skinless chicken breasts
- 3 tablespoons chopped fresh rosemary
- 5 Roma tomatoes, quartered
- 10 Greek olives
- 8 small red potatoes, quartered
- 2-8 garlic cloves
- 1 teaspoon Herbes de Provence (optional)
- 1 tablespoon white wine
  Rosemary sprig

- Coat a 10-inch cast iron skillet with 1 teaspoon olive oil. Thinly slice 1 lemon and place lemon slices in a single layer in skillet.

- Use zester to remove and shred zest from remaining lemon. Juice lemon and combine 1 teaspoon olive oil, lemon zest, lemon juice, salt, pepper, and minced garlic in a large bowl. Add chicken (breasts can be left whole or sliced) and toss to coat. Arrange chicken in a single layer on top of lemon slices.

- Combine 1 teaspoon olive oil, remaining salt and pepper, chopped rosemary, tomatoes, olives, potatoes, and whole garlic cloves (peeled or unpeeled) in a bowl and toss to coat. Arrange potato mixture over chicken.

- Sprinkle Herbes de Provence over the top and drizzle with white wine. Top with a rosemary sprig. Bake at 400° for 1 hour, basting chicken during last 10 minutes of cooking.

*These robust garlic and tangy lemon flavors require a fairly tart Chardonnay with a strong citrus finish.*

Wine lets no lover unrewarded go.

*Alexander Pope*

 Georges Bizet: *L'Arlesienne Suite #1*

146   MAIN MOTIFS

# GARLIC CHICKEN

*Serves 8 to 10*

- Place chickens in a 2-gallon plastic zipper bag. Combine water, rosemary or dill, vinegar, lemon juice, garlic, bay leaves, and lemon slices and pour over chicken. Seal bag securely (you can use 2 bags and divide the marinade between them). Marinate the chicken in the refrigerator for 2 hours, turning occasionally.

- Remove chickens from marinade, reserving lemon slices but discarding remainder. Place chickens breast side up in a large roasting pan. Combine oil and paprika; pour over chicken. Place lemon slices on chickens.

- Bake uncovered at 450° for 10 minutes. Reduce heat to 350°, cover, and continue baking for 75 minutes.

| | |
|---|---|
| 2 | (3½-pound) frying chickens |
| 8 | cups water |
| ½ | cup chopped fresh rosemary or dill |
| ¾ | cup white vinegar |
| ½ | cup lemon juice |
| 13 | large garlic cloves, minced |
| 5 | bay leaves |
| 2 | lemons, thinly sliced |
| ¾ | cup vegetable oil or olive oil |
| 1 | tablespoon paprika |

Wine is earth's answer to the sun.

*Margaret Fuller*

Maurice Ravel: "Oiseaux Tristes"

# LEMON-DIJON CHICKEN

*Serves 6*

⅓ cup lemon juice
5 tablespoons olive oil
2 tablespoons Dijon mustard
1 small clove garlic, pressed
¼ teaspoon hot pepper sauce
6 boneless, skinless chicken breasts
2 cups chicken broth
2 teaspoons cornstarch
1 tablespoon water
1 tablespoon butter

- Whisk together lemon juice, 4 tablespoons olive oil, mustard, garlic, and pepper sauce. Arrange chicken in a single layer in a glass dish. Pour marinade over, turning to coat evenly. Marinate at room temperature for 1 hour (if chicken breasts are not very cold when you begin to marinate them, do so in the refrigerator). Drain chicken, reserving marinade.

- Heat 1 tablespoon oil in a large skillet over medium-high heat. Add chicken and cook until chicken is completely done, about 10 minutes, turning occasionally. Transfer chicken to a platter.

- Add chicken broth and reserved marinade to skillet; bring to a boil. Allow mixture to boil for 10 minutes. Mix cornstarch and water; add to skillet. Cook over high heat, stirring constantly, about 5 minutes or until sauce thickens slightly. Stir in butter.

- Return chicken to skillet and simmer until heated through, about 2 minutes. Serve chicken with sauce.

Beethoven: *Symphony #3 in E-Flat, Op. 55*

## MEXICAN RED CHICKEN

*Serves 4*

- Put chicken breasts and taco seasoning in a plastic zipper bag. Shake to coat chicken thoroughly. Remove from bag.

- Sauté chicken in olive oil until sealed and partly cooked. Pour salsa and water over chicken. Cover and simmer until cooked through, about 20 minutes.

- Transfer chicken and sauce to an ovenproof dish. Cover with shredded cheese. Bake at 400° until cheese melts.

| | |
|---|---|
| 4 | boneless, skinless chicken breasts |
| 1 | package taco seasoning |
| | Olive oil |
| 2 | cups Salsa Diablo, see page 65 |
| 1 | cup water |
| ¾ | pound shredded Monterey Jack cheese or pepper Jack |

*Turn this into a casserole by cubing the chicken breasts before coating with taco seasoning; reduce simmering time to about 10 minutes.*

Igor Stravinsky: *The Firebird*

# CHICKEN WINGS WITH GREEN TOMATOES AND COUSCOUS

*Serves 4*

| | |
|---|---|
| 1 | medium eggplant |
| 1 | medium onion |
| 2 | large green tomatoes |
| 12 | chicken wings |
| 2 | tablespoons olive oil |
| 1 | tablespoon cumin |
| 1 | tablespoon cinnamon |
| ½ | teaspoon salt |
| ½ | teaspoon black pepper |
| 1 | (32-ounce) can diced red tomatoes |
| 1 | cup couscous |
| 1¼ | cups water |

- Cut eggplant lengthwise into quarters. Slice each quarter crosswise into 1-inch pieces. Place eggplant in a bowl of heavily salted water (use heavy plate to keep pieces submerged). Allow to soak for about 20 minutes. Drain and rinse before using.

- Slice the onion and green tomatoes into 8 wedges each. Set aside.

- Remove the wingtips or tuck under wings to form a triangle shape. Brown the chicken wings in 1 tablespoon oil in a nonstick skillet. Remove from pan with slotted spoon or tongs and place in a 10-inch by 15-inch baking dish.

What is better than to sit at the end of the day and drink wine with friends, or substitutes for friends?

*James Joyce*

 Johann Strauss, Jr.: *Wings of the Phoenix Waltz, Op. 125*

150   MAIN MOTIFS

## CHICKEN WINGS *continued*

- Add remaining oil to skillet. Sauté onion wedges for 5 minutes. Add eggplant and sauté for 2 minutes. Add green tomatoes and sauté 5 minutes more. Add the sautéed vegetables to the baking dish.

- Stir cumin, cinnamon, salt, and pepper into the can of tomatoes; pour over the chicken. Cover pan with foil and bake at 375° for 25 minutes. Remove foil and bake an additional 20 minutes.

- In small saucepan, bring water to boil. Stir in couscous. Cover saucepan and remove from heat. Allow to stand 5 minutes. Fluff with a fork. Mound couscous in the center of a platter. Surround with chicken, vegetables, and sauce.

# CHICKEN-BLACK BEAN CASSEROLE

*Serves 6 to 8*

- ⅔ cup lime juice
- ⅓ cup olive oil
- ½ teaspoon black pepper
- 2 teaspoons garlic powder
- 2 teaspoons salt
- 1½ pounds boneless, skinless chicken breasts
- 4 cups cooked rice
- 2 (15-ounce) cans black beans
- 1 cup finely chopped fresh cilantro
- 1 teaspoon onion powder
- 1 teaspoon chili powder
- 1 teaspoon cumin seeds

- In medium bowl, whisk lime juice, oil, pepper, and 1 teaspoon each of garlic powder and salt. Cut chicken into bite-size pieces. Add to lime juice mixture and stir until coated. Cover and refrigerate 2 hours.

- Drain chicken and transfer to large nonstick skillet coated with nonstick spray. Cook over medium heat until juices run clear when chicken is pierced with a fork.

- In a 2-quart casserole, combine rice, beans, cilantro, onion powder, chili powder, cumin seeds, and remaining 1 teaspoon each of garlic powder and salt. Add chicken and mix well. Cover and bake at 350° for 40 to 45 minutes or until heated through.

"Bye Bye Blackbird" as performed by Carmen MacRae

# CHICKEN INDIRA

*Serves 4*

- Mix yogurt, lemon juice, garlic, cumin, coriander, black pepper, cloves, and crushed chile in a plastic zipper bag. Cut the chicken breasts into cubes or strips. Add to plastic bag, distributing yogurt mixture so that all chicken pieces are coated. Marinate in refrigerator for several hours, turning occasionally.

- Remove chicken from bag and drain excess yogurt. Heat oil in a skillet. Add the chicken pieces and sauté over high heat for about 5 minutes or just until done. Serve with Yogurt Nehru.

| | |
|---|---|
| 1 | cup plain yogurt |
| 2 | tablespoons lemon juice |
| 3 | cloves garlic, pressed |
| 1 | teaspoon cumin |
| 1 | teaspoon coriander |
| 1 | teaspoon black pepper |
| ¼ | teaspoon ground cloves |
| 1 | dried red chile, crumbled |
| 5 | boneless, skinless chicken breasts |
| 1 | tablespoon peanut oil |
| | Yogurt Nehru, see below |

*Makes 1½ cups*

- Place a coffee filter inside a medium strainer and suspend it over a large cup or small bowl. Spoon yogurt into filter and drain in refrigerator for 2 hours or overnight.

- Peel and seed cucumber. Shred onto several thicknesses of paper towel; blot liquid away. In a small skillet, toast the cumin seeds for 1 minute. Add pepper flakes; toast an additional 30 seconds or until fragrant.

- Combine strained yogurt, cucumber, cumin seeds, and pepper flakes. Season to taste with salt and pepper. This sauce will keep for 3 days.

🍷 A Zinfandel with black cherry or black raspberry fruit will handle these spicy flavors well.

*Yogurt Nehru*

| | |
|---|---|
| 1½ | cups yogurt (use yogurt with high fat content) |
| 1 | small cucumber |
| 1 | tablespoon cumin seeds |
| 1 | teaspoon red pepper flakes |
| | Salt and black pepper |

From wine what sudden friendship springs!

*John Gay*

# SATELLITE CHICKEN

*Serves 6 to 8*

| | |
|---|---|
| 24 | ounces cream cheese, softened |
| 1 | bunch green onions, chopped |
| 2-3 | teaspoons Cajun seasoning |
| 5 | cloves garlic, pressed |
| 1 | tablespoon fresh basil, chopped |
| | Salt and black pepper |
| 8 | boneless, skinless chicken breasts |
| 16 | slices thinly cut bacon |

- Put cream cheese into a medium bowl. Mix in green onions, seasoning, garlic, and basil. Salt and pepper to taste.

- Butterfly the chicken breasts. Place ⅛ of the cheese mixture in the center of each butterflied breast. Fold lengthwise. Wrap the bacon around the chicken breast to enclose completely; secure with toothpicks.

- Grill over a slow fire or with the rack at least 8 inches from coals until bacon is very well done and chicken is cooked through.

*To butterfly a chicken breast, put chicken breast on a work surface. Place your hand flat on the top. Using a sharp knife, slice into the breast horizontally, stopping about ¼-inch before the edge. Open breast like a book and flatten slightly.*

Quickly, bring me a beaker of wine, so that I may wet my mind and say something clever.

*Aristophanes*

"Chasin' The Bird" as performed by Charlie Parker

MAIN MOTIFS

# CHICKEN WITH TARRAGON CREAM

Serves 3 to 4

- Place chicken thighs in single layer in baking dish. In heavy saucepan, melt butter and add onion. Cook until translucent. Add flour, stirring for 1 minute. Gradually add cream and stock, stirring constantly until a white sauce is formed. Add vermouth, tarragon, and salt and pepper to taste.

- Pour sauce over chicken and bake at 350° for 45 minutes or until thoroughly cooked. Sprinkle with parsley just before serving.

| 8 | chicken thighs |
| 1 | tablespoon butter |
| ½ | onion, finely diced |
| 1 | tablespoon flour |
| ½ | cup whipping cream |
| ½ | cup chicken stock or canned low-salt broth |
| ¼ | cup dry vermouth |
| 3 | tablespoons minced fresh tarragon (or 2 teaspoons dried) |
| | Salt and black pepper |
| ½ | cup minced fresh parsley |

Johannes Brahms: *Sonata #2 in A For Violin & Piano, Op. 100*

# EXTRAORDINARY CHICKEN

*Serves 8*

| | |
|---|---|
| 4 | cups cooked chicken, cubed |
| 1 | (16-ounce) can artichokes, quartered |
| 8 | ounces whole button mushrooms, trimmed |
| 1 | cup butter |
| 1 | small onion, chopped |
| 3 | cloves garlic, pressed |
| ½ | cup flour |
| ½ | teaspoon cayenne pepper |
| 1 | teaspoon salt |
| 1 | tablespoon chopped fresh parsley |
| 1 | teaspoon chopped fresh dill |
| 1 | cup half & half or 1 can evaporated skimmed milk |
| 2 | cups milk, regular or low-fat |
| 1 | cup shredded sharp cheddar cheese |
| 1 | cup shredded Gruyère cheese |
| 1 | cup breadcrumbs |

- Put chicken into a greased 3-quart baking dish. Top with artichokes and mushrooms.

- Melt butter in a 2-quart saucepan. Add onion and garlic; sauté until clear. Add flour, cayenne pepper, salt, parsley, and dill; cook 1 minute, stirring constantly. Gradually stir in half & half and milk. Cook over medium heat until thick and smooth, stirring constantly. Add cheeses and stir until all cheese melts.

- Pour cheese sauce over chicken, artichokes, and mushrooms. Sprinkle breadcrumbs over top. Bake at 350° for 30 minutes.

*Serve with spinach fettuccini and plenty of French bread.*

 Franz Joseph Haydn: *String Quartet in C, Op. 33* ("The Bird")

# CORNISH HEN WITH BLACKBERRY SAUCE

*Serves 2*

- Sprinkle both sides of hen halves with thyme, allspice, salt, and pepper. Heat oil in a skillet over medium-high heat. Add Cornish hen, skin side down, and cook until brown, about 6 minutes per side. Transfer to baking sheet and roast about 20 minutes or until juices run clear when thigh is pricked with fork.

- In same large skillet, pour off all but 2 tablespoons fat. Sauté shallots over medium heat until soft. Add broth, wine, blackberries, and sugar; boil until sauce thickens enough to coat spoon, scraping up browned bits and crushing berries. Strain sauce into small bowl. Season to taste with salt, pepper, and more sugar if desired. Serve Cornish hen halves with sauce under, over, or on the side.

| | |
|---|---|
| 1 | large Cornish hen, split lengthwise |
| 2 | teaspoons fresh thyme or ½ teaspoon dried |
| ½ | teaspoon ground allspice |
| | Salt and black pepper |
| 2 | tablespoons olive oil |
| 4 | shallots, chopped |
| 2 | cups chicken stock or canned low-salt broth |
| ⅔ | cup Merlot |
| ⅔ | cup fresh or frozen blackberries |
| 2 | teaspoons sugar |

*This sauce is also excellent with quail or squab.*

*A full-bodied Merlot works well both in this dish and poured on the side.*

---

Georg Frideric Handel: *Il Penseroso:* "Sweet Bird" ("Penseroso's Aria")

# CORNISH HENS WITH ROSEMARY-MUSTARD SAUCE

*Serves 2 to 4*

| | |
|---|---|
| 2 | Cornish hens |
| 2 | tablespoons olive oil |
| 2 | tablespoons Dijon mustard, coarse style |
| 1 | tablespoon minced rosemary |
| 2 | teaspoons minced garlic |
| 2 | tablespoons lemon juice |
| 1 | tablespoon grated lemon zest |
| | Salt and black pepper |
| 4 | sprigs rosemary |

- Rub each hen with 1 tablespoon oil and place on rack in roasting pan.

- Mix mustard, rosemary, garlic, lemon juice, and lemon zest; add salt and pepper to taste. Place 2 sprigs rosemary inside the cavity of each hen. Brush sauce over the outside.

- Roast at 400° for 10 minutes. Reduce oven to 350°. Continue cooking, basting every 10 minutes, for 40 minutes or until juices run clear.

It is good food and not fine words that keeps me live.

*Moliere*

Dilys Elwyn-Edwards: Three Welsh Bird Songs

# DUCK BREASTS WITH WINE AND MARMALADE SAUCE

*Serves 4*

- Sprinkle duck breasts generously with seasoning. Dredge in flour that has been seasoned with salt and pepper; shake off excess and allow to stand at room temperature.

- Fry the bacon until very crisp; remove to paper towels and drain. Sauté onions in hot bacon grease until limp; remove and set aside. Fry floured duck breasts in hot fat, turning once, until golden.

- Mix wine and marmalade until thoroughly combined. Crumble bacon and add along with onions to the sauce. Stir well. Pour the sauce over the duck breasts; cover and reduce heat to medium. Allow to simmer for 3 to 5 minutes. Do not overcook duck; the breasts should still be pink in center for best flavor.

Fileted breasts from 2 large ducks
Seasoning such as Greek or Cajun
Flour
Salt and black pepper
12 ounces bacon
1 large onion, chopped
1 cup dry red wine
¾ cup orange marmalade

Heitor Berlioz: *Symphonie Fantastique, Op. 14:* II. A Ball

# ITALIAN STUFFED PEPPERS

*Serves 4*

| | |
|---|---|
| 4 | bell peppers (mixed colors) |
| 1 | cup coarse fresh breadcrumbs |
| 1 | cup milk |
| 8 | ounces sweet Italian sausages, casings removed |
| 1 | egg |
| 1 | tablespoon chopped fresh sage |
| | Salt and pepper |
| 2 | tablespoons olive oil |
| 1 | tablespoon fine dry breadcrumbs |

- Wash peppers and place on lightly oiled baking sheet. Roast at 400° until quite tender. Use paper towels or dish towel to rub off skin. Halve the peppers lengthwise; remove stem and seeds.

- Moisten the fresh breadcrumbs in the milk, squeezing gently and discarding excess liquid. Mix moist crumbs and sausage together. Add egg and sage; season with salt and pepper.

- Spoon mixture into pepper halves and place stuffing side up on foil-covered baking sheet. Drizzle oil over stuffing; sprinkle with dry breadcrumbs. Bake at 350° for about 20 to 25 minutes or until sausage is thoroughly cooked.

 "Don't Explain" as performed by Billie Holiday

# GRILLED PORK SKEWERS

*Serves 8 to 10*

- Cut all fat off pork chops; cut them into 1¼-inch cubes. Put meat in a bowl and add soy sauce. Marinate in refrigerator for 3 hours.

- Cut onions and peppers into chunks. Wash mushrooms and trim tough stems. Drain pork cubes. Thread the meat and vegetables onto skewers, alternating meat, onion, pepper, mushroom.

- Mix the olive oil, thyme, rosemary, oregano, lemon zest, and lemon juice in a small bowl. Use a brush to baste the skewers as they cook on grill or under hot broiler for 20 to 30 minutes.

*Use metal skewers which have been coated with nonstick spray or bamboo skewers which have been soaked in water for 1 hour.*

| | |
|---|---|
| 6 | butterflied pork chops |
| 12 | ounces soy sauce |
| 2 | small red onions |
| 4 | green peppers |
| 8 | ounces fresh button mushrooms |
| ¼ | cup olive oil |
| 1 | tablespoon fresh thyme |
| 1 | tablespoon chopped fresh rosemary |
| 1 | tablespoon chopped fresh oregano |
| | Juice and grated zest from 1 lemon |

 "Lyonnaise Potatoes and Some Pork Chops" as performed by Gene Krupa

# ROASTED PORK LOIN WITH LEMON AND FRESH HERBS

*Serves 8*

| | |
|---|---|
| 1 | (3-pound) boneless pork loin roast |
| ½ | teaspoon salt |
| 2 | small sprigs lemon thyme |
| 1 | large sprig rosemary |
| 2 | large sprigs oregano |
| 1 | tablespoon grated lemon zest |
| 2-4 | cloves garlic, peeled |
| ½ | cup fresh parsley |
| 4-6 | leaves lemon basil |
| 1 | teaspoon cracked black pepper |
| 4 | tablespoons lemon juice |

The discovery of a new dish does more for human happiness than the discovery of a new star.

*Anthelme Brillat-Savarin*

- Sprinkle salt over pork loin and let rest for 10 minutes. Place several thicknesses of plastic wrap, large enough to wrap roast, on work surface. Lay sprigs of thyme, rosemary, and oregano in center of plastic wrap; top with the roast.

- Using small processor or blender, mince lemon zest, garlic, parsley, lemon basil, and pepper with 1 tablespoon of the lemon juice until a chunky paste forms, adding more lemon juice if necessary. Spread paste over roast. Gather the plastic wrap to prevent spilling, and add remaining lemon juice. Wrap roast tightly. Refrigerate at least 8 hours.

- Unwrap the roast. Remove herb sprigs and place in bottom of an appropriately sized roasting pan. Place roast on top of herbs in pan, adding as much of the minced herb mixture as possible.

- Roast at 400° for 1 hour; reduce temperature to 350° and cook an additional ½ to 1 hour (depending on size of roast). Allow roast to rest for 10 minutes; carve into ½-inch thick slices. Heat pan juices in a saucepan; reduce slightly. Pour juices over the sliced meat.

*This pork is also delicious served cold. Slice thinly and serve with small rolls for tea sandwiches.*

# PORK TENDERLOIN WITH FIGS

Serves 6 to 8

- Place tenderloins in a glass baking dish. Liberally sprinkle with seasonings; add basil and thyme. Surround the tenderloins with the figs and other dried fruit. Lay rosemary sprigs on top of tenderloins.

- Mix olive oil, teriyaki sauce, Worcestershire sauce, and balsamic vinegar. Drizzle over meat and fruit. Pour red wine over all. Marinate for 4 to 6 hours.

- Bake at 325° for 45 to 60 minutes. To serve, slice pork and transfer to platter. Surround with fruit and top with sauce, passing extra sauce alongside.

*Try a Cabernet Sauvignon with this, a complex one with flavors of cedar, spice, currant, chocolate, cherry, plum, blackberry, and vanilla.*

| | |
|---|---|
| 2 | (1-pound) pork tenderloins Greek seasoning and garlic-pepper seasoning |
| 1 | tablespoon sliced fresh basil |
| 2 | teaspoons fresh thyme leaves |
| 8 | ounces dried Calimyrna figs |
| 8 | ounces chunky mixed dried fruits |
| 4 | sprigs rosemary |
| 3 | tablespoons olive oil |
| ½ | cup teriyaki sauce |
| 2 | tablespoons Worcestershire sauce |
| 2 | tablespoons balsamic vinegar |
| 2 | cups red wine |

"Plum" as performed by Stanley Turrentine

# PORK TENDERLOIN WITH BRANDY CREAM SAUCE *Serves 2 to 3*

- 1 (12-ounce) pork tenderloin
- 1 teaspoon fresh thyme
- ¼ teaspoon ground allspice
- Salt and black pepper
- 2 tablespoons vegetable oil
- 1 cup half & half
- ½ cup brandy

- Season pork with thyme, allspice, salt, and pepper. Let stand for 30 minutes.

- Heat oil in an ovenproof skillet. Add pork and cook over medium high heat until brown on all sides. Put skillet in oven at 325° for 30 minutes or until pork is cooked through. Transfer meat to platter and tent with foil.

- Add half & half and brandy to skillet. Boil over high heat, scraping up browned bits. Cook until liquid is reduced to ½ cup, about 8 minutes. Slice pork and serve with sauce.

Hell is full of musical amateurs: music is the brandy of the damned.

*George Bernard Shaw*

Wolfgang Amadeus Mozart: *Concerto in A for Clarinet & Orchestra*

# PORK LOIN WITH CREAMY LEEK SAUCE

*Serves 4*

- Boil both stocks together until reduced to ⅔ cup (about 25 minutes). Set aside.

- Heat oil in an ovenproof skillet. Season pork with salt and pepper (eliminate salt if using salted beef broth); brown on all sides over high heat. Transfer skillet to oven and roast at 400° until just cooked, about 25 minutes. Transfer meat to carving board and tent with foil.

- Add leeks and shallots to skillet. Sauté until tender, about 8 minutes. Add reduced stock and port; boil until reduced by half, scraping up any browned bits. Add whipping cream and boil until the mixture reaches a sauce consistency, about 4 minutes. Whisk in butter 1 tablespoon at a time. Slice pork and spoon sauce over, saving some to pass alongside.

2 cups chicken stock or canned low-salt broth
1 cup beef stock or canned broth (preferably unsalted)
1 tablespoon olive oil
1 (1½-pound) boneless pork loin roast
Salt and black pepper
1 large leek, sliced (white and pale green parts only)
3 shallots, chopped
1 cup ruby Port wine
½ cup whipping cream
2 tablespoons butter

John Novacek: "Hog Wild Rag"

# PORK MEDALLIONS WITH COGNAC-MUSTARD CREAM

*Serves 2 to 3*

| | |
|---|---|
| 1 | (12-ounce) pork tenderloin |
| 1 | tablespoon butter |
| 1 | teaspoon olive oil |
| ¼ | cup cognac |
| 1 | cup half & half |
| 1 | tablespoon Dijon mustard |
| 1 | teaspoon cracked black pepper |

- Trim points off ends of tenderloin and reserve for another use. Slice the tenderloin crosswise into ½-inch thick rounds.

- Melt butter with olive oil in a large skillet. Brown the pork medallions over medium-high heat, turning once. Remove to plate.

- Add cognac to skillet and boil for 2 minutes, scraping up any browned bits. Whisk in half & half, mustard, and cracked pepper. Simmer until sauce begins to thicken, about 3 minutes.

- Return pork medallions and any juices which have collected on plate to skillet. Simmer until pork is fully cooked, about 3 to 5 more minutes. Serve medallions in sauce.

Ludwig Van Beethoven: *Concerto #5 in E-Flat for Piano & Orchestra, Op. 73*

## *Serves 2 to 4*  SCALOPPINE MARSALA

- Cover veal cutlets or chicken breasts with waxed paper and pound lightly with a mallet or rolling pin until very thin. Cut meat into 3-inch square pieces and dredge in grated Parmesan cheese. Brown in hot olive oil in large skillet. Add stock, wine, nutmeg, marjoram, salt, and pepper; cover and simmer until very tender. Transfer meat to hot platter; sprinkle with lemon juice and tent with foil.

- Melt butter in small saucepan; add flour and cook for 2 minutes. Add some of the hot sauce from the large skillet, stirring constantly, then add contents of saucepan to remaining sauce in large skillet. Whisk constantly for 5 minutes or until thickened into a smooth, thin sauce.

- Pour a little sauce over meat; serve remainder alongside.

| | |
|---|---|
| 1 | pound veal cutlets or chicken breasts |
| | Grated Parmesan cheese |
| 2 | tablespoons olive oil |
| 2 | cups beef stock or canned broth (preferably unsalted) |
| $2/3$ | cup Marsala wine |
| $1/4$ | teaspoon nutmeg |
| 2-3 | sprigs sweet marjoram or $1/4$ teaspoon dried |
| | Salt and pepper |
| | Lemon juice |
| 2 | tablespoons butter |
| 2 | tablespoons flour |

 Pyotr Ilyich Tchaikovsky: *Capriccio Italien*

# VEAL WITH GREEN PEPPERCORN SAUCE

*Serves 2*

| | |
|---|---|
| 4-5 | ounces veal scaloppine (cutlets) |
| | Salt and freshly ground black pepper |
| ½ | cup flour |
| 2 | tablespoons olive oil |
| 1 | clove garlic |
| ¼ | cup sherry |
| 1 | cup whipping cream |
| 1 | tablespoon green peppercorns in brine |
| | Grated lemon zest |

- Lightly season the veal with salt and pepper. Dredge in flour and shake off excess, reserving all leftover flour.

- Heat olive oil in a sauté pan or skillet over medium heat. Crush the garlic clove with the flat side of a knife; sauté in olive oil until light brown. Remove garlic from skillet and reserve.

- Sauté the veal in the same skillet until it is light brown on both sides. Transfer meat to plate. Add the remaining flour to the oil and cook until frothy, about 2 minutes. Deglaze the pan with sherry and stir briefly until sauce thickens. Add the whipping cream and peppercorns. Reduce heat to simmer. Dice the reserved garlic and add to sauce. Carefully return veal to skillet, covering pieces with sauce. Simmer for 2 additional minutes. Serve garnished with grated lemon zest.

 "Veal Chop and Pork Chop" as performed by Percy "Brother" Randolph

# TIPSY STEW

*Serves 6*

- In a 6-quart Dutch oven, brown stew meat in hot fat or oil. Add bay leaf, chopped carrots, chopped onions, and chopped celery. Continue cooking until vegetables begin to brown. Add vermouth, thyme, beef broth, and pepper. Bring to boil. Cover, reduce heat, and simmer until meat is just tender.

- Add sliced onions, sliced carrots, and cubed potatoes to pot. Return to boil. Cover, reduce heat, and cook an additional 20 minutes or until vegetables are tender.

- Mix cornstarch with Port until smooth. Add to stew and cook for 5 minutes, stirring frequently.

| | |
|---|---|
| 2 | pounds stew beef, cut into 1-inch cubes |
| 1 | tablespoon bacon fat or olive oil |
| ½ | bay leaf |
| ¼ | cup finely diced carrot |
| ¼ | cup finely diced onion |
| ¼ | cup finely diced celery |
| 1 | cup dry white vermouth |
| 1 | teaspoon fresh thyme leaves |
| 1 | (14-ounce) can beef broth, reduced to 1 cup |
| | Freshly ground pepper |
| 2 | cups sliced onions |
| 2 | cups sliced carrots |
| 5 | small potatoes, cubed |
| 1 | tablespoon cornstarch |
| ½ | cup ruby Port wine |

Wine is the only natural beverage that feeds not only the body, but the soul and spirit.

*Robert Mondavi*

 Johann Sebastian Bach: *Cantata #78:* "Wir eilen mit schwachen, doch emsigen schritten" ("We hasten with faltering, yet eager footsteps")

# PAPRIKA STEW

*Serves 6 to 8*

3 tablespoons oil
3 pounds stew beef, cut into 1-inch cubes
1 large onion
1 large green pepper
1 large clove garlic
2 tablespoons flour
1 (14-ounce) can beef broth
1 (28-ounce) can diced tomatoes in juice
1 (28-ounce) can crushed tomatoes in puree
1 bay leaf
3 tablespoons paprika
1 medium head cauliflower
1 tablespoon butter

- Heat oil in a Dutch oven; add beef and cook over high heat until liquid evaporates and meat begins browning. Add onion and green pepper; continue cooking for about 5 minutes or until the onion begins to brown. Keep scraping up browned bits from the bottom of the pan (this is a rich, dark, heavily-flavored stew). Add garlic and flour; cook and stir for 2 minutes.

- Stir in beef broth, again scraping up any browned bits, and both cans of tomatoes with all juices. Add 1 tomato can of water, the bay leaf, and paprika. Bring to a boil; reduce heat, cover, and simmer until beef is very tender. Stir frequently to avoid scorching (add a bit more water if necessary).

- Clean cauliflower and break into florets. Steam or boil until very tender. Drain and return cauliflower to pan with butter. Using potato masher, smash cauliflower thoroughly (it will be a bit chunky).

- When beef is tender, remove cover and turn heat to medium-high, stirring gently, to thicken sauce slightly. Serve stew over cauliflower.

# STIFADO

*Serves 6 to 8*

- Bring a medium saucepan of water to a boil. Add the pearl onions and simmer for 1 minute. Drain and rinse with cool water. Using a small, sharp knife, cut off the root end of each onion and squeeze from the top so that the skin slips off. In a Dutch oven, brown the onions in olive oil over medium-high heat. When nicely colored, remove onions with slotted spoon and set aside.

- In the same pan, cook the meat over high heat, stirring frequently, until well-browned. Add wine, tomatoes, tomato paste, and spices. Stir well and return to boil. Reduce heat to simmer and cook until meat is nearly tender, about 1 to 1½ hours. Add the onions and cook for an additional 20 minutes. Season to taste with salt and pepper.

*This stew from Greece is typically served by itself on a flat plate with plenty of crusty peasant bread to sop up the juices.*

| | |
|---|---|
| 1-2 | cups yellow or white pearl onions |
| ¼ | cup olive oil |
| 2-3 | pounds arm roast, cut into 2-inch pieces |
| 2 | cups dry red wine |
| 1 | (26-ounce) can diced tomatoes in juice |
| 3 | tablespoons tomato paste |
| 1 | tablespoon ground cinnamon |
| 1 | teaspoon ground clove |
| 1 | teaspoon ground allspice |
| | Salt and pepper |

 Ludwig Van Beethoven: *Symphony #9 in D minor, Op. 125*

# FILET MIGNON WITH RED WINE-SHALLOT SAUCE

*Serves 2*

½ cup finely chopped shallots
3 tablespoons butter, cut into 6 pieces
1 cup beef stock or broth (preferably unsalted)
1 cup dry red wine
¼ cup brandy
½ tablespoon olive oil
2 (8-ounce) filet mignon steaks
Freshly ground pepper

- In a small saucepan, sauté the shallots in ½ tablespoon (1 piece) butter until soft. Add beef broth; cook on medium high heat until reduced to ¼ cup. Add wine and cook until reduced to ½ cup. Add brandy and cook for 2 minutes. Remove from heat and allow to stand.

- Melt ½ tablespoon butter (1 piece) with oil in skillet. Sear steaks over high heat for about 1 minute on each side. Lower heat to medium high and cook to desired doneness. Remove steaks to platter or plates and tent with foil.

- Add wine sauce to skillet, scraping up any browned bits. Whisk remaining 2 tablespoons of butter in 1 piece at a time over medium-high heat. Spoon sauce over steaks and top with freshly ground pepper.

***Variations:*** *Rib-Eye with Rosemary-Wine Sauce: Place 2 sprigs fresh rosemary about 6 inches apart on a piece of plastic wrap. Top each sprig with a 12-ounce rib-eye. Place another sprig of rosemary on each steak. Wrap tightly in plastic wrap and allow to stand at room temperature for 30 minutes. When preparing the reduction sauce, omit the brandy. Unwrap the steaks and add rosemary sprigs to pan with sauce. Return sauce to low heat and allow to simmer. Cook steaks and finish sauce as directed above*

 Wolfgang Amadeus Mozart: *Concerto #21 in C for Piano & Orchestra*

# ROASTED BEEF SHANKS AND SHALLOTS WITH WINE

*Serves 4*

- Toss beef, shallots, and garlic with oil in baking dish. Spread meat out to single layer, covering garlic cloves with meat. Roast at 425° for 20 minutes or until well-browned. Remove shallots and set aside.

- Put meat and garlic into a Dutch oven. Add stock, red wine, Port, brandy, bay leaf, rosemary, and thyme. Bring to boil; reduce heat, cover, and simmer until meat is tender, about 1½ hours.

- Uncover the Dutch oven and add the shallots. Cook on medium high until liquid is slightly reduced, about 10 minutes. Mix cornstarch and water until smooth. Add half the cornstarch mixture and stir until sauce begins to thicken. Add remaining cornstarch for a thicker sauce. Serve over mashed potatoes, wide noodles, or couscous.

| | |
|---|---|
| 2 | pounds beef shanks (sliced about 1-inch thick) or 1½ pounds stew beef cut into 2-inch pieces |
| 8 | large or 12 small shallots, peeled |
| 4 | cloves garlic, peeled |
| 2 | tablespoons olive oil |
| 4 | cups beef stock or broth (preferably unsalted) |
| 1 | cup red wine |
| ½ | cup ruby Port wine |
| ¼ | cup brandy |
| 1 | bay leaf |
| 2 | teaspoons chopped fresh rosemary |
| 2 | teaspoons fresh thyme leaves |
| 1 | tablespoon cornstarch |
| 2 | tablespoons water |

A bone to the dog is not charity. Charity is the bone shared with the dog, when you are just as hungry as the dog.

*Jack London*

 Darius Milhaud: *Le Boeuf Sur Le Toit*

BEEF 173

# SPICED BEEF TENDERLOIN

*Serves 4*

| | |
|---|---|
| 1 | (1½-pound) beef tenderloin roast |
| 1 | lemon |
| 1 | sprig rosemary, leaves stripped |
| 3 | cloves garlic, pressed |
| 1 | tablespoon cracked black pepper |
| ¼ | cup olive oil |
| ½ | cup dry red wine |

- Place tenderloin in a plastic zipper bag. Remove and reserve zest from lemon. Cut lemon in half; slice two thin slices from the cut side of each half. Squeeze juice from remainder of halves and strain. Add lemon juice, lemon slices, and lemon zest to zipper bag with meat, along with rosemary leaves, pressed garlic, and cracked pepper. Pour in the oil and wine, seal the bag, and refrigerate overnight (at least 6 hours).

- Place tenderloin with all juices in a shallow baking dish. Bake at 400° for approximately 1 hour (medium-rare). Allow roast to rest on carving board for 5 minutes. Slice thinly and serve with pan juices on side.

 Ludwig Van Beethoven: *Symphony #7 in A, Op. 92*

# LAMB WITH LENTILS

*Serves 2*

- In a large skillet, brown lamb in oil. Add shallots and cook for 2 additional minutes. Add water. Bring to boil, cover, and reduce heat. Cook for about 20 minutes or until lamb is nearly tender.

- Add lentils, thyme, rosemary, and tomatoes. Stir well. Return to boil; simmer until lentils are fully cooked and lamb is tender, about 30 minutes. Add olives about 5 minutes before dish is finished. Serve over couscous or in shallow soup plates.

| | |
|---|---|
| 2 | cups cubed lamb |
| 2 | tablespoons olive oil |
| 2 | large shallots, sliced |
| 6 | cups boiling water |
| 1 | cup brown lentils, rinsed |
| 2 | sprigs thyme |
| 1 | sprig rosemary |
| ¼ | cup coarsely chopped sun-dried yellow tomatoes (red will work) |
| ¼ | cup coarsely chopped, pitted Niçoise or other brine-cured olives |
| | Prepared couscous |

However mean your life is, meet it and live it: do not shun it and call it hard names. Cultivate poverty like a garden herb, like sage. Do not trouble yourself much to get new things, whether clothes or friends. Things do not change, we change. Sell your clothes and keep your thoughts.

*Henry David Thoreau*

Max Bruch: *Scottish Fantasy for Violin, Orchestra & Harp, Op. 46*

# ROSEMARY-SCENTED LAMB WITH PENNE

*Serves 2*

- 2 cloves garlic, chopped
- 5 ounces lamb, cut into thin strips
- ½ red or yellow bell pepper, cut into strips
- ¼ cup dry white wine
- 1½ cups crushed tomatoes with puree
- Sprig of rosemary
- 2 tablespoons heavy cream
- Salt and black pepper
- ½ pound penne, cooked
- ¼ cup Asiago or Parmesan cheese
- 1 teaspoon chopped rosemary
- 1 teaspoon chopped sage
- 1 teaspoon chopped oregano

- Sauté the garlic, lamb, and bell pepper until the lamb is tender and cooked to your preference. Over high heat, deglaze the pan with wine, cooking until liquid is almost evaporated. Add the tomatoes and rosemary. Simmer for 15 minutes.

- Stir in the cream, salt, and pepper. Cook until heated through. Toss with warm penne and garnish with cheese, rosemary, sage, and oregano. Serve immediately.

. . . wine is life, and my life and wine are inextricable.

*MFK Fisher*

 "Counting My Blessings" as performed by Bing Crosby

# GRILLED LAMB CHOPS

*Serves 6*

- Rub chops with salt and pepper. Coat on all sides with olive oil and allow to rest for 5 minutes.

- Blend or process garlic, rosemary, lemon zest, and lemon juice until a smooth paste forms. Spread paste over chops; wrap each chop tightly in plastic wrap and refrigerate for at least 4 hours.

- Unwrap chops and allow to stand for 20 minutes. Grill for 3 to 5 minutes per side for rare or medium-rare chops (lamb should be pink inside).

| | |
|---|---|
| 6 | (1½-inch thick) lamb t-bone chops |
| | Salt and freshly ground black pepper |
| | Olive oil |
| 3 | cloves garlic |
| 3 | tablespoons chopped fresh rosemary |
| | Zest and juice from 1 lemon |

*Grilled Lamb Chops Greek-Style:* Use small thin rib chops (the kind found on a rack of lamb). About 20 small chops will serve 3 to 5 people. Rub chops with oil and grill over hot fire for 1 to 2 minutes per side. Just before serving, sprinkle with plenty of dried oregano and drench with lemon juice. Serve immediately. These chops make excellent "walking around" food at a party; just think of them as lamb lollipops.

Aaron Copland: *Billy The Kid*

# RACK OF LAMB WITH HAZELNUT-WALNUT CRUST *Serves 2*

| | |
|---|---|
| 1 | (1 pound) rack of lamb |
| | Salt and black pepper |
| 1 | cup hazelnuts |
| ½ | cup walnuts |
| 1 | teaspoon chopped fresh rosemary |
| 1 | cup fresh breadcrumbs |
| | Melted butter |

- Sprinkle lamb with salt and pepper. Allow to stand for 30 minutes.

- Put hazelnuts in a round cake pan and bake at 400° for a few minutes until lightly toasted. Allow to cool. Rub the skins off using your fingers; transfer hazelnuts, walnuts, and rosemary to small bowl of food processor or blender. Process until the mixture resembles moist crumbs. Combine nut crumbs and breadcrumbs.

- Place rack of lamb in shallow baking pan, bone side down. Press the crumb mixture onto the top of the meat, covering evenly. Drizzle melted butter over crumbs. Bake lamb at 400° for 30 minutes for rare, 40 minutes for medium. Slice between bones into rib chops and serve immediately.

Good wine, well drunk, can lend majesty to the human spirit.

*MFK Fisher*

# ACCOMPANIMENTS
*Salads, Side Dishes, & Breads*

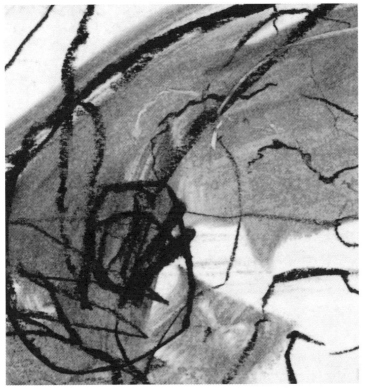

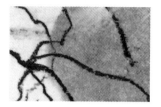

# A MENU FOR SUMMER

One cannot think well, love well,
sleep well, if one has not dined well.

*Virginia Woolf*

---

*Soup*
White Corn Soup with Sautéed Scallops

*Salad*
Mixed Greens with Warm Goat Cheese

*Main Plate*
Roasted Pork Loin with Lemon and Fresh Herbs
Mashed Potatoes with Caramelized Onions & Roasted Garlic
Roma-Zucchini Wheel

*Dessert*
Fresh Peach Cake

---

 Sir William Walton: *Belshazzar's Feast*

# CREAMY APPLE-BEET SALAD

*Serves 4 to 6*

- Peel apple and cut it in half. Remove core. Slice each half as thinly as possible. Slice beets thinly.

- Gently mix apple and beet slices with sour cream until they are thoroughly coated. Sprinkle onion over top.

1 medium apple (Gala, Fuji, or Jonathan)
2 medium cooked beets or 1½ cups canned whole beets
⅓ cup sour cream
1 tablespoon finely chopped onion

# CARROT-GREEN ONION SALAD

*Serves 4 to 6*

| | |
|---|---|
| 1 | pound carrots, peeled and coarsely grated |
| 3 | green onions, chopped |
| 2 | tablespoons minced parsley |
| 1½ | tablespoons white wine vinegar |
| 1 | tablespoon grated lemon zest |
| 1 | teaspoon Dijon mustard |
| ¼ | cup olive oil |
| | Salt and black pepper |

- Mix carrots, onions, and parsley in large bowl.

- Whisk vinegar, lemon zest, and mustard in a small bowl. Gradually whisk in the olive oil. Season with salt and pepper.

- Pour dressing over carrots in large bowl. Toss until carrots are thoroughly coated. Refrigerate at least 2 hours. This dish will keep for 3 days.

**Variations:** For Carrot-Turnip Salad, mix carrots with ½ pound of peeled and shredded turnips. Toss with 2 tablespoons olive oil and 2 tablespoons lemon juice. Top with freshly ground pepper.

Traditional: "Down by the Sally Gardens"

# CABBAGE SALAD

*Serves 10*

- Wash cabbage and remove core. Slice the cabbage as thinly as possible. Peel and coarsely shred carrots.

- Pour olive oil over cabbage and carrots. Sprinkle lemon juice on top. Season with salt and pepper and toss to coat thoroughly.

1 small head cabbage
½ pound carrots
¼ cup olive oil
2 tablespoons lemon juice
Salt and black pepper

 Samuel Barber: *First Essay for Orchestra, Op. 12*

# SHREDDED SALAD

*Serves 6 to 8*

| | |
|---|---|
| 1 | small head cabbage |
| 1 | red or yellow bell pepper |
| 1 | green bell pepper |
| ½ | purple onion |
| ⅓ | cup olive oil |
| 2 | tablespoons red wine vinegar |
| 1 | clove garlic, minced |
| 2 | tablespoons fresh herbs (oregano, basil, parsley, or rosemary) |
| 1 | teaspoon dried oregano |
| 2 | teaspoons cracked black pepper |
| 1 | teaspoon salt |

- Wash and core cabbage; shred coarsely or slice thinly with knife. Wash, seed, and julienne both bell peppers. Cut onion into slivers. Mix vegetables together in a large bowl.

- Whisk together olive oil, vinegar, garlic, fresh herbs, dried oregano, cracked pepper, and salt. Pour over cabbage mixture. Toss thoroughly. Cover and refrigerate at least 4 hours. This salad will keep for 4 days.

*This is a very versatile salad. Add whatever vegetables you have in stock and delete any you are out of, even cabbage. Try finely diced celery, shredded zucchini or summer squash, finely chopped radish, minced hot peppers, or thinly sliced green beans.*

 Samuel Barber: *Second Essay for Orchestra, Op. 17*

# CRISPY SLAW WITH SOY VINAIGRETTE

*Serves 6*

- Combine cabbage, snow peas, and carrots in a large bowl. Pour Soy Vinaigrette over cabbage mixture and toss to coat thoroughly. Let stand for 30 minutes. Toss again and serve.

- Whisk soy sauce, peanut oil, vinegar, wine, and lime juice in a small bowl. Add sugar and whisk until sugar dissolves. Whisk in ginger, sesame oil, and garlic. This dressing will keep for 2 days.

2 cups finely sliced Napa cabbage
1 cup julienned snow peas
1 cup julienned carrots
Soy Vinaigrette

*Soy Vinaigrette*
2 tablespoons soy sauce
1 tablespoon peanut or vegetable oil
1 tablespoon rice vinegar
1 tablespoon sweet rice wine (mirin) or sherry
1 tablespoon lime juice
1½ teaspoons sugar
1 teaspoon grated ginger
1 teaspoon dark sesame oil
1 clove garlic, minced

---

Samuel Barber: *Third Essay for Orchestra, Op. 47*

# CAULIFLOWER SALAD  *Serves 6*

| | |
|---|---|
| 1 | small head cauliflower |
| ½ | cup sliced green onion |
| 1 | tablespoon olive oil |
| 1 | teaspoon lemon juice |
| | Freshly ground black pepper |

- Clean cauliflower and break into large florets. Steam or boil until crisp tender.

- Break the cauliflower into bite-size pieces and put in bowl. Toss with green onion, olive oil, and lemon juice while still warm. Allow to cool; refrigerate for 2 hours or overnight.

- Stir before serving and sprinkle with freshly ground black pepper. Serve at room temperature.

Music can change the world.
   *Ludwig von Beethoven*

 Pyotr Ilyich Tchaikovsky: *The Nutcracker:* "Waltz of the Flowers"

# BROCCOLI CRUNCH

*Serves 6*

- Cook bacon until crisp. Remove from heat and crumble.

- Trim tough ends from broccoli. Cut the florets and break into bite-size pieces. Dice the stems. Chop onion finely. Mix broccoli, onion, raisins, cheese, and peanuts in large bowl.

- Stir mayonnaise and sugar together until sugar dissolves. Blend in vinegar.

- Just before serving, add bacon and mayonnaise mixture to salad. Toss gently and serve.

| | |
|---|---|
| 8 | slices bacon |
| 1 | bunch broccoli |
| ¼ | cup red onion |
| ¼ | cup raisins |
| 1 | cup shredded cheddar cheese |
| ½ | cup honey roasted peanuts or toasted walnuts (optional) |
| 1 | cup mayonnaise |
| ¼ | cup sugar |
| 2 | tablespoons white vinegar |

 James Scott: "Evergreen Rag"

# SUCCOTASH SALAD

*Serves 12*

½ cup mayonnaise
5 tablespoons buttermilk
1 tablespoon Dijon mustard
1 tablespoon lemon juice
1 tablespoon sugar
1 teaspoon shredded lemon zest
1 teaspoon hot pepper sauce
1 large serrano chile, seeded and minced
1 pound fresh or frozen lima beans
1 pound fresh or frozen corn kernels
2 large red bell peppers
½ cup green onions, thinly sliced

- Combine mayonnaise, buttermilk, mustard, lemon juice, sugar, lemon zest, hot pepper sauce, and minced chile. Mix thoroughly and refrigerate for at least 1 hour or overnight.

- Cook lima beans in boiling water for 5 minutes; drain and allow to cool. Cook fresh corn in boiling water for 2 minutes; drain and allow to cool. (If using frozen corn, simply allow to thaw and drain.)

- Char red peppers on grill or gas burner or under broiler until blackened all over. Place in paper bag; close bag and leave for 10 minutes. Peel, seed, and dice red peppers.

- Mix vegetables together in a large bowl. Pour dressing over and toss gently until everything is thoroughly combined.

**Variations:** *This recipe is perfectly designed for variations. Substitute any of your favorite summer vegetables; just blanch or grill, dice, and add to the bowl.*

# BLACK-EYED PEA SALAD

*Serves 4 to 6*

- Rinse and drain peas. Transfer to medium bowl and combine with celery and both onions.

- Combine oil, vinegar, mayonnaise, pepper sauce, salt, and pepper. Pour over peas and stir gently to coat. Refrigerate for at least 1 hour.

- Just before serving, add diced tomatoes.

| | |
|---|---|
| 2 | cups cooked or canned black-eyed peas |
| 1 | stalk celery, finely diced |
| 1 | tablespoon finely chopped onion |
| 1 | green onion, sliced |
| 1 | tablespoon olive oil |
| 1 | tablespoon red wine vinegar |
| 1 | tablespoon mayonnaise |
| ½ | teaspoon hot pepper sauce |
| ¼ | teaspoon salt |
| | Freshly ground black pepper |
| 1 | tomato, diced |

---

EDIBLE, adj. Good to eat, and wholesome to digest, as a worm to a toad, a toad to a snake, a snake to a pig, a pig to a man, and a man to a worm.

*Ambrose Bierce*

# CORN, BLACK BEAN, AND HEARTS OF PALM SALAD

*Serves 10 to 12*

| | | |
|---|---|---|
| 2 | (16-ounce) cans black beans, rinsed and drained | • Mix black beans, corn, hearts of palm, tomato, onion, and cilantro in large bowl. Pour vinaigrette over vegetables and mix gently until well coated. Season with salt and pepper. Serve chilled or at room temperature. |
| 1 | (16-ounce) package frozen corn kernels, thawed | |
| 1 | (14-ounce) jar hearts of palm, diced | |
| 2 | medium tomatoes, chopped | |
| ½ | cup sliced green onion | |
| ¼ | chopped cilantro (packed) | |
| 1 | fresh jalapeño pepper, minced (optional) | |
| | Lime Vinaigrette | |
| | Salt and black pepper | |

**Lime Vinaigrette**

| | | |
|---|---|---|
| ¼ | cup oil | • Whisk all ingredients together in a small bowl or measuring cup. |
| 2 | tablespoons lime juice | |
| 2 | teaspoons cumin | |
| 1 | teaspoon shredded lime zest | |

 George Butterworth: *Banks of Green Willow Idyll*

# MESCLUN WITH WARM GOAT CHEESE

*Serves 6*

- Slice cheese into ½-inch thick rounds (you should have 12). Place rounds in shallow dish. Sprinkle with half of the herbs and onions; turn and sprinkle with remaining herbs. Drizzle ¼ cup olive oil over top. Allow to stand at room temperature for 1 hour.

- Coat each cheese round with breadcrumbs and transfer to baking sheet lined with foil and sprayed with nonstick cooking spray. Bake at 350° until cheese just begins to melt, about 10 minutes.

- Toss greens with vinaigrette. Divide among 6 salad plates. Place 2 warm cheese rounds on center of each salad. Grind pepper on top; garnish with whole chives.

**Variations:** A simpler version can be prepared very quickly. Slice the cheese into rounds and place rounds on a nonstick baking sheet or in nonstick cake pans which have been coated with nonstick spray. Broil on high for 1-2 minutes, removing when rounds collapse and begin to brown. Use spatula to transfer 2 rounds to each salad. Cheese rounds can also be placed on top of toasted baguette slices before broiling. This same mixed salad is also delicious when the cheese is replaced by pâté. Spread toast points or toasted baguette slices with a thick layer of pâté and arrange on the salads.

| | |
|---|---|
| 2 | (6-ounce) logs goat cheese |
| 2 | tablespoons chopped fresh parsley |
| 1 | tablespoon minced fresh oregano or 1 teaspoon dried |
| 1 | tablespoon minced fresh tarragon or 1 teaspoon dried |
| 2 | tablespoons chopped green onions |
| ½ | cup olive oil |
| 1 | cup coarse dry breadcrumbs (not seasoned) |
| 10 | cups mixed greens, including some endive, radicchio, or other bitter greens |
| ⅓ | cup French Vinaigrette, see page 317 |
| | Freshly ground black pepper |
| | Whole chives |

Albert W. Ketelbey: *In a Monastery Garden*

# SPRING GREENS WITH CLEMENTINES AND RED ONION

*Serves 6*

8 cups mixed baby greens
1½ cups fresh or canned clementine, tangerine, or mandarin orange sections
6 extremely thin slices of purple onion, separated into rings
Honey-Mustard Dressing or Blush Vinaigrette

- Method 1: Toss greens, clementines, and onion rings in a large bowl with enough dressing to lightly coat. Divide among 6 salad plates.

- Method 2: Divide greens among 6 salad plates. Arrange clementine sections around the outer edge of the plates; arrange rings of onion on the center of the greens. Drizzle with one of the dressings below or with a similar prepared dressing.

Some people have a foolish way of not minding, or pretending not to mind, what they eat. For my part, I mind my belly very studiously, and very carefully; for I look upon it, that he who does not mind his belly will hardly mind anything else.

*Samuel Johnson*

 Percy Aldridge Grainger: "My Robin is to the Greenwood Gone"

## SPRING GREENS *continued*

- To make this very flexible dressing, decide whether you want a sweet flavor or tart flavor to be more predominant. Mix together a few tablespoons of honey and mustard until you get a mix that tastes right to you. Add 1 or 2 teaspoons of balsamic vinegar, again tasting for proper quantity. Whisk in some olive oil. The less you add, the stronger the honey-mustard flavors will be; the more you add, the subtler those flavors will be. Season to taste with salt and pepper.

- Whisk together wine and vinegar in a 2-cup glass measure. Whisk in onion and allow to stand for 30 minutes. Slowly add olive oil, pouring in a thin stream and whisking constantly. Season to taste with salt and pepper.

### Honey-Mustard Dressing

Honey
Dijon mustard
Balsamic vinegar
Olive oil
Salt and black pepper

### Blush Vinaigrette

| | |
|---|---|
| ¼ | cup white Zinfandel or other blush, rose, or white wine |
| 1 | teaspoon balsamic vinegar |
| 1 | tablespoon grated onion |
| ¾ | cup olive oil |
| | Salt and black pepper |

# BABY GREENS WITH PEAR, BLEU CHEESE, AND WALNUTS

*Serves 4*

| | |
|---|---|
| 1 | creamy pear, any soft variety |
| 6 | cups mixed baby greens |
| ½ | cup crumbled bleu cheese |
| ½ | cup walnut halves, lightly toasted |
| 3 | tablespoons olive oil |
| 1 | tablespoon balsamic vinegar |
| | Salt and black pepper |

- Peel the pear and cut in half lengthwise. Remove the core. Slice the pear halves lengthwise.

- Toss the greens with bleu cheese, walnuts, oil, and vinegar. Season with salt and pepper. Divide among 4 salad plates. Top salads with pear slices.

# BABY GREENS WITH FETA AND ORANGE VINAIGRETTE

*Serves 8 to 12*

- Put salad greens into large bowl. Add pine nuts, croutons, and feta. Toss lightly.

- Add half of Orange Vinaigrette; toss well. Add additional dressing as desired or pass alongside.

*Makes ⅔ cup*
- In a small bowl, combine garlic, mustard, and vinegar. Add marmalade and stir well. Whisk in oil, salt, and pepper.

| | |
|---|---|
| 3 | (4-ounce) packages baby greens |
| ¾ | cup toasted pine nuts |
| 2 | cups seasoned croutons |
| 1 | cup crumbled feta |

Orange Vinaigrette

**Orange Vinaigrette**

| | |
|---|---|
| 1 | clove garlic, minced |
| ½ | teaspoon Dijon mustard |
| 2 | tablespoons balsamic vinegar |
| 1-3 | tablespoons orange marmalade |
| 2 | tablespoons olive oil |
| ¼ | teaspoon salt |
| | Freshly ground black pepper |

Those who dance are thought to be quite insane by those who cannot hear the music.

*Angela Monet*

SALADS 195

# AUTHENTIC GREEK SALAD  *Serves 6*

| | |
|---|---|
| 2 | large tomatoes |
| 1 | large hothouse cucumber |
| 4 | ounces feta cheese |
| 18 | Greek olives, preferably Kalamata |
| ¼ | small red onion |
| 1 | tablespoon dried oregano |
| | Salt and black pepper |
| 2 | tablespoons olive oil |

- Cut each tomato into 8 wedges and place in serving bowl. Peel cucumber and halve lengthwise. Cut crosswise into chunky slices about ½-inch thick. Add to bowl on top of tomato (do not mix together). Crumble, cube, or slice feta cheese and place on top of cucumber. Add olives around the edges of the bowl. Cut the onion lengthwise into paper-thin slivers; sprinkle over feta. Put dried oregano in the palm of your hand; use fingers of other hand to crush the herb. Sprinkle over feta. Add salt and pepper to the salad.

- The salad should not be assembled more than ½ hour in advance or the cucumbers will get soggy. Refrigerate for a cold salad or leave at room temperature. Just before serving, sprinkle olive oil over the salad and gently toss until the cheese, oregano, and oil are distributed throughout. You may wish to present the salad at the table in its layered form and then toss. Serve plenty of crusty peasant bread for sopping the delicious tomato-oregano-flavored oil.

# CORNBREAD SALAD

*Serves 8 to 12*

- In a medium bowl, combine eggs, tomatoes, onion, bell pepper, and pickles. Crumble the cornbread into another bowl. Whisk together pickle juice and mayonnaise.

- Put half of cornbread into the bottom of a serving dish. Top with half the egg-vegetable mixture. Cover with a layer of half the pickle-mayonnaise mixture. Repeat layering once more. Chill for 2 to 3 hours. Just before serving, scatter crumbled bacon over top.

*Use additional pickle-mayonnaise mixture if desired, combining 4 parts mayonnaise to 1 part pickle juice.*

| | |
|---|---|
| 5 | hard-boiled eggs, chopped |
| 2 | medium tomatoes, chopped |
| 1 | cup chopped green onion |
| 1 | cup diced green bell pepper |
| ½ | cup sweet pickles, finely chopped |
| | Iron Skillet Cornbread, baked and cooled, see page 243 |
| ¼ | cup sweet pickle juice |
| 1 | cup mayonnaise |
| 12 | strips of bacon, cooked and crumbled |

# SPA SALAD

*Serves 4 to 6*

| | |
|---|---|
| 4 | cups cooked brown rice |
| ½ | cup sliced ripe olives |
| 6 | green onions, sliced |
| 1 | cup frozen peas, thawed |
| 12 | cherry tomatoes, quartered |
| ¼ | cup sliced fresh basil |
| ⅓ | cup raw sunflower seeds or toasted pine nuts |
| 4 | tablespoons olive oil |
| 1½ | tablespoons balsamic vinegar |
| | Salt and black pepper |

- Toss rice with olives, onions, peas, tomatoes, basil, and seeds or nuts. Add oil and vinegar and toss again. Season with salt and pepper.

**Variations:** To make a Bulghur Salad, substitute 4 cups cooked bulghur wheat for rice.

# MEDITERRANEAN RICE SALAD

*Serves 2*

- Put rice and chicken broth in a saucepan; cover and cook until tender. Fluff with a fork; spoon rice into a medium bowl.

- Mix olive oil and lemon juice with rice. Add olives, arugula, green onion, pine nuts, and cheeses. Season with salt and pepper and mix well. Serve at room temperature.

½ cup basmati rice
¾ cup chicken broth
1 tablespoon olive oil
2 teaspoons lemon juice
¼ cup chopped Kalamata olives
1 ounce fresh arugula, chopped
1 green onion, minced
¼ cup toasted pine nuts
2 tablespoons crumbled feta cheese
2 tablespoons grated Romano cheese
Salt and black pepper

> Always carry a flagon of whiskey in case of snakebite and furthermore always carry a small snake.
>
> *W.C. Fields*

 Manuel De Falla: *Nights in the Gardens of Spain*

# ORZO SALAD

*Serves 6*

1½ cups orzo pasta
⅓ cup chopped oil-packed sun-dried tomatoes, drained
5 tablespoons olive oil
¼ cup balsamic vinegar
2 large garlic cloves, minced
¼ cup chopped Kalamata olives
1 cup finely chopped radicchio
½ cup toasted pine nuts
½ cup chopped fresh basil
Salt and black pepper

- Cook orzo pasta in boiling water until tender but still firm. Drain.

- In a large bowl, mix hot pasta, tomatoes, oil, vinegar, garlic, and olives. Allow to cool to room temperature.

- Mix in radicchio, pine nuts, and basil. Season with salt and pepper.

Too many pieces of music finish too long after the end.

*Igor Stravinsky*

# CAULIFLOWER-POTATO SALAD WITH MARINATED RED ONIONS AND BLEU CHEESE

*Serves 6 to 8*

- Whisk olive oil, horseradish, and vinegar in a medium bowl. Mix in onion and season with salt and pepper. Let stand at room temperature for 2 hours.

- Wash and core cauliflower. Break head into bite-size florets (keep them small because they will be added to the salad raw). Steam potatoes in their jackets for about 20 minutes. Allow to cool; slice thinly.

- Place cauliflower florets in a serving bowl. Add marinated onions and toss well. Add the potato slices and bleu cheese; toss gently until thoroughly mixed. Serve at room temperature.

9 tablespoons olive oil
5 tablespoons cream-style horseradish
3 tablespoons white wine vinegar
1 red onion, halved and thinly sliced
Salt and black pepper
1 head cauliflower
2 pounds small red potatoes
½ cup crumbled bleu cheese

Leonard Bernstein: *Candide:* "Make Our Garden Grow"

# WARM SAUSAGE AND POTATO SALAD

*Serves 4 to 6*

| | |
|---|---|
| 1 | cup sun-dried tomatoes (not oil-packed) |
| 3 | links Italian sausage |
| 1½ | pounds red potatoes |
| 1 | cup sliced celery |
| ½ | cup chopped red onion |
| | Classic Vinaigrette, see page 316 |
| ¼ | cup chopped fresh fennel |

- Put tomatoes in a small bowl and cover with boiling water. Set aside.

- Cook sausages in a skillet; transfer to paper towels and allow to cool. Slice the sausages on the diagonal and set aside.

- Cook potatoes in their jackets in boiling water until tender. While the potatoes are cooking, chop the sun-dried tomatoes. Cut hot potatoes into ⅓-inch slices and immediately put potatoes, tomatoes, celery, and onion in a large serving bowl. Add enough Classic Vinaigrette to coat and toss gently.

- Put sausage slices into a nonstick skillet over high heat. Cook, stirring constantly, just until the slices are beginning to brown, about 2 minutes. Transfer to paper towels to blot grease. Add sausage to salad and toss gently. Sprinkle with fennel and serve immediately.

# PESTO PASTA SALAD

*Serves 8*

- Cook pasta in boiling water until just tender. Drain, reserving ½ cup cooking liquid.

- Toss pasta with Classic Pesto and reserved cooking liquid until thoroughly mixed. Add tomatoes; season with salt and pepper and toss gently. Sprinkle with Asiago cheese.

1½ pounds farfalle (bow-tie) or radiatore pasta
1 cup Classic Pesto, see page 326
3 cups halved cherry tomatoes
Salt and black pepper
½ cup grated Asiago cheese

# CONFETTI PASTA SALAD

*Serves 8*

| | |
|---|---|
| 4 | tablespoons olive oil |
| 4 | garlic cloves, minced |
| 1 | (12-ounce) package spiral, shell, or other shaped pasta |
| 6 | radishes, sliced |
| 2 | stalks celery, sliced |
| ½ | green bell pepper, diced |
| ½ | red bell pepper, diced |
| 4 | green onions, sliced |
| 1 | tablespoon capers |
| ½ | cup sliced ripe olives |
| 1 | small cucumber, peeled and diced |
| 2 | tablespoons minced fresh basil or 2 teaspoons dried |
| 1 | tablespoon chopped fresh oregano or 1 teaspoon dried |
| 1 | tablespoon chopped dill or 1 teaspoon dried |
| ½ | teaspoon cayenne pepper |
| | Salt and freshly ground black pepper |
| ½ | cup grated Parmesan cheese (optional) |

- Put olive oil and garlic into serving bowl; allow to stand while pasta cooks.

- Cook pasta according to package directions until just tender. Drain and add to serving bowl; toss with olive oil-garlic mixture.

- Add radish, celery, green and red bell pepper, green onion, capers, olives, and cucumber to pasta. Toss to combine. Sprinkle basil, oregano, dill, and cayenne pepper over the top. Season with salt and pepper.

- Toss gently but thoroughly until all ingredients are combined. This salad tastes best if refrigerated for 12 to 24 hours. Just before serving, sprinkle with cheese if desired.

 Robert Schumann: *Carnaval, Op. 9*

# LINGUINE SALAD WITH MARINATED TOMATOES

*Serves 6 to 8*

- Snap off the tough ends from asparagus. Cut into 1-inch pieces, reserving tips. Bring water to boil in a large saucepan or Dutch oven. Add asparagus tips; cook for 1 minute and remove with slotted spoon to cold water. Drain and reserve. Cook pasta according to package directions until just tender. During last 2 minutes of cooking, add remaining asparagus. Drain and rinse with cold water.

- Toss drained pasta and asparagus with bell pepper, onions, parsley, dill, and basil. Pour Classic Vinaigrette over salad and toss again until dressing coats all pasta. Transfer to serving bowl. Spoon Marinated Tomatoes onto center of pasta salad. Scatter top with reserved asparagus tips and Parmesan cheese, if desired.

- Mix together shallot, vinegar, and oil. Add tomatoes and bleu cheese, if desired. Let stand at room temperature for 30 minutes.

½ pound asparagus
1 pound fresh linguine
1 red bell pepper, thinly sliced
2 green onions, thinly sliced
¼ cup finely chopped fresh parsley
3 tablespoons finely chopped fresh dill
8-10 fresh basil leaves, sliced
Classic Vinaigrette, see page 316
2 tablespoons freshly grated Parmesan cheese (optional)
Marinated Tomatoes

***Marinated Tomatoes***
1 small shallot, minced
2 tablespoons balsamic vinegar
1 tablespoon olive oil
2 large tomatoes, cut into wedges
½ cup bleu cheese (optional)

Heitor Berlioz: *Harold in Italy, for Viola & Orchestra, Op. 16*

# OVEN-GRILLED VEGGIES

*Makes 2 to 10 cups*

Nonstick cooking spray
Assorted vegetables (see preparations for each vegetable below)
Balsamic vinegar and sliced fresh basil (optional)

- Select and prepare 2 to 10 cups of vegetables. Line a baking sheet (or use 2 or 3 for large batches) with foil; spray with nonstick spray. Arrange a single layer of vegetables on the foil. Spray vegetables lightly with nonstick spray.

- Preheat broiler to hot. Put baking sheet as close to heat source as possible. Broil until veggies are lightly blackened. Turn and broil other side until blackened and tender. Transfer veggies to large bowl and reuse baking sheet if necessary for additional batches. Use veggies plain or toss with balsamic vinegar and sliced fresh basil.

I am not a vegetarian because I love animals; I am a vegetarian because I hate plants.

*A. Whitney Brown*

 "Farmer's Market" as performed by Art Farmer

# OVEN-GRILLED VEGGIES *continued*

Asparagus: wash and snap off tough end of stem

Green Beans: wash and trim off stem end

Zucchini: wash and trim ends; slice on diagonal into ovals or slice lengthwise into long, thin slices

Yellow Squash: wash and trim ends; cut small squash in half lengthwise; quarter larger squash lengthwise or slice

Eggplant: wash and trim ends; cut crosswise or lengthwise into ⅓-inch slices

Mushrooms: brush or rinse off dirt; leave small mushrooms whole; halve larger ones

Peppers: wash, halve, and remove stem and seeds; cut each half lengthwise into 2 or 3 pieces (especially good with red or yellow bell peppers and sweet banana peppers, but the same technique works with hot peppers as well)

Carrots: peel and cut into ¼-inch diagonal slices or cut crosswise in half and slice each half lengthwise into rectangles

Shallots: peel and cut in half lengthwise

Green Onions: wash and trim root end and any tough green ends

Onions: peel small onions and cut from top to bottom into 6 wedges, each containing a piece of the root end to hold the wedge together

*Always make extras; there are dozens of ways to use them. Slice leftover veggies into strips and toss with hot pasta or use in sandwiches, wraps, or salads.*

# MÉLANGE OF BRIGHT VEGETABLES

*Serves 4*

| 2 | medium zucchinis |
| 2 | medium carrots |
| 5 | medium or 10 slender stalks asparagus |
| 2 | teaspoons butter, melted |
| 2 | teaspoons olive oil |
| 4 | drops balsamic vinegar |
| 1-2 | tablespoons minced fresh parsley |
| | Salt and pepper |

- Cut zucchinis and carrots into matchstick-size pieces or julienne in processor. Place carrots in bottom of steamer insert. Add zucchini on top. Snap off the tough ends of the asparagus. Slice crosswise, starting at bottom, into circles the thickness of a penny. Leave tips whole or slice lengthwise in half. Put asparagus slices on top of zucchini; top with tips. Bring water in steamer saucepan to boil. Insert steamer; cover and steam for 2 minutes. Toss steamed vegetables with butter, oil, vinegar, and parsley. Season to taste with salt and pepper.

 Pablo Saizasate: *Zigeunerweisen, Op. 20*

# GREEK ISLAND VEGETABLES

*Serves 6 to 8*

- Grate or mince onion, or cut into chunks and blend with 1 tablespoon water. Heat olive oil in a 3-quart saucepan, Dutch oven, or large skillet. Add onion and cook on medium-low until very tender and translucent (blending onion saves cooking time here). Do not allow browning, but eventually the onion will acquire a warm yellow color; texture must be "melting" before you continue.

- Using flat or 4-sided grater, grate the tomatoes, holding stem end against your palm. Once the skin is pierced, grating will be very quick. Grate until only the core remains in your hand. Discard core. Added grated tomatoes to onions; stir well and cook until tomatoes and onions blend together into a sauce. Add tomato paste and stir well. If sauce doesn't seem to have enough liquid to cook the vegetable, add a bit of water.

- Leave small vegetables such as green beans and okra whole. Trim larger vegetables and cut into chunks. Add raw vegetable to sauce; stir until well coated. Cover and cook over medium-low heat until very tender, stirring often to avoid scorching. Season with salt and pepper.

| | |
|---|---|
| 1 | large onion |
| ¼ | cup olive oil |
| 1½ | pounds fresh tomatoes |
| 1 | tablespoon tomato paste |
| 1½ | pounds fresh vegetables (choose 1 single vegetable: whole green beans, zucchini, yellow squash, okra, eggplant, cauliflower, cabbage, or potatoes) |
| | Salt and black pepper |

> Georg Frideric Handel: *Concerto #1 in B-Flat for Oboe, Strings & Continuo*

# ROASTED ASPARAGUS  *Serves 4 to 6*

| | |
|---|---|
| 1 | pound fresh asparagus |
| 4 | cloves garlic, chopped |
| ¼ | cup olive oil |
| | Kosher salt |
| | Fresh lemon wedges |
| | Crumbled feta cheese |

- Wash asparagus and snap off tough ends. Lay lengthwise in a glass baking dish. Sprinkle with garlic. Drizzle olive oil over all; shake dish until asparagus and garlic are well coated with oil. Roast at 400° for 10 to 12 minutes. Sprinkle with your choice of kosher salt, lemon juice, and feta cheese, using any or all.

**Variations:** *Create Bleu-Green Beans by using tender green beans in this recipe and replacing feta with bleu cheese.*

Johann Sebastian Bach: *Cantata #208:* "Schape konnen signer weiden" ("Sheep may safely graze")

# TUSCAN BEANS WITH GREENS

*Serves 8 to 10*

- Wash and trim greens, removing any tough stems. Stack the leaves and chop or slice into strips. Set aside.

- Heat olive oil in skillet over medium heat. Add garlic and rosemary and sauté for 1 minute. Add the beans with their liquid; simmer 5 minutes. Add greens and cook, stirring frequently, until greens are wilted. Add some chicken broth if necessary to keep beans moist and slightly soupy. Season with salt.

- Put beans into serving dish. Drizzle with olive oil and grind black pepper over the top. Sprinkle with Parmesan cheese, if desired.

*Dried cannellini beans can be cooked according to package directions and substituted for canned beans.*

2 (15-ounce) cans cannellini beans (also called white kidney beans)
5 tablespoons olive oil
6 cloves garlic, finely chopped
3 tablespoons chopped fresh rosemary
1 large bunch greens (chard, spinach, kale, mustard, turnip, or collard)
Low-salt chicken broth
Salt
Additional olive oil
Freshly ground black pepper
Parmesan cheese (optional)

---

Pyotr Ilyich Tchaikovsky: *The Nutcracker:* "A Pine Forest in Winter"

SIDE DISHES

# FRESH BEETS AND GREENS

*Serves 4 to 6*

1 bunch fresh beets with greens attached
Olive oil
Red wine vinegar

- Twist the stems of the beet greens until they separate from the beets. Scrub the beets and place in a saucepan. Cover with cold water. Rinse the greens several times under running water, picking out any wilted pieces. Put the greens in the same saucepan, laying them on top of the beets. You may have to curl the long red stems around the inside edge of the pan to fit them in.

- Cover the saucepan and bring to a boil. Reduce the temperature to a slow boil and cook until beets are tender. Small beets will take 20 to 30 minutes; allow 45 to 60 minutes for large beets.

- Using tongs, remove the greens, allowing excess liquid to drip back into the pan. Place greens on one side of serving dish or platter. Drain the beets and allow to cool for a few minutes. As soon as they are cool enough to handle, peel them by rubbing the skins off (they should slip off easily). Trim root and stem ends; cut beets into wedges. Place the beets on the platter beside the greens. Drizzle with olive oil and red wine vinegar to taste. Serve at room temperature or chill. These will keep in refrigerator for 3 to 4 days.

**Variations:** For Beet Salad, cook as directed. Chop greens and cut peeled beets into ¼-inch dice. Toss with 2 tablespoons of finely chopped onions, olive oil, red wine vinegar, salt, and black pepper to taste.

---

I like children. Properly cooked.

*W. C. Fields*

# BRUSSELS SPROUTS WITH CHIVES AND LEMON ZEST

*Serves 8*

- Combine chives, butter, and lemon zest in medium bowl. Set aside.
- Boil Brussels sprouts in salted water until tender, about 8 minutes. Drain well. Return to pot; add butter mixture and stir until butter melts and sprouts are coated. Season with salt and pepper.

½ cup chopped fresh chives or green onions

¼ cup butter

1 tablespoon shredded lemon zest

2 pounds fresh or frozen Brussels sprouts, halved

Salt and black pepper

Claude Debussy: *Images oubliers*

# HONEYED CARROTS   *Serves 6*

| | |
|---|---|
| 1 | pound carrots |
| 1 | cup water |
| 1 | tablespoon butter |
| 1 | tablespoon honey |

- Peel carrots and cut into ¼-inch x 3-inch sticks. Put carrots and water into medium nonstick skillet. Bring to a boil, reduce heat, and cover. Simmer for five minutes.

- Remove cover; add butter and honey. Cook uncovered on high until liquid evaporates and carrots are tender and just beginning to brown.

**Variations:** *Replace honey with 1 tablespoon chopped crystallized ginger to make Ginger Carrots.*

Thomas Augustine Arne: "Where the Bee Sucks"

# CARROTS WITH LEEKS

*Serves 4*

- Trim top and bottom of leek, saving the white and pale green parts only. Quarter the leek lengthwise and rinse well. Slice crosswise into ¼-inch pieces. Peel carrots and cut into sticks.

- Melt butter with oil in a nonstick skillet. Add leeks and sauté over medium-high heat until they begin to brown. Add carrots and broth; stir well. Cover and reduce heat to medium-low. Cook until the carrots are barely tender, about 5 minutes. Remove lid and cook over medium heat until liquid is absorbed.

1 medium leek
½ pound carrots
1 tablespoon butter
½ tablespoon vegetable oil
¼ cup low-salt chicken broth
Salt and black pepper

Torelli: *Concerto for Trumpet, Strings, and Basso Continuo in D Major*

# ROASTED CORN WITH GREEN CHILE BUTTER  *Serves 8 to 12*

12 large ears of fresh yellow corn
Green Chile Butter
Salt and black pepper

- Husk corn and remove silks.
- Preheat broiler to high. Put corn in large pot of boiling water. Boil for 5 minutes. Drain corn and lay ears on foil lined baking sheet. Broil on high about 3 minutes each side or until blackened spots appear.
- Slather Green Chile Butter over ears. Sprinkle with salt and pepper. Pass any remaining butter alongside.

*Green Chile Butter*
½ cup butter, softened
1 small can diced green chiles, drained
¼ cup chopped fresh cilantro
1 tablespoon toasted cumin seeds

- In processor or blender, puree butter, chiles, and cilantro. Mix in cumin seeds. Transfer to bowl or crock. Refrigerate for several hours (will keep in refrigerator for 1 week).

**Variations:** *For Lime Chicken with Green Chile Butter, marinate 6 chicken breasts in ½ cup lime juice. Grill or broil until cooked through. Put 2 tablespoons Green Chile Butter on top of each breast and serve hot. Or slice the cooked chicken and layer onto crusty rolls which have been spread with Green Chile Butter.*

 Aaron Copland: *El Salon Mexico*

# WHITE CORN WITH CRISPY SAGE

*Serves 4 to 6*

- Melt butter with oil in a large skillet. Add the sage leaves and sauté over medium-high heat. The leaves will turn very green, then pale, and then they'll begin to crisp. When crisp, remove with slotted spoon to paper towel.

- Add corn to skillet and sauté over medium-high heat for about 3 minutes, stirring frequently. Season to taste with salt and pepper. When corn is just beginning to brown, remove from heat and transfer to serving dish. Top with sage leaves.

| | |
|---|---|
| 1 | tablespoon butter |
| 1 | teaspoon olive oil |
| 20 | fresh sage leaves |
| 4 | cups sweet white corn kernels, fresh or frozen |
| | Salt and black pepper |

Always carry a corkscrew and the wine shall provide itself.

*Basil Bunting*

 Claude Debussy: *Preludes, Book II:* "Brouillards" ("Mists")

# GREEN BEANS WITH GARLIC AND PINE NUTS

*Serves 4 to 6*

| | |
|---|---|
| 1 | pound fresh or frozen whole green beans |
| 1 | cup water |
| 1 | tablespoon olive oil |
| 1 | tablespoon butter |
| 3 | medium cloves garlic, peeled and sliced |
| ¼ | cup pine nuts |

- In covered skillet over medium heat, cook green beans with 1 cup of water until they are crisp tender, rearranging once or twice. Drain and return to pan. Add oil, butter, and garlic; sauté beans for 1 minute. Add pine nuts and sauté 1 additional minute.

**Variations:** A quick variation of this dish is Pesto Green Beans. Cook beans as directed above. After draining, return to pan with 2 tablespoons Classic Pesto (see page 326) and toss until coated.

The French cook; we open tins.

*John Galsworthy on English cuisine*

 Ottorino Respighi: *The Pines of Rome:* "I pini di Villa Borghese"

# GARDEN FRESH RATATOUILLE

*Serves 12 to 16*

- Peel (optional) eggplants and cut into 1-inch cubes. Immerse in heavily salted water for 20 minutes to draw out bitterness. Drain, rinse, and drain again. Pat dry. Place on foil-lined baking sheet which has been sprayed with nonstick cooking spray. Broil until brown. Set aside.

- Heat oil in a skillet over low heat. Add garlic and cook over low heat for 1 minute. Add onion; increase heat to medium and sauté until tender.

- Cut yellow squash and zucchini lengthwise in half, then crosswise into 1-inch pieces. Add to skillet with chopped tomatoes; stir well and continue to cook on low. Stem and seed peppers; cut each into thin strips and add to skillet. Simmer for about 5 minutes. Add eggplants and herbs; cover and simmer for 40 to 45 minutes, stirring occasionally (watch for sticking).

- Remove cover and simmer until some of the liquid has evaporated, about 10 to 15 minutes. For best results, make this dish a day ahead and refrigerate to allow flavors to develop. Simply reheat to serve.

*For a main dish, top ratatouille with feta cheese and serve with crusty bread and a salad.*

| | |
|---|---|
| 2 | large eggplants |
| ¼ | cup olive oil |
| 6-8 | cloves garlic, pressed |
| 1 | large onion, chopped |
| 6-8 | yellow squash, ends trimmed |
| 4 | large zucchini, ends trimmed |
| 1 | small red bell pepper |
| 1 | small yellow bell pepper |
| 3 | large tomatoes, chopped |
| ⅓ | cup chopped mixed fresh rosemary, oregano, thyme, basil, and parsley (if fresh herbs are not available, substitute 1½ tablespoons Herbes de Provence or Italian seasoning) |

"Marseilles" as performed by Jimmy Buffett

SIDE DISHES

# CREAMY SPINACH

*Serves 4*

2 tablespoons butter
1 small onion, coarsely chopped
1 (16-ounce) bag frozen leaf spinach or 1 thawed block of frozen spinach
4 ounces cream cheese
Hot pepper sauce
Salt and black pepper

- Melt butter in a large saucepan. Add the chopped onions and cook over high heat, stirring frequently, until tender and lightly browned. Stir in the spinach and reduce heat to medium-high.

- Cover and cook, stirring occasionally, until spinach is thawed. Cook for 1 additional minute. Add cream cheese and stir over low heat until melted. Season to taste with hot pepper sauce, salt, and pepper.

*This dish makes a perfect bed for a grilled or baked chicken breast.*

---

Wine is the intellectual part of any meal . . . food is the material underpinnings.

*Alexandre Dumas*

# SQUASH ACADIEN

*Serves 2 to 4*

- Trim ends of squash and cut into thin slices. Put squash in bowl or glass baking dish; pour buttermilk over. Soak in buttermilk for 30 minutes, stirring a few times. Put cornmeal and seasonings into a cake pan or pie plate and mix well.

- Line a baking sheet with foil and spray liberally with nonstick cooking spray. Remove squash slices one at a time from the buttermilk, allowing excess to drip back into bowl, and coat both sides with cornmeal mixture. Place on prepared sheet.

- Bake squash at 400° for 30 minutes. Turn slices and bake an additional 10 to 15 minutes or until browned and crispy. Serve hot.

2 large yellow squash
2 cups buttermilk
1 cup cornmeal (or more)
1 tablespoon Cajun seasoning
1 teaspoon salt
½ teaspoon black pepper

Kenny G: *Silhouette:* "Summer Song"

# SQUASH PECAN

*Serves 12 to 16*

| | |
|---|---|
| 3 | pounds yellow squash |
| ½ | cup melted butter |
| 2 | teaspoons sugar |
| 2 | eggs, beaten |
| 1 | cup mayonnaise |
| ¾ | cup mild cheddar cheese, grated |
| | Salt and black pepper |
| 1 | cup pecans, broken or chopped |
| ½ | cup buttered breadcrumbs |
| | Butter for coating baking dish |

- Trim ends and cut squash into thick slices. Boil until it is very tender; drain thoroughly.

- Mix together in a large bowl the butter, sugar, eggs, mayonnaise, cheese, salt, and pepper. Add the squash and mash everything together with a potato masher or pulse a few times in a food processor. Leave the squash rather chunky.

- Pour the mixture into a buttered 10-inch by 13-inch glass baking dish. Top with the crumbs and pecans. Bake for 20 minutes at 400°.

Aaron Copland: *Appalachian Spring:* "The Gift to Be Simple"

# WARM CHERRY TOMATOES WITH PINE NUTS

*Serves 4 to 6*

- Heat oil in large skillet over medium heat. Add garlic and tomatoes; sauté, stirring occasionally, about 5 minutes or until tomatoes look as if they're ready to burst. Add pine nuts, basil, vinegar, salt, and pepper. Serve warm or at room temperature.

3 tablespoons olive oil
2 cloves garlic, minced
1½ pounds cherry tomatoes
⅓ cup toasted pine nuts
2 tablespoons chopped fresh basil
1 tablespoon balsamic vinegar
Salt and black pepper

Ottorino Respighi: *The Pines of Rome:* "I pini della via appia"

# ROASTED TOMATOES AND GARLIC

*Makes 1 cup*

| | |
|---|---|
| 2 | pounds ripe tomatoes, halved |
| 12 | cloves garlic, peeled |
| 1 | tablespoon olive oil |
| 1 | teaspoon salt |
| ½ | teaspoon freshly ground black pepper |
| 1 | teaspoon dried thyme, crushed |

- Spread tomatoes evenly on a rimmed baking sheet which has been lined with parchment paper (or spray sheet heavily with nonstick cooking spray). Roast at 300° until skins can be easily removed, about 20 minutes. Carefully peel tomatoes. Return to baking sheet.

- Arrange garlic cloves over tomatoes. Drizzle with olive oil and season with salt, pepper, and thyme. Return baking sheet to oven.

- Continue roasting at 300°, occasionally pouring off accumulated juices, until tomatoes are dry but not crunchy, about 2 to 3 hours. The rich flavor makes these tomatoes perfect to combine with other vegetables, or in salads and sauces.

 Lee Ritenour: *Stolen Moments:* "Uptown"

# ROMA-ZUCCHINI WHEEL

*Serves 2*

- Heat oil in medium skillet. Add onions and sauté until transparent; add garlic and cook 1 minute more. Add zucchini to skillet. Cook 3 to 5 minutes or until crisp tender, stirring often.

- In quiche dish or pie plate, overlap alternating slices of zucchini and tomato, drizzling remaining oil, garlic, and onion in the skillet over the vegetables. Sprinkle with herbs, salt, black pepper, and red pepper. Lay sliced or sprinkle shredded provolone over the tomato and zucchini; sprinkle with grated Romano cheese.

- Bake at 350° for 15 to 20 minutes or until top is lightly browned.

| | |
|---|---|
| 1 | tablespoon olive oil |
| ½ | cup chopped onion |
| 2 | cloves garlic, chopped |
| 2 | medium zucchini, sliced ¼-inch thick |
| 6 | Roma tomatoes, sliced thinly |
| 1 | teaspoon each chopped fresh thyme, basil, and oregano (or ⅛ teaspoon dried) |
| | Salt and black pepper |
| | Red pepper flakes (optional) |
| 4 | ounces Provolone or mozzarella cheese |
| 1 | tablespoon grated Romano cheese |

Lee Ritenour: *Festival:* "Night Rhythms"

# GLAZED TURNIPS

*Serves 6*

1 pound turnips
1 tablespoon butter
2 tablespoons brown sugar

- Peel turnips and cut into ½-inch wedges. Put in medium saucepan with just enough water to cover.
- Bring to boil; reduce heat, cover, and simmer until turnips are nearly cooked. Uncover and add butter and brown sugar. Increase heat to high and cook, stirring occasionally, until liquid is absorbed. Continue cooking until turnips just begin to brown.

"Tulip or Turnip" as performed by Bobby Troup

# TURNIP SOUFFLÉ

*Serves 6*

- Peel turnips and cut into 1-inch cubes. Transfer to a medium saucepan and add water to cover by 2 inches. Boil over high heat until turnips are very tender. Drain turnips, reserving ¼ cup cooking liquid. Allow reserved liquid and turnips to cool for 30 minutes.

- Puree turnips, reserved liquid, half & half, butter, and egg yolk in blender or processor. Season to taste with salt, pepper, and nutmeg; return mixture to saucepan. Using an electric mixer, whip egg white with a pinch of salt until stiff but not dry. Mix ⅓ of egg white into turnips to lighten mixture. Fold remaining egg white into turnips in 2 additions.

- Transfer turnip mixture to a buttered 2-quart glass or ceramic baking dish. Bake at 375° for 15 to 20 minutes or until golden.

1 pound turnips
½ cup half & half
2 tablespoons butter
1 egg, separated
Salt, black pepper, and nutmeg
Additional butter for coating dish

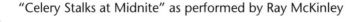

"Celery Stalks at Midnite" as performed by Ray McKinley

SIDE DISHES

# GORGONZOLA GRITS  *Serves 6 to 8*

| | |
|---|---|
| 3 | cups milk |
| 3 | garlic cloves, minced |
| 1 | cup quick-cooking grits (not instant) |
| ½ | cup Gorgonzola or other bleu cheese |
| 6 | tablespoons butter, cut into 6 pieces |
| ½ | cup whipping cream |
| 3 | large eggs, lightly beaten |
| 1 | (4-ounce) can chopped green chiles, drained |
| 2 | tablespoons shredded Parmesan cheese |
| 2 | teaspoons chopped fresh basil |
| 1 | teaspoon fresh thyme leaves |
| | Salt and pepper |
| | Butter for coating dish |

- In medium saucepan, boil garlic in milk for 2 minutes. Gradually stir in grits. Cover, reduce heat, and simmer, stirring occasionally, for about 10 minutes or until mixture is smooth and thick.

- Add Gorgonzola cheese and butter, whisking until butter is melted. Whisk in whipping cream, eggs, chiles, Parmesan cheese, basil, and thyme. Season to taste with salt and pepper.

- Transfer mixture to a buttered 1½-quart soufflé dish. Bake at 325° for 70 minutes (center may still be slightly soft).

An empty stomach is not a good political advisor.

*Albert Einstein*

 Basia: *The Sweetest Illusion:* "The Prayer of a Happy Housewife"

# SWEET ONION RISOTTO

*Serves* 6

- Heat oil and butter in medium saucepan over medium heat. Add onion and garlic; sauté 1 minute. Stir in rice.

- Add ½ cup broth; cook and stir until liquid is nearly absorbed. Add remaining broth ½ cup at a time, each time stirring constantly until liquid is nearly absorbed before continuing.

- When mixture is creamy and rice is tender, remove from heat and stir in feta cheese, herbs, and Parmesan cheese. Sprinkle with freshly ground black pepper.

| | |
|---|---|
| 1 | teaspoon olive oil |
| 1 | teaspoon butter |
| 2 | cups chopped Vidalia or other sweet onion |
| 2 | large cloves garlic, minced |
| 1½ | cups Arborio rice |
| 4 | cups chicken stock or canned low-salt broth |
| ½ | cup crumbled feta cheese |
| ⅓ | cup mixed fresh herbs (parsley, basil, oregano, thyme, or your favorites) |
| ¼ | cup freshly grated Parmesan cheese |
| | Freshly ground black pepper |

 Giacomo Puccini: *Turandot:* "Nessun Dorma"

SIDE DISHES

# ROASTED RED POTATOES

*Serves 4*

1½ pounds small red potatoes
1 tablespoon butter
1 tablespoon olive oil
Salt and black pepper
2 tablespoons minced fresh thyme, rosemary, oregano, or marjoram (or 1 teaspoon dried herbs)

- Preheat oven to 375°. Wash potatoes and cut into quarters or eighths, depending on size. Put butter and oil into a glass or ceramic baking dish and place in preheated over for 1 minute. Remove dish from oven.

- Add potatoes, salt, pepper, and herbs to the baking dish. Toss to coat with butter mixture. Roast at 375° for 45 minutes, basting occasionally with a pastry brush, until potatoes are nicely browned and tender when pierced with the tip of a knife.

*If using a metal baking pan, increase oven to 400°.*

**Variations:** Parmesan Potatoes: Toss potatoes with butter-oil mixture and 2 tablespoons minced fresh rosemary; add salt and pepper to taste. Bake as directed, sprinkling potatoes with ⅓ cup grated Parmesan cheese and returning dish to oven for 2 additional minutes.

Bay-Roasted Potatoes: Warm 2 tablespoons olive oil in a small skillet. Add 4 bay leaves and cook for 2 minutes. Remove from heat and let stand 15 minutes. Toss with 1½ pounds red potatoes; season with salt and pepper and cook as above.

 "Home Fries" as performed by Joshua Redman

# CREAMY POTATOES WITH FRESH HERBS

*Serves 6*

- In a blender or food processor, puree cottage cheese and yogurt until smooth. Pour into a large bowl and mix in dill and chives. Season to taste with salt and pepper.

- Add potatoes and toss gently to coat completely. Pour potato mixture into a 1½-quart baking dish which has been sprayed with nonstick cooking spray.

- Bake at 350° for 30 minutes or until bubbly. Just before serving, sprinkle with parsley.

1 cup cottage cheese, regular or low-fat
1 cup plain yogurt
1 tablespoon chopped fresh dill
1 tablespoon chopped fresh chives
Salt and freshly ground black pepper
4 cups cooked, cubed potatoes
¼ chopped fresh parsley

 Johann Sebastian Bach: "Chaconne" *(from Violin Partita #2)*

# JALAPEÑO POTATOES

*Serves 6 to 8*

| | |
|---|---|
| 4 | medium russet potatoes |
| 1 | (2-ounce) jar pimientos |
| 1 | small bell pepper, julienned |
| 1 | jalapeño pepper, seeded and minced |
| | Salt and black pepper |
| ¼ | cup butter |
| 2 | cloves garlic, minced |
| 1 | tablespoon flour |
| 1 | cup half & half or evaporated skimmed milk |
| 1½ | cups pepper Jack |
| | Butter for coating pan |

- Boil potatoes in their jackets in salted water until tender but not falling apart. When cool enough to handle, peel and slice the potatoes.

- Place half of the potatoes in a buttered glass baking dish. Sprinkle with half the pimientos, bell pepper, and jalapeño pepper. Add salt and pepper to taste. Repeat layers once more.

- Melt butter in medium saucepan; add garlic and cook over low heat for 2 minutes. Sprinkle flour over garlic and cook and stir for 2 more minutes. Add milk gradually and cook, stirring constantly, until sauce thickens. Add cheese and stir until melted. Pour over potatoes.

- Bake at 350° for 45 minutes or until golden.

 Basia: *The Sweetest Illusion:* "More Fire Than Flame"

# POTATOES WITH CHEESE, GARLIC, AND PESTO

*Serves 6*

- Place potatoes in 10-inch x 13-inch glass baking dish. Mix cream, tomatoes, shallots, garlic, pesto, and pepper in large bowl. Pour sauce over potatoes and toss gently to coat. Sprinkle cheese on top.

- Bake at 375° until potatoes are tender and cheese is golden brown, about 50 minutes. Allow dish to stand for 10 minutes before serving.

| | |
|---|---|
| 2 | pounds russet potatoes, peeled and cut into 1-inch pieces |
| 1 | cup whipping cream |
| 2 | tablespoons minced sun-dried tomatoes in oil (drained) |
| 2 | tablespoons minced shallots |
| 2 | tablespoons minced garlic |
| 2 | tablespoons Classic Pesto, see page 326 |
| ¼ | teaspoon white pepper |
| ¾ | cup shredded Provolone or mozzarella cheese |
| ¾ | cup shredded Jarlsberg cheese or Swiss cheese |

Beethoven: *Romance for Violin #2 in F Major, Opus 50*

SIDE DISHES 233

# PEAR-GINGER MUFFIN TOPS

*Makes 12*

| | |
|---|---|
| 1½ | cups oats |
| ½ | cup sugar |
| 6 | tablespoons butter, melted |
| 1⅓ | cups flour |
| 1 | tablespoon baking powder |
| 1 | teaspoon ground ginger |
| ⅔ | cup milk |
| 1 | egg, lightly beaten |
| ¼ | cup finely chopped crystallized ginger |
| 1 | large or 2 medium Bartlett pears, peeled, cored, and finely chopped |

- Combine oats and sugar. Mix ¼ cup oat mixture with 1 tablespoon melted butter for streusel topping; set aside.

- To remaining oat mixture, add flour, baking powder, and ground ginger; mix well. Combine milk, egg, and remaining melted butter. Stir into dry ingredients, mixing just until moistened. Add crystallized ginger and pear.

- Use a ¼ cup measuring cup to drop batter into greased muffin top pans or onto a greased cookie sheet (batter is thick enough not to spread off sheet). Sprinkle with streusel topping, pressing lightly onto the muffin top. Bake at 400° for 20 to 22 minutes or until golden brown.

**Variations:** *For Sweet Potato-Pecan Muffin Tops, add a dash of ground cloves. Delete crystallized ginger and pear; replace with 1 cup cooked, mashed sweet potato and ⅓ cup broken pecans.*
*For Blueberry-Lemon Muffin Tops, delete both forms of ginger and pear; substitute 2 tablespoons of shredded lemon zest and 1 cup fresh or frozen blueberries.*

 Johannes Brahms: *Sonata #3 in D minor for Violin & Piano, Op. 108*

# MORNING GLORY MUFFINS

*Makes 20 muffins or 4 small loaves*

- Mix dry ingredients together in a large bowl. Gently stir in carrots, apples, pecans, raisins, and coconut.

- Blend vanilla, eggs, oil, and applesauce together. Add to flour mixture; stir just until moistened.

- Spray 20 muffin cups or 4 small loaf pans with nonstick cooking spray. Fill ⅔ full with muffin batter. Bake at 350° for 20 to 22 minutes.

*These muffins get quite dark in the oven.*

| | |
|---|---|
| 2 | cups flour |
| 1 | cup sugar |
| 2 | teaspoons baking soda |
| ½ | teaspoon baking powder |
| 2 | teaspoons cinnamon |
| ¼ | teaspoon nutmeg |
| ¼ | teaspoon salt |
| 2 | cups grated carrots |
| 2 | large Granny Smith apples, peeled and diced |
| ½ | cup toasted pecans |
| ¾ | cup golden raisins |
| ¼ | cup lightly toasted coconut |
| 2 | teaspoons vanilla |
| 1 | egg, beaten |
| 4 | egg whites, beaten |
| ⅓ | cup oil |
| ⅓ | cup unsweetened applesauce |

Music washes away from the soul the dust of everyday life.

*Berthold Auerbach*

 Georg Frideric Handel: *The Messiah:* "Glory to God"

# HARVEST MUFFINS

*Makes 48 miniature muffins*

| | |
|---|---|
| 1 | cup chopped dried fruit (dates, apricots, figs, raisins, prunes, or your favorites) |
| 1 | teaspoon baking soda |
| 1 | cup boiling water |
| 1 | cup sugar |
| 1 | tablespoon butter |
| 1 | egg |
| 1¼ | cups flour |
| 1 | teaspoon vanilla |
| ½ | cup chopped walnuts (optional) |

- Mix dried fruit and baking soda. Add boiling water and let stand for 15 minutes.

- Cream sugar, butter, and egg until light. Add flour, alternating with the dried fruit and liquid mixture. Stir in vanilla and nuts (optional). Batter will be quite thin.

- Spray miniature muffin tins with nonstick cooking spray. Drop batter in by spoonfuls, filling about ⅔ full. Bake at 350° for about 12 minutes or until a toothpick inserted in the center of a muffin comes out clean.

*This recipe makes about 18 regular-sized muffins. Increase baking time to 18 to 20 minutes.*

Charles Ives: Three Places in New England

# BABY BANANA CAKES

*Makes 24*

- Cream together sugar and shortening until light; add eggs one at a time, beating after each addition. Mix mashed bananas and milk. Stir together salt, soda, baking powder, and flour. Add dry ingredients to sugar mixture alternately with the bananas, beginning and ending with dry ingredients. Stir in vanilla and any optional ingredients.

- Spray muffin tins with nonstick cooking spray. Fill cups ⅔ full with banana cake batter. Bake at 350° for about 18 minutes or until top of cake springs back when you touch it. The cakes will pull away from the edges of the muffin cups.

*These little cakes are delicious with buttercream frosting (try vanilla, chocolate, caramel, or cream cheese). If you prefer not to frost them, mix up a little cinnamon-sugar and sprinkle that on top of cakes before baking.*

| | |
|---|---|
| 1½ | cups sugar |
| ½ | cup shortening |
| 2 | eggs |
| ¼ | cup milk |
| 3 | ripe bananas, mashed |
| | Pinch salt |
| 1 | teaspoon baking soda |
| 1 | teaspoon baking powder |
| 2 | cups sifted flour |
| 1 | teaspoon vanilla |
| | Chopped walnuts, raisins, chocolate chips, coconut (optional) |

---

"I Ain't Gonna Give Nobody None O' This Jelly Roll" as performed by Fats Waller

# BREAD OF THE ISLANDS

*Makes 3 loaves*

| | |
|---|---|
| ¾ | cup butter |
| 2 | cups sugar |
| 3 | eggs |
| 3½ | cups flour |
| 1 | teaspoon salt |
| 1 | tablespoon baking powder |
| ⅔ | cup milk |
| 2 | teaspoons lemon juice |
| 1 | teaspoon baking soda |
| 1 | teaspoon vanilla |
| 3 | bananas, peeled and mashed |
| 1 | cup peeled and diced mango |
| ½ | cup peeled and diced papaya |

Better halfe a loafe than no bread.

*Camden*

- Cream butter with electric mixer until light. Add sugar and continue creaming until light. Add eggs 1 at a time, mixing after each addition, until mixture is fluffy.

- Mix together flour, salt, and baking powder. Stir with fork.

- Put milk in measuring cup. Add lemon juice and let stand for 5 minutes until milk sours. Add baking soda and vanilla.

- Add about 1 cup of flour mixture to creamed butter in mixer. Mix to combine. Add half of the milk mixture and half the bananas. Mix to combine. Add half of remaining flour, all of remaining milk mixture and remaining bananas. Add remaining flour. Stir in mango and papaya.

- Divide batter evenly into 3 greased or sprayed 4-inch x 9-inch loaf pans. Bake at 350° for 40 minutes or until bread is golden brown and center is set. Allow to cool before cutting into 1-inch slices. The texture will be a bit sticky but delicious.

**Variations:** Add ¾ cup grated coconut with mango and papaya. To spike the bread, pierce the tops with a fork about 20 times and pour ¼ cup rum over each loaf. Allow to stand for at least 2 hours or refrigerate overnight. Bread will keep in refrigerator for 3 days.

Claude Debussy: "L'Isle Joyeuse"

# A TO Z BREAD

*Makes 2 loaves or 1 Bundt ring*

- Stir sugar, flour, salt, baking soda, and cinnamon together in a medium bowl. Set aside.

- In a large bowl, beat eggs lightly. Blend applesauce into eggs. Stir in vanilla. Add flour mixture and stir well (batter will be very stiff). Fold in zucchini and pecans.

- Coat 2 loaf pans or 1 Bundt pan liberally with nonstick cooking spray (or grease and flour pans). Pour batter into pan(s). Bake at 300° for 30 minutes. Increase heat to 325° and bake an additional 20 minutes. Turn oven off and leave bread inside for 10 to 15 more minutes. Serve hot or cold.

| | |
|---|---|
| 2 | cups sugar |
| 3 | cups flour |
| 1¼ | teaspoons salt |
| 1 | teaspoon baking soda |
| 3 | teaspoons cinnamon |
| 3 | eggs or ¾ cup egg substitute |
| 1 | cup unsweetened applesauce |
| 3 | teaspoons vanilla |
| 2 | large zucchini, shredded |
| 1 | cup chopped pecans |

 Leos Janacek: *String Quartet #2* ("Intimate Letters")

# TOMATO BREAD  *Makes 12 to 16 pieces*

1 loaf French bread
1 large very ripe tomato
  Olive oil
  Salt

- Slice bread in half horizontally. Place bread halves cut side up in broiler and toast until golden brown.

- Cut the tomato crosswise in half. Rub 1 tomato half onto each bread half, squeezing pulp and juice onto bread as you rub. Drizzle with olive oil and salt to taste.

- Cut each half on the diagonal into 2-inch pieces and serve immediately.

There's music in all things, if men had ears.

*Byron*

 "Jam for your Bread" as performed by Red Mitchell

# ANGEL BISCUITS

*Makes 5 to 6 dozen*

- Dissolve yeast in warm water. Sift together flour, baking soda, baking powder, sugar, and salt. Cut in shortening with pastry blender or two knives until mixture resembles coarse crumbs.

- Add buttermilk and yeast. Stir until dough is thoroughly moistened. Turn onto floured board and knead 1 to 2 minutes. Roll or pat dough out to ½-inch thickness; cut with a 2-inch biscuit cutter.

- Transfer biscuits to ungreased baking sheet. Brush with melted butter if desired. Bake at 400° for 12 to 15 minutes or until golden brown.

| | |
|---|---|
| 1 | package active dry yeast |
| 2 | tablespoons very warm water |
| 5 | cups flour |
| 1 | teaspoon baking soda |
| 3 | teaspoons baking powder |
| 2 | tablespoons sugar |
| 1½ | teaspoons salt |
| 1 | cup shortening |
| 2 | cups buttermilk |
| | Melted butter (optional) |

Music is well said to be the speech of angels.

*Thomas Carlyle*

 Cesar Franck: *Messe solennelle, Op. 12:* "Panis Angelicus"

# CLASSIC BUTTERMILK BISCUITS

*Makes 12 to 14*

| | |
|---|---|
| 2 | cups flour |
| 2 | teaspoons baking powder |
| ¼ | teaspoon baking soda |
| ¾ | teaspoon salt |
| ¼ | cup shortening |
| 1 | cup buttermilk |

- Sift together flour, baking powder, baking soda, and salt. Cut in shortening with pastry blender or two knives until mixture resembles coarse crumbs. Add buttermilk and stir with a fork just until dough leaves sides of bowl.

- Turn dough onto a lightly floured board. Knead gently just until smooth. Roll or pat dough out to ½-inch thickness. Cut with a 2-inch biscuit cutter.

- Transfer biscuits to ungreased baking sheet. Bake 10 to 12 minutes at 400° until golden.

*To make biscuits with regular milk, omit baking soda and increase baking powder to 3 teaspoons. Use about ¾ cup milk in place of buttermilk.*

***Variations:*** *Add extra ingredients along with the buttermilk or milk. Add 2 tablespoons shredded lemon zest for Lemon Biscuits. Make Cheddar-Onion Biscuits with ¼ cup chopped green onions and ½ cup shredded cheddar. Add 2 tablespoons toasted cumin or caraway seeds for savory Seed Biscuits. For Bleu Cheese Biscuits, add ½ cup crumbled bleu cheese and ½ cup chopped walnuts. Sweet Potato-Sage Biscuits need 1 cup of cooked or canned sweet potato and 1 tablespoon chopped fresh sage. Add 2 to 4 tablespoons of any combination of chopped fresh herbs for Fresh Herb Biscuits. The possibilities are as unlimited as your imagination.*

 Johann Sebastian Bach: *Flute Sonata in G Minor*

# IRON SKILLET CORNBREAD

*Makes 1 round*

- Put bacon drippings into medium black iron skillet and place in oven at 400°. Allow to heat while you mix other ingredients.

- Mix buttermilk, baking powder, baking soda, and salt in a medium bowl. Add enough cornmeal to make a batter the consistency of cake batter (not too thick). Add egg and mix well.

- Remove skillet from oven and immediately pour batter into pan. The hot fat should cause the bottom and sides of batter to puff up and begin to cook. Return skillet to oven and bake until cornbread is golden brown. Invert onto rack or plate; cut into wedges.

3 tablespoons bacon drippings
1 cup buttermilk
2 heaping teaspoons baking powder
½ teaspoon baking soda
½ teaspoon salt
   Cornmeal
1 egg, lightly beaten

 Harry Warren & Mack Gordon: "At Last"

# HOT WATER CORNBREAD

*Makes 4 to 6*

½ cup boiling water
1 cup white cornmeal
Salt to taste
Oil for frying

- Add boiling water to cornmeal which has been liberally salted. Stir vigorously. The boiling water will cause the cornmeal to puff slightly.

- Oil your hands and pinch off about ¾ cup mixture. Shape into a 3-inch by 2-inch oval. Continue shaping until you have used all of the mixture.

- Pour oil into a large skillet to a depth of ¾ inch. Heat oil over high heat until smoking. Drop ovals into hot oil. Fry until dark brown and crunchy, turning once.

**Variations:** *For a taste of the Southwest, add 2 tablespoons canned chopped green chiles and 1 teaspoon ground cumin to batter.*

Lee Ritenour: *Festival:* "Rio Sol"

# SPICY CORN BITES

*Makes* 72

- Butter 3 (24-cup) mini-muffin tins (or work in batches).

- Mix eggs, corn, whipping cream, salsa, butter, and cheese in a large bowl until thoroughly combined. Stir together flour, cornmeals, and baking powder in a medium bowl. Add to corn mixture and stir until just moistened (batter will be lumpy).

- Fill mini-muffin cups ⅔ full; sprinkle a few shreds of cheese on top of each. Bake at 450° until golden and muffins spring back when touched, about 8 minutes.

Butter for coating pan
4 eggs, beaten
1 (16-ounce) can cream-style corn
½ cup whipping cream
¾ cup salsa
1 tablespoon butter, room temperature
1 cup shredded cheddar cheese
¾ cup flour
½ cup white cornmeal
2¼ cups yellow cornmeal
4 tablespoons baking powder
Additional shredded cheese

"Raging Waters" as performed by Al Jarreau

# SOUTHWESTERN SPOONBREAD

*Serves 6 to 8*

| | |
|---|---|
| 1 | (16-ounce) can cream-style corn |
| ¾ | cup buttermilk |
| ⅓ | cup vegetable oil |
| 3 | large eggs |
| 1 | cup cornmeal |
| ½ | cup flour |
| 1 | teaspoon baking powder |
| ½ | teaspoon soda |
| 1 | teaspoon salt |
| 1 | tablespoon cornmeal |
| 1 | cup grated cheddar cheese |
| 1 | cup sautéed chopped onion |
| 2 | tablespoons chopped, pickled jalapeño peppers |
| ¼ | pound ground beef, browned (optional) |

- Combine corn, buttermilk, oil, and eggs in large bowl; stir thoroughly. In a medium bowl stir together 1 cup cornmeal, flour, baking powder, baking soda, and salt. Add cornmeal mixture to large bowl and stir until thoroughly moistened.

- Sprinkle 1 tablespoon cornmeal on bottom of iron skillet. Place in 400° oven and heat until the cornmeal turns brown. Add half the batter to the skillet. Sprinkle with cheese, onion, peppers, and beef. Top with remaining batter. Bake at 400° until brown, about 30 minutes.

*The bread does not have to be layered. Instead, add the cheese, onion, peppers, and beef to the batter just before pouring into skillet. This bread can also be baked in muffin cups; reduce cooking time to approximately 20 minutes.*

 Donald Fagen: *Kamakiriad:* "Teahouse on the Tracks"

# ICEBOX ROLLS

*Serves 36*

- Bring the milk, shortening, and sugar to a boil, stirring until the sugar melts. Cool until just warm. Add enough flour to make mixture the consistency of cake batter. Stir in the yeast. Cover, put in warm place, and let rise until double in bulk, about 2 hours.

- Add the baking soda, baking powder, salt, and enough flour to make soft dough. Cover and refrigerate for several hours or overnight.

- Two hours before baking, roll dough out to ½-inch thickness and cut with a 2-inch round biscuit cutter. Dip each circle into melted butter and fold in half. Place folded edge down on a greased baking sheet, leaving rolls very close together so they will rise up, not out. Cover and let rise for 2 hours.

- Bake at 450° until golden brown.

| | |
|---|---|
| 1 | quart whole milk |
| 1 | cup shortening |
| ½ | cup sugar |
|  | Flour |
| 2 | teaspoons dry yeast |
| 1 | teaspoon baking soda |
| 1 | heaping teaspoon baking powder |
| 1 | rounded tablespoon salt |
|  | Melted butter |

Donald Fagen and Walter Becker: *Kamakiriad:* "Snowbound"

# BAKER'S CHOICE BREAD

*Makes 1 loaf*

- 1½ tablespoons yeast or 1 packet
- 2⅔ cups bread flour
- 1⅓ cups total of your choice of cornmeal, rye flour, whole wheat flour, 4 or 7-grain cereal, toasted sunflower seeds, millet or other seeds, herbs such as dill, rosemary, or basil
- 1 teaspoon salt
- 1 tablespoon olive oil (or more)
- Honey to taste (at least 2 tablespoons)
- 1⅓ cups warm water (reduce if using extra oil or honey or if humidity is high)

- This recipe uses a bread machine that makes a 2-pound loaf. The bread can be made on "automatic," but try "manual" finishing of the loaves for best texture. Set for French bread/manual.

- Add ingredients in this order: yeast, bread flour, additional grains and seeds, salt, oil, honey, and warm water. As soon as "manual" cycle finishes, remove mixture.

- Knead in additional bread flour or olive oil to create fairly stiff dough. Form into a long "baguette" loaf, a round loaf, long rolls, or whatever you prefer. Place on a baking sheet liberally dusted with cornmeal.

- Place baking sheet in warm, humid area and let rise until doubled in volume, about 30 to 40 minutes. Place in 400° oven. For a crispy crust, drop 2 ice cubes onto oven floor every 2 minutes for a total of 6 cubes (close oven door to keep steam in). After 20 minutes, reduce heat to 325° and bake until done, usually not more than 10 additional minutes. Cool on rack or cloth before cutting.

*To prepare dough manually, mix yeast, honey, and warm water together and allow to stand for 15 minutes. In mixer with dough hook or by hand, stir in flour, other grains or seeds, salt and oil. Knead with machine or by hand until smooth and elastic. Lightly coat a bowl with olive oil; put dough in bowl, turning to coat both sides. Allow to rise until doubled in size. Continue with the third step above.*

A crust eaten in peace is better than a banquet partaken in anxiety.

*Aesop*

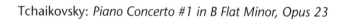
Tchaikovsky: *Piano Concerto #1 in B Flat Minor, Opus 23*

# FINALES: Sweet Indulgences

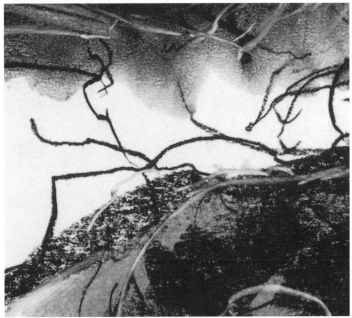

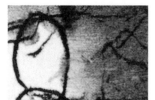

# TEA PARTY

A man hath no better thing under the sun, than
to eat, and to drink, and to be merry.

*Ecclesiastes*

Lemon-Berry Tea Tartlets

Jewel Tartlets

Ham Cream Tartlets

Crème Wafer Cookies with Buttercream Filling

A to Z Bread

Earl Grey Cake

 Pyotr Ilyich Tchaikovsky: *The Nutcracker:* "The Enchanted Palace of the Kingdom of Sweets"

# ORANGE-CAMPARI GRANITA

*Serves 6*

- Stir juice, Campari, and sugar together in a medium bowl until the sugar is completely dissolved. Pour mixture into a 7-inch x 11-inch x 2-inch glass baking dish. Place in freezer for 6 hours or overnight.

- About 20 minutes before serving, place 6 martini glasses, wine glasses, or short dessert stems in the freezer. To serve, remove frosted glasses and dessert from freezer. Using a dinner fork, rake the tines across the surface of the frozen dessert to form crystals. Scoop the crystals into the glasses and garnish with mint sprigs or fresh fruit.

**Variations:** For Pear-Pernod Granita, substitute 1½ cups pear nectar and ½ cup water for juice, and ⅓ cup Pernod or other anise-flavored liqueur for Campari. For Lemon-Espresso Granita, use 2 cups of freshly brewed espresso or triple-strength coffee, ⅓ cup limoncello or other lemon flavored liqueur, and increase sugar to ½ cup.

2 cups freshly squeezed or good quality pasteurized orange juice, strained
⅓ cup Campari
⅓ cup sugar

Wine has lit up for me the pages of literature, and revealed in life romance lurking in the commonplace.

*Alfred Duff Cooper*

 Pyotr Ilyich Tchaikovsky: *The Nutcracker:* "Waltz of the Snowflakes"

DESSERTS 251

# STRAWBERRY SORBET  *Makes 4 cups*

| | |
|---|---|
| ⅔ | cup boiling water |
| ½ | cup sugar |
| 4 | cups fresh or frozen strawberries, sliced |
| 2 | tablespoons orange juice |
| 1 | teaspoon grated lemon zest |
| 1 | tablespoon lemon juice |

- Combine boiling water and sugar in a large bowl, stirring until sugar dissolves. Allow to cool. Stir in strawberries, orange juice, lemon zest, and lemon juice.

- Transfer mixture to a 13-inch x 9-inch x 2-inch glass baking dish. Freeze until almost firm. Break up sorbet and spoon into a mixing bowl. Beat at medium speed with an electric mixer until smooth. Return mixture to pan; smooth out and freeze until firm.

- To serve, let stand at room temperature 10 to 15 minutes; garnish with mint or fresh fruit.

Antonio Vivaldi: *The Four Seasons, Op. 8:* "Winter"

# PEACH SORBET

*Makes 5 cups*

½ cup sugar
¼ cup light corn syrup
2 cups water, divided
1 pound fresh or frozen peaches, peeled and sliced
2 tablespoons lemon juice
½ cup peach nectar
⅛ teaspoon almond extract

- Combine sugar, corn syrup, and 1 cup water in saucepan; bring to boil, stirring constantly. Reduce heat and simmer 3 minutes. Allow to cool.

- Place peaches and remaining 1 cup water in container of blender or processor. Whirl or pulse until smooth, scraping down sides.

- Combine peach mixture, cooled syrup, lemon juice, nectar, and extract. Pour into a 13-inch x 9-inch x 2-inch pan. Freeze until almost firm. Spoon mixture into mixing bowl and beat at medium speed until slushy. Return to pan and freeze 8 hours or overnight.

- To serve, allow mixture to stand for 10 minutes. Garnish with mint, biscotti, or fresh fruit.

Duke Ellington: "A Beggar's Holiday"

# WHITE WINE SHERBET   *Serves 10 to 12*

- 2 packets unflavored gelatin
- 4 cups white wine (the better the wine, the better the sherbet)
- 1 cup sugar
- 1 cup water
- 1½ tablespoons grated orange zest
- 1½ tablespoons grated lemon zest
- ½ cup orange juice
- ¼ cup lemon juice
- 3 egg whites

- Begin preparations 1 day ahead. Sprinkle gelatin over ½ cup wine to soften; let stand 5 minutes.

- In small saucepan combine sugar with 1 cup water. Stir over low heat to dissolve sugar. When sugar has dissolved, bring syrup to boiling; boil gently without stirring for 5 minutes. Remove from heat and add gelatin, stirring until dissolved.

- In a large bowl, combine gelatin mixture, orange zest, lemon zest, orange juice, lemon juice, and remaining wine. Transfer to a 13-inch x 9-inch x 2-inch pan; place in freezer until frozen around edges, about 3 hours. In the small bowl of an electric mixer, beat egg whites at high speed until soft peaks form. Turn wine mixture into a large mixing bowl and beat at medium until smooth. Fold egg whites into wine mixture just until combined.

- Return mixture to pan and freeze until firm, about 4 hours or overnight.

*Try this recipe with red wine for a Sangría Sherbet.*

Claude Debussy: *Preludes, Book I:* "Des pas sur la niege" ("Steps on the snow")

# FRESH PEACH ICE CREAM

*Makes 2 quarts*

- In a large bowl, stir together peaches, sugar, and lemon juice. Mix in canned milk, cream, salt, and extract. Pour into container of ice cream freezer; fill to freeze line with milk.

- Process ice cream according to manufacturer's instructions.

6 cups pureed peaches (about 10 to 12 peeled peaches, stones removed)
3 cups sugar
Juice of 2 lemons
1 (12-ounce) can evaporated skimmed milk, chilled
1½ cups whipping cream, whipped until thick but not forming peaks
Pinch of salt
⅛ teaspoon almond extract
Milk (regular or as light as 1% fat)

 "Ice Cream" as performed by Buglin' Sam DeKemee

# HEAVENLY CHOCOLATE ICE CREAM

*Makes 1 gallon*

- 12 (1¾-ounce) Milky Way Bars, cut into pieces
- 1 (14-ounce) can sweetened condensed milk, regular or low-fat
- 3 quarts (or more) milk
- 1 (5½-ounce) can chocolate syrup

- Combine candy and sweetened condensed milk in a large saucepan; cook over low heat, stirring constantly, until candy melts. Cool, stirring occasionally. Add 1 quart of milk to candy mixture. Beat until thoroughly blended.

- Pour mixture into freezer container of 1-gallon hand-turned or electric ice cream freezer. Stir in chocolate syrup. Add enough milk to fill freezer contain to within 4 inches from top. Freeze according to manufacturer's instructions.

Life is magically delicious.

*Jean-Camille Kollmorgen*

 Pyotr Ilyich Tchaikovsky: *The Nutcracker:* "Chocolate (Spanish Dance)"

# STRAWBERRY YOGURT PIE

*Serves 6*

- Beat cheese in bowl until smooth. Stir in yogurt, honey, and vanilla.

- Sprinkle gelatin over ¼ cup water in saucepan; let soften 1 minute. Stir over low heat to dissolve gelatin. Stir gelatin mixture and remaining ½ cup water into cheese mixture. Spread evenly in prepared crust.

- Place a sheet of waxed paper on work surface. In microwave or in small saucepan over low heat, melt the chocolate with the cream. Stir well and allow to cool slightly. Transfer to deep custard cup. Reserve 6 large whole strawberries; slice remainder. Dip whole strawberries into chocolate, covering about ¾ of each berry. Arrange chocolate-dipped berries around perimeter of pie. Arrange sliced berries in a flower shape in center of pie. Chill for 2 hours.

| | |
|---|---|
| 8 | ounces Neufchâtel or Light Cream Cheese |
| 8 | ounces strawberry yogurt |
| 1 | tablespoon honey |
| 1 | teaspoon vanilla |
| 1 | packet unflavored gelatin |
| ¾ | cup water |
| 1 | prepared chocolate crumb pie crust |
| 3 | tablespoons chopped semi-sweet chocolate or semi-sweet chips |
| 1 | tablespoon whipping cream |
| 1½ | cups sliced strawberries |
| 6 | large whole strawberries |

Johann Sebastian Bach: *Cantata #170:* "Vergnugte Run" ("Continued Peace")

# PEANUT BUTTER-CHOCOLATE FAST FUDGE

*Makes 32 pieces*

| | |
|---|---|
| 1 | pound powdered sugar |
| ½ | cup cocoa |
| ¼ | cup milk |
| ½ | cup butter |
| 1 | tablespoon vanilla |
| ½ | cup crunchy peanut butter |
| | Butter for coating pan |

- Blend sugar and cocoa in an 8-cup measure or deep 2-quart glass baking dish. Add milk and butter to top but do not stir. Microwave on high for 2 minutes.

- Remove from microwave and stir well to mix. Add vanilla and stir until thoroughly blended. Add peanut butter and stir until streaky.

- Spoon fudge into a buttered 8-inch x 8-inch square baking dish. Transfer to freezer for 20 minutes or refrigerator for 1 hour. Cut into 1-inch x 2-inch bars.

 "My Favorite Things" as performed by John Coltrane

# MEXICAN PRALINES

*Makes 32 to 96*

- Cook sugar, syrup, milk, and pecans over medium heat until sugar dissolves. Continue cooking mixture until it reaches a temperature of 235° to 240° or soft ball stage (a small amount dropped into a cup of cold water can be shaped with fingers into a soft ball).

- Remove from heat. Add vanilla and butter; stir until butter melts. Allow to cool 5 minutes. Stir or beat mixture until it becomes thick.

- Drop mixture by spoonfuls onto waxed paper. Make a variety of sizes by dropping candy from a larger or smaller spoon. Allow to cool completely. Peel pralines from waxed paper and wrap each individually in plastic wrap.

| | |
|---|---|
| 2 | cups sugar |
| ½ | cup light Karo syrup |
| ½ | cup milk |
| 2 | cups pecans |
| ¼ | cup butter |
| 1 | tablespoon Mexican vanilla |
| 1 | teaspoon cinnamon |

"The Candyman" as performed by Sammy Davis, Jr.

# MARTHA WASHINGTON CANDY

*Makes 36 to 48*

½ cup butter
2 pounds powdered sugar
1 can sweetened condensed milk
1 teaspoon vanilla
   Chopped pecans (optional)
   Shredded coconut (optional)
4 cups semi-sweet chocolate chips
¼ cup whipping cream

- Melt butter and combine with sugar, condensed milk, and vanilla. Add pecans or coconut if desired.

- Butter hands. Pinch off small pieces of sugar mixture and roll between palms to form balls. Melt chocolate chips with whipping cream or paraffin. Cool slightly. Drop balls 1 at a time into melted chocolate. Remove with bamboo skewer and place on waxed paper.

**Variations:** Make Chocolate Truffles by chilling Chocolate Truffle Sauce (see page 309) until quite stiff. Pinch off small pieces and roll them between palms into 1-inch balls. Chill balls again if necessary. Dip as directed above. These are best stored in the refrigerator.

Tell me what you eat, and I will tell you what you are.

*Brillat-Savarin*

 "Candy" as performed by Nat King Cole

# MOUNTAIN OF DIVINITY

*Makes 1 big old mountain*

- Combine sugar, syrup, and water in a medium saucepan over low heat. Stir until sugar is dissolved. Continue to cook and stir until syrup reaches 235° to 240° or soft ball stage (a small amount dropped in a cup of cold water will form a soft ball).

| | |
|---|---|
| 3 | cups sugar |
| ½ | cup light corn syrup |
| ½ | cup water |
| 2 | egg whites |
| 1 | teaspoon vanilla |
| 2 | cups chopped pecans or hazelnuts |

- Beat egg whites at high speed until stiff. Continue beating on high and slowly pour half the syrup over the egg whites. Stir with a spatula. Resume beating and return other half of syrup to low heat. Cook until syrup reaches 255° or hard ball stage (a small amount dropped in a cup of cold water makes a cracking sound and will form a hard ball).

- Again, gradually add hot syrup to egg white mixture, beating constantly. Add vanilla and nuts. Beat until mixture is thick enough to drop from a spoon.

- Choose a round serving platter. Drop dollops of the candy by spoonfuls onto the platter, covering the center area. Add another layer of candy on top of the first, covering a smaller area. Continue until the mounded dollops become a "mountain." Serve with a knife for slicing off pieces of divinity.

Alan Hovhaness: "The Mysterious Mountain"

CANDIES

# PEANUT BUTTER MIRACLES

*Makes 24*

1 cup sugar
1 cup peanut butter
1 egg
1 teaspoon vanilla

- With an electric mixer or by hand, cream together sugar and peanut butter. In a small bowl, beat egg and add vanilla. Combine the peanut butter mixture and the egg.

- Roll dough into ¾-inch balls. Place on ungreased baking sheet and flatten each ball with a floured fork. Bake at 350° for 10 minutes. Remove from oven and allow cookies to cool before removing from pan.

*From the beautiful light texture the baked cookies have, it is difficult to believe that they are flourless.*

The Vice Presidency is sort of like the last cookie on the plate. Everybody insists he won't take it, but somebody always does.

*Bill Vaughan*

 "Sweet and Lovely" as performed by Al Bowfly

# FORGOTTEN COOKIES

*Makes 48*

- Beat egg whites until stiff. Gradually add ⅔ cup sugar and beat until very stiff. Fold in chips and nuts.

- Spray baking sheets with nonstick cooking spray. Drop mixture by spoonfuls, flattening each mound slightly with the back of the spoon. Place baking sheets in a 350° oven and turn oven off. Leave cookies overnight or for at least 2 hours. Store in an airtight container.

2 egg whites
⅔ cup sugar
1 cup semi-sweet or milk chocolate chips
1 cup chopped pecans

**Variations:** Create Cherry-Almond Kisses by replacing chips with 1 cup chopped candied cherries and use chopped slivered almonds instead of pecans. Or simply use mint-flavored chocolate chips to make Chocolate-Mint Meringues.

 "Love is the Sweetest Thing" as performed by Al Bowfly

# CRÈME WAFER COOKIES

*Makes 18 sandwich cookies*

| | |
|---|---|
| 1 cup butter, softened | |
| 2 cups sifted flour | |
| ½ cup whipping cream | |
| Sugar | |
| Buttercream Filling | |

- Mix butter, flour, and cream together with electric mixer until thoroughly combined. Chill dough at least 1 hour.

- Roll dough out ⅛-inch thick. Cut into 1½-inch rounds, using small biscuit cutter. Sprinkle wafers with sugar on both sides and place on ungreased baking sheet. Prick each cookie 4 times with a fork.

- Bake cookies at 375° for 7 to 9 minutes or until slightly puffy and set but not brown (they should remain very pale). To serve, spread bottoms of half the cookies with Buttercream Filling. Top with remaining wafers.

### Buttercream Filling

¼ cup butter, softened
1 egg yolk (optional)
¾ cup powdered sugar
1 teaspoon vanilla, almond, or lemon extract

- Beat butter with mixer until light. Blend in egg yolk (the egg adds richness, but the filling will be fine without it if you prefer not to consume raw egg) and add sugar. Beat until smooth. Mix in extract. Use as filling for Crème Wafers or as frosting for cake or cupcakes.

 "The Teddy Bear's Picnic" as performed by Henry Hall

# CHEWY OATMEAL BROWNIES

*Makes 20*

- Combine flour, sugar, and eggs in a large mixing bowl; mix well. Mix together butter and cocoa; stir into flour mixture. Add oats and pecans and blend well.

- Spread batter in a buttered 8-inch x 8-inch x 2-inch pan. Bake at 350° for 30 minutes or until toothpick inserted near center comes out mostly clean with just a few fudgy crumbs clinging. Cool and cut into 2-inch x 1½-inch bars.

½ cup self-rising flour
1 cup sugar
2 eggs, beaten
½ cup melted butter
½ cup cocoa
½ cup quick-cooking oats
½ cup chopped pecans
Butter for coating pan

 "Have Yourself a Merry Little Christmas" as performed by Tom Scott

# HONEY-SPICE BARS

*Makes 4 dozen*

¾ cup brown sugar
1 egg
1 cup honey
1 tablespoon shredded orange zest
2¾ cups flour
½ teaspoon baking soda
½ teaspoon salt
1 teaspoon allspice
1 teaspoon cinnamon
1 teaspoon ground ginger
1 cup slivered almonds, toasted
1 cup dried apple, snipped into small pieces
1 cup dried cranberries
1 cup powdered sugar
1-2 tablespoons orange juice

- Beat brown sugar and egg in bowl of electric mixer until smooth; mix in honey and orange zest. In a medium bowl, mix dry ingredients. Gradually beat dry ingredients into honey mixture on low speed. With spoon, stir in dried fruit and nuts. Mixture will be very thick and sticky.

- Line a 9-inch x 13-inch baking pan with foil or parchment, allowing long sides to extend over edges of the pan. Coat with nonstick cooking spray. With oiled hands, pat batter evenly into the prepared pan. Bake at 350° for 28 to 32 minutes or until light golden brown. Cool 10 minutes on rack.

- In a small bowl, mix powdered sugar with enough orange juice to make a thin glaze. Turn cake out of pan onto work surface and remove foil. Spread glaze over top and let stand for 15 to 20 minutes until glaze is set. Cut into 1-inch x 2-inch bars.

*To fancy these up a bit, reserve 1 tablespoon of glaze and use it to glue pieces of dried fruit or nuts to the tops of the bars.*

**Variations:** *The possibilities are endless for variations on this recipe. Choose any dried fruits and nuts which please you. Change spices or use additional ingredients such as coconut.*

 "Santa Claus is Coming to Town" as performed by Dave Valentin

# RASPBERRY-CHOCOLATE BARS

*Makes 4 dozen*

- Beat butter, egg yolk, and water. Stir together flour, sugar, and baking powder. Add to butter mixture; combine thoroughly and press into bottom of greased 13-inch x 9-inch x 2-inch baking pan. Bake at 350° for 10 minutes. Sprinkle with baking chips and return to oven for 1 minute. Spread melted raspberry chocolate over top. Allow to cool for 5 minutes. Spread Meringue-Nut Topping over cake. Return pan to oven and bake at 350° for 30 to 35 minutes or until golden on top. Cut into 1½-inch squares.

- Beat eggs until thick and lemon-colored. Beat in sugar, melted butter, and vanilla. Stir in nuts.

*If raspberry-flavored chips are not available, use regular semi-sweet chips along with ⅓ cup seedless raspberry jam.*

| | |
|---|---|
| ½ | cup butter |
| 1 | egg yolk |
| 2 | tablespoons water |
| 1¼ | cups flour |
| 1 | teaspoon sugar |
| 1 | teaspoon baking powder |
| 1 | (10-ounce) package raspberry-flavored chocolate chips |
| | Meringue-Nut Topping |

*Meringue-Nut Topping*

| | |
|---|---|
| 2 | whole eggs |
| ¾ | cup sugar |
| 6 | tablespoons melted butter |
| 2 | teaspoons vanilla |
| 2 | cups finely chopped nuts (pecans, walnuts, almonds, or hazelnuts) |

---

Nicolai Rimsky-Korsakov: *Scheherazade*, Op. 35:
"Le jeune Prince et la Princesse"

# CREAM CHEESE BROWNIES WITH STRAWBERRY GLAZE

*Serves 12 to 16*

**Brownie Crust**
- 6 ounces unsweetened chocolate
- 3 cups sugar
- 1½ teaspoons vanilla extract
- 1½ teaspoons salt
- ¾ cup shortening
- 6 large eggs
- 1¾ cups flour
- Butter for coating pan

- Melt unsweetened chocolate and shortening in a 3-quart saucepan over medium-low heat, stirring frequently. Remove from heat and allow to cool for 10 minutes. With an electric mixer, beat in sugar. Add eggs and vanilla and beat well. Gradually mix in flour and salt.

- Butter a 13-inch x 9-inch x 2-inch pan; line the bottom with waxed paper. Pour in the batter and bake at 350° for 35 to 40 minutes. Pick inserted near center should come out clean. Cool pan on rack for 10 minutes. Run a small knife around the edges and turn the brownie out of the pan onto rack. Peel off waxed paper and cool completely.

**Cream Cheese Layer**
- 8 ounces Neufchâtel or light cream cheese
- 2 teaspoons powdered sugar

- Using an electric mixer, beat cheese with sugar until soft and fluffy. Taste the mixture and add more sugar if desired. Spread the cream cheese mixture over the cooled brownie crust.

 Claude Debussy: *Preludes, Book II:* "La terrasse des audiences du clair de lune" ("The audience terrace by moonlight")

# CREAM CHEESE BROWNIES *continued*

- Mash half the strawberries in a measuring cup. If the mashed strawberries result in less than ½ cup, add water to make ½ cup. Add sugar and cornstarch; mix well. Bring mixture to a boil in a small saucepan. Continue boiling until mixture becomes clear and shiny, about 2 minutes. Cool the glaze slightly.

- Slice remaining strawberries and arrange them on top of the cream cheese layer. Pour the cooled glaze over the berries.

- Put whipping cream into freezer for 20 minutes. Beat whipping cream in large bowl of electric mixer. When it begins to thicken, add liqueur and sugar. Beat until very thick and creamy. Spread on top of glaze. Refrigerate until serving. Cut into 12 to 16 squares or rectangles.

*Strawberry Glaze*

| | |
|---|---|
| 1 | quart fresh strawberries |
| 1 | cup sugar |
| | Water |
| 2 | tablespoons cornstarch |

*Whipped Cream Godiva*

| | |
|---|---|
| 1 | pint whipping cream |
| 1 | tablespoon Godiva or other chocolate liqueur |
| 1 | tablespoon powdered sugar |

# CAPPUCCINO BROWNIES

*Serves 12*

| | |
|---|---|
| 3 | tablespoons instant espresso powder or instant dark roast coffee |
| 1 | tablespoon water |
| 2 | cups brown sugar, packed |
| ¾ | cup unsalted butter |
| 2 | large eggs |
| 2 | tablespoons coffee-flavored liqueur |
| 2 | tablespoons Irish cream liqueur |
| 2 | cups flour |
| 2 | teaspoons baking powder |
| ½ | teaspoon salt |
| 5 | ounces white chocolate, cut into ¾-inch pieces |
| ¾ | cup broken pecans, toasted |
| | Vanilla ice cream |
| | White Chocolate-Espresso Sauce, see page 311 |
| | Chocolate-Caramel Sauce, see page 310 |

- Mix coffee powder and water in heavy saucepan. Stir over medium heat until coffee dissolves. Add sugar and butter; stir or beat until butter melts. Cool to room temperature, stirring occasionally.

- Whisk eggs and liqueurs into cooled coffee mixture. In a large bowl, mix flour, baking powder, and salt. Add coffee mixture to flour and stir to combine. Stir in white chocolate and pecans.

- Butter a 10-inch cake pan or an 8-inch x 11-inch baking dish. Line with parchment. Pour batter into prepared pan and bake at 375° for about 35 minutes or until toothpick inserted near center comes out with just a few fudgy crumbs attached. Cool in pan on rack. Run small knife around sides of pan and turn out onto work surface. Peel off parchment.

- Cut into 12 wedges or squares. Top each serving with a good scoop of vanilla ice cream, drizzled with your choice of sauce. For a truly decadent experience, ladle the White Chocolate-Espresso Sauce onto the dessert plate. Top with brownie and ice cream; spoon Chocolate-Caramel Sauce on top. Brownies would keep for a week if they weren't so irresistible.

A work of art has an author and yet, when it is perfect, it has something which is anonymous about it.

*Simone Weil*

 "Java Jive" as performed by Manhattan Transfer

# WARM PEAR AND CHERRY CONSERVE WITH TRIPLE GINGER

*Makes 3 cups*

- Peel and core the pears; cut into ½-inch cubes. Combine pears, cherries, wine, vinegar, sugar, fresh ginger, pepper, salt, ground ginger, and walnuts in a large, heavy saucepan. Simmer until slightly thickened, stirring occasionally, about 25 minutes. Cool to room temperature. Cover and refrigerate overnight.

- To serve, heat until just warm. Stir in crystallized ginger and divide among bowls or use to top waffles or French toast. The conserve will keep for about 1 week.

**Variations:** Make Ham Steak with Ginger-Pear Conserve by spreading 1 cup of conserve onto a thick ham slice and baking at 400° for 20 minutes.

| | |
|---|---|
| 2 | pounds Bosc pears |
| 1 | cup dried cherries |
| ¼ | cup dry red wine |
| ¼ | cup red wine vinegar |
| ½ | cup sugar |
| 2 | tablespoons peeled and grated fresh ginger |
| ½ | teaspoon black pepper |
| ¼ | teaspoon salt |
| 2 | teaspoons ground ginger |
| ½ | cup walnut pieces |
| ⅓ | cup chopped crystallized ginger |

 "Clarinet Marmalade" as performed by Original Dixieland Jazz Band

# POACHED SPICED PEARS

*Serves 4*

| | |
|---|---|
| 1 | (750-milliliter) bottle dry red wine |
| 2¼ | cups sugar |
| 2 | cups water |
| ½ | cup orange juice |
| 3 | teaspoons shredded orange zest |
| 1 | teaspoon ground cardamom |
| 1 | cinnamon stick |
| 4 | Bosc pears, peeled but stems intact |

- Combine wine, sugar, water, orange juice, 2 teaspoons orange zest, cardamom, and cinnamon stick in heavy large saucepan. Stir over medium heat until mixture simmers and sugar dissolves. Add pears and return to simmer. Reduce heat and maintain simmer until pears are tender, about 25 minutes.

- Transfer pears to plate. Boil liquid in saucepan until it is reduced to 2 cups. Ladle sauce onto dessert plates. Place 1 pear upright in center of each plate. Garnish with remaining orange zest.

*For a different presentation, cut pears in half after cooking and scoop out small core with a teaspoon. Leaving the stem end of each pear intact, slice the pear halves from about ½-inch below the stem vertically through the rest of the pear. Place pear halves on serving plate and press slightly to fan pear. This method gives you 8 servings.*

**Variations:** *For a dangerously rich dessert, create Poached Pears with Mascarpone and Chocolate by coring whole pears after cooking, leaving pears intact, and stuffing cavities with 1 cup mascarpone cheese which has been blended with 1 tablespoon of Cointreau or other orange-flavored liqueur. Spoon Chocolate Truffle Sauce (see page 309) over pears.*

 "Merry Christmas Baby" as performed by B. B. King

# BITTERSWEET CHOCOLATE-ORANGE FONDUE WITH FRESH FRUITS

*Serves 2 to 4*

- Bring whipping cream and orange zest to simmer in heavy medium saucepan. Reduce heat to low and add chopped chocolate and 1 tablespoon Grand Marnier. Whisk until smooth. Remove from heat and add remaining 2 tablespoons of Grand Marnier. Pour into fondue pot over candle or canned heat; a preheated ceramic serving bowl will also keep fondue hot.

- Peel banana and cut in half lengthwise; cut each half on the diagonal into 4 chunks per half. Peel both kiwis and cut each crosswise into 4 thick slices. Arrange banana, kiwi, strawberries, and apricots on a platter. Dip fruits individually into the fondue mixture.

⅓ cup whipping cream
1½ teaspoons shredded orange zest, packed
8 ounces bittersweet chocolate, chopped
3 tablespoons Grand Marnier or other orange-flavored liqueur
1 banana
2 kiwis
8 strawberries
8 dried apricots

A waltz and a glass of wine invite an encore.

*Johann Strauss*

Heitor Berlioz: *Symphonie Fantastique, Op. 14:* IV. March to the Scaffold

# BLACKBERRY PINWHEEL COBBLER

*Serves 8*

| | |
|---|---|
| 1 | cup butter |
| 1 | cup sugar |
| 1 | cup water |
| 1½ | cups self-rising flour |
| ⅓ | cup milk, room temperature |
| 2 | cups blackberries, fresh or frozen |
| 1 | teaspoon cinnamon |
| | Additional sugar |

- Melt ½ cup butter in a round or oval glass baking dish; set aside. Heat sugar and water until sugar melts; set aside.

- Make cobbler dough by cutting remaining ½ cup butter into flour until mixture resembles fine crumbs. Add milk and stir with a fork until dough leaves sides of bowl. Turn out on floured surface and knead 3 or 4 times. Roll out to 11-inch x 9-inch x ¼-inch thick rectangle.

- Spread berries over dough; sprinkle with cinnamon. Beginning at 1 long side, roll dough up jelly-roll fashion. Cut log into 1¼-inch thick slices. Carefully place slices in prepared dish with melted butter. Pour syrup around slices so that the crust can absorb the syrup.

- Bake at 350° for 1 hour. During the last 15 minutes of cooking, sprinkle a few teaspoons of additional sugar over the crust. Serve warm or cold.

*Double the syrup recipe for a juicier cobbler.*

 "Blackberry Winter" as performed by Keith Jarrett

# PAVLOVA

*Serves 12*

- Using electric mixer, beat egg whites until soft peaks form. Add sugar very slowly, beating continuously, until firm but not stiff. Beat in cornstarch, vanilla, and white vinegar.

- Cover a cookie sheet with heavy-duty foil. Run water over the pan and allow all the water to drain off (but do not dry the foil). Pile the egg white mixture in the center of the cookie sheet. The mound should be at least 2 inches high. Use a frosting spatula to smooth the sides into a circle and smooth the top.

- Bake at 300° for 1 hour. Turn off heat, but leave the meringue in the oven for 5 hours or until cold.

- Beat whipping cream until stiff peaks form. Spread over the top of the meringue. Peel and cut up fresh fruits such as clementines, grapes, kiwi, bananas, mangos, or berries. Arrange fruit on top of Pavlova. Refrigerate until it is time to serve.

6 egg whites
1½ cups powdered sugar
1 tablespoon cornstarch
1 teaspoon vanilla
1 teaspoon white vinegar
8 ounces chilled whipping cream
Assorted fresh fruits

Al Jarreau, Jay Graydon, Nathan East, Marcel East: *High Crime:* "Fallin"

# CHERRY PIE WITH CRUNCHY OATMEAL CRUST

*Serves 12 to 16*

**Pie Filling**
- 2 cans tart cherries
- 1½ cups sugar
- 4 tablespoons tapioca
- 1 teaspoon almond extract
- 5 drops red food coloring (optional)

- Drain juice from cherries into saucepan. Add sugar and tapioca. Bring to a rolling boil and add extract and food coloring. Add cherries; remove from heat and cool.

**Crunchy Oatmeal Crust**
- 1 cup flour
- 1 cup brown sugar
- 1 cup dry oatmeal
- ¾ cup butter
- 1 cup chopped pecans

- Blend together flour, sugar, and oatmeal. Cut or rub in butter. Take half of mixture and divide between 2 (9-inch) pie plates. Add pie filling. Mix pecans into remaining half of flour and brown sugar mixture. Sprinkle over the pies. Bake at 325° for 25 minutes. Allow to cool. Cut into wedges to serve.

"I'll Be Home for Christmas" as performed by Diane Schuur

# LOUISIANA SWAMP PIE
*Makes 2 pies*

- Beat eggs well. Add sugar, melted butter, vinegar, and vanilla; mix well. Stir in coconut, pecans, and raisins. Transfer pie crusts into 2 pie plates. Pour in filling, dividing evenly between the 2 crusts.

- Bake at 300° for 50 to 55 minutes or until toothpick inserted into center of pie comes out clean. This pie freezes well and is best served at room temperature (refrigerate leftovers).

| | |
|---|---|
| 4 | eggs |
| 2 | cups sugar |
| 1 | cup butter, melted |
| 1 | teaspoon vinegar |
| 2 | teaspoons vanilla |
| 1 | cup coconut |
| 1 | cup chopped pecans |
| 1 | cup golden raisins |
| 2 | (9-inch) pie crusts |

---

Doug Duffey: *The Doug Duffey Band Live:* "Back Home in Louisiana"

# GRAND FINALE PIE

*Makes 2 pies*

| | |
|---|---|
| ¼ | cup butter |
| 1 | cup chopped pecans |
| 7 | ounces flaked coconut |
| 8 | ounces cream cheese |
| 1 | (14-ounce) can sweetened condensed milk (regular, low-fat, or no fat) |
| 8 | ounces whipping cream or nonfat whipped topping |
| 2 | (8-inch) pie shells, baked |
| | Buttery Caramel Sauce, see variation page 310 |

- In heavy iron skillet, melt butter and add pecans and coconut. Cook on low, stirring often, until brown. Set aside.

- Mix cream cheese and condensed milk in a large bowl. Use electric mixer to whip cream to soft peaks. Beat into cream cheese mixture. Pour cream mixture into pie crusts, dividing evenly. Sprinkle coconut mixture over the top and drizzle with caramel sauce. Freeze the pies for at least 4 hours. Remove from freezer, cut each pie into 6 to 8 wedges, and serve immediately.

Music . . . the favorite passion of my soul.

*Thomas Jefferson*

 Telemann: *Concerto for Trumpet, Strings, and Basso Continuo in D Major*

# BANANA-CARAMEL PIE

*Serves 6 to 8*

- Pour condensed milk into an 8-inch glass pie plate. Cover with foil. Fill a shallow 2-quart casserole with ¼-inch hot water. Place covered pie plate in casserole and bake at 375° for 45 minutes or until condensed milk is thick and caramel colored, adding hot water to the water bath as necessary.

- Cut bananas crosswise into ⅛-inch thick slices and place in bottom of pie crust. Spread caramelized milk over bananas. Cool for 30 minutes. Combine whipping cream and sugar; beat until very stiff. Spread over caramel layer and sprinkle with crumbled candy. Chill 3 hours or overnight before serving.

| | |
|---|---|
| 1 | (14-ounce) can sweetened condensed milk (regular, low-fat, or no fat) |
| 2-3 | bananas |
| 1 | (9-inch) pie crust, baked |
| 1 | cup whipping cream (or nonfat whipped topping) |
| ¼ | cup powdered sugar |
| | Crumbled Heath bars |

Torelli: *Concerto for Trumpet, Strings and Basso Continuo in D Major*

# PECAN FUDGE PIE

*Serves 10 to 12*

- 12 ounces semisweet chocolate chips
- 4 eggs
- ½ teaspoon salt
- 2 teaspoons vanilla extract
- 1 cup light corn syrup
- 2 tablespoons butter
- 1½ cups broken pecans
- 1 deep-dish pie shell
- Vanilla ice cream (optional)

- In small saucepan, melt chocolate pieces over low heat, stirring occasionally. In mixing bowl, beat eggs, salt, vanilla, corn syrup, and butter. Slowly add melted chocolate, stirring constantly with wire whisk. Fold in pecans.

- Pour mixture into pie shell. Bake at 350° for 50 to 60 minutes or until center is set. Cool pie before cutting into 10 to 12 wedges. Top each serving with vanilla ice cream if desired.

 "More Than You Know" as performed by Kenny Rankin

# IRISH COFFEE PIE

*Makes 2 pies*

- Dissolve coffee in ¼ cup boiling water; add enough cold water to make 1 cup. Dissolve gelatin in coffee mixture. Whisk in ⅔ cup sugar, egg yolks, and salt. Heat slowly until mixture is slightly thickened but not congealed, whisking occasionally. Add whiskey and Kahlúa; allow to cool.

- Whip egg whites until stiff but not dry, adding remaining ⅔ cup sugar gradually. Fold egg whites into coffee mixture. Beat cream until very stiff; fold into coffee mixture. Pour filling into pie crusts, dividing evenly. Chill until set, at least 4 hours. Garnish with chocolate shavings, if desired.

| | |
|---|---|
| 2 | tablespoons instant coffee |
| 1 | cup water |
| 2 | tablespoons unflavored gelatin |
| 1⅓ | cups sugar |
| 6 | eggs, separated |
| | Pinch salt |
| ¾ | cup Irish whiskey |
| ½ | cup Kahlúa or other coffee-flavored liqueur |
| 2 | cups whipping cream |
| 2 | graham cracker crusts |
| | Shaved chocolate for garnish (optional) |

No man can be a patriot on an empty stomach.

*William Cowper*

 "Black Coffee" as performed by Peggy Lee

# THREE-CITRUS TART WITH MANGOES AND PAPAYAS

*Serves 6 to 8*

| | |
|---|---|
| 1 | (9-inch) refrigerated pie crust |
| ¼ | cup sugar |
| 1½ | tablespoons flour |
| ½ | teaspoon baking powder |
| ¼ | teaspoon salt |
| 3 | large egg whites |
| 1 | large egg |
| 2 | tablespoons each fresh lemon, lime, and orange juice |
| ¾ | teaspoon each grated lemon, lime, and orange zest |
| 1 | (26-ounce) jar chilled mango slices in syrup |
| 1 | (26-ounce) jar chilled papaya spears in syrup |
| | Thinly shredded lemon, lime, and orange zest for garnish |

- Place the pie crust on work surface and roll or pat it out slightly to increase diameter about ¾ inch. Put pie crust into a 9-inch tart pan with removable bottom, pressing dough up sides to top of rim. Bake crust at 450° until set and just starting to turn golden, about 15 minutes. Cool on rack.

- Mix sugar, flour, baking powder, and salt in small bowl. Whisk egg whites, whole egg, juices, and zest in medium bowl. Add flour mixture and whisk until smooth. Pour into baked crust. Bake at 350° until filling is set, about 15 minutes. Cool on rack; chill in refrigerator.

- Drain syrup from mangoes and papayas into small saucepan. Boil until syrup is reduced to ¾ cup. Place mango and papaya slices decoratively on top of tart. Chill sauce and pie separately.

- To serve, remove tart pan side. Cut the tart into 6 to 8 wedges; place each on a dessert plate. Spoon 2 tablespoons sauce over and around each tart slice; sprinkle entire plate with shredded zest.

 Sergei Prokofiev: *The Love for Three Oranges*

# CHOCOLATE-AMARETTO CHEESECAKE

*Serves* 16

- In processor or mixer, blend cream cheese, sugar, cocoa, flour, Amaretto, and vanilla until smooth. Mix in eggs and combine thoroughly.

- Spray a 9-inch springform pan with nonstick cooking spray. Sprinkle ¼ cup chocolate crumbs on bottom of pan. Pour cream cheese mixture into pan. Bake at 300° for 45 to 50 minutes or until center is almost set. Sprinkle with remaining ¼ cup crumbs. Let cool completely on wire rack; cover with plastic wrap and refrigerate for 8 hours or overnight.

- Release pan sides and cut cheesecake into 16 thin wedges. Top each with a dollop of whipped cream and a sprinkling of almonds.

| | |
|---|---|
| 32 | ounces cream cheese (regular, low-fat, or no fat) |
| 2 | cups sugar |
| ⅔ | cup unsweetened cocoa |
| ⅔ | cup flour |
| 3 | tablespoons Amaretto or other almond-flavored liqueur |
| 2 | tablespoons vanilla extract |
| 3 | eggs or ½ cup egg substitute |
| ½ | cup chocolate cookie crumbs |
| | Whipped cream or nonfat whipped topping |
| | Sliced almonds, toasted |

Giuseppe Tartini: *Violin Sonata in G Minor* ("The Devil's Trill")

CAKES 283

# EXTRAVAGANT POUND CAKE

*Serves 20*

| | |
|---|---|
| 1 | cup butter |
| ½ | cup shortening |
| 4 | cups sugar |
| 6 | eggs |
| 1 | teaspoon rum extract |
| 1 | teaspoon coconut extract |
| 3 | cups flour |
| ½ | teaspoon baking powder |
| ⅛ | teaspoon salt |
| 1 | cup milk |
| ½ | cup water |
| 1 | teaspoon almond extract |

- Cream butter and shortening in bowl of electric mixer until they resemble mayonnaise. Add 3 cups sugar and beat until light and fluffy. Beat in eggs 1 at a time; mix in rum and coconut extracts.

- Stir together flour, baking powder, and salt. Add half of flour to mixing bowl with the milk; mix well. Add the remaining flour and mix until combined. Pour into greased and floured tube pan.

- Bake cake at 350° for 75 minutes. Remove pan from oven; allow to cool for 20 minutes. While cake is cooling, make a glaze by boiling 1 cup sugar with ½ cup water for 1 minute. Add almond extract. Remove cake from pan and pour hot glaze over hot cake. Allow cake to cool before serving.

 "We've Saved the Best for Last" as performed by Kenny G

# COLD OVEN POUND CAKE

*Serves* 12 *to* 16

- Cream shortening and sugar; add eggs and beat until light and fluffy. Stir together flour, soda, and salt. Add 1 cup of flour to sugar mixture and blend well. Mix in ½ cup buttermilk. Repeat additions, ending with 1 cup flour. Add all extracts and beat until smooth. Pour into greased and floured tube pan. Put cake into cold oven. Turn oven to 300° and bake for 1½ hours.

| | |
|---|---|
| 1 | cup butter-flavored shortening |
| 3 | cups sugar |
| 6 | eggs |
| 1 | cup buttermilk |
| 3 | cups flour |
| ¼ | teaspoon baking soda |
| ¼ | teaspoon salt |
| 2 | teaspoons coconut extract |
| 2 | teaspoons butter extract |
| 2 | teaspoons vanilla extract |

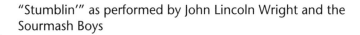

"Stumblin'" as performed by John Lincoln Wright and the Sourmash Boys

# CREAM CHEESE POUND CAKE

*Serves 12 to 16*

| | |
|---|---|
| 8 | ounces cream cheese, softened |
| 1 | cup margarine, softened |
| ½ | cup butter, softened |
| 3 | cups sugar |
| 6 | eggs |
| 3 | cups cake flour |
| 2 | teaspoons vanilla |

- Beat cream cheese, margarine, butter, and sugar in a large bowl until smooth and light. Add eggs, one at a time, alternating with flour. Blend well after each addition. Mix in vanilla.

- Pour batter into a greased and floured Bundt pan. Bake at 375° for 30 minutes. Reduce heat to 325° and continue cooking until a toothpick inserted near center comes out clean, about 40 to 50 minutes more. Cool in pan on rack.

 "Blame It on my Youth" as performed by Kenny Rankin

# RUM CAKE

*Serves 16 to 20*

- Butter and flour a 10-inch tube pan. Mix together cake mix, eggs, cold water, vegetable oil, and rum. Sprinkle pecans in bottom of pan; pour batter over. Bake 1 hour at 325°. Remove from oven.

- While still warm, prick the top of the cake all over with a large fork. Pour Rum Glaze over the top and leave in the pan until ready to serve. Unmold gently onto a cake plate.

- Melt butter in saucepan. Stir in water and sugar. Boil 5 minutes, stirring constantly. Remove from heat; stir in rum.

| | |
|---|---|
| 1 | yellow pudding cake mix |
| 3 | eggs |
| ½ | cup cold water |
| ⅓ | cup vegetable oil |
| ½ | cup dark rum |
| 1 | cup chopped pecans |
| | Rum Glaze |

*Rum Glaze*

| | |
|---|---|
| ¾ | cup unsalted butter |
| ⅓ | cup water |
| ¾ | cup sugar |
| ¾ | cup dark rum |

 "Rum and Coca Cola" as performed by The Andrews Sisters

# GOLDEN SIN

*Serves 16*

| | |
|---|---|
| 1½ | cups sugar |
| 3 | cups cake flour |
| 2 | teaspoons baking powder |
| ½ | cup butter, melted |
| 3 | eggs |
| 2 | teaspoons vanilla extract |
| 8 | ounces cream cheese |
| 1 | (16-ounce) box powdered sugar |

- Using an electric mixer, beat together 1½ cups sugar, flour, baking powder, butter, 1 egg, and 1 teaspoon vanilla. Batter will be very stiff. Spray a 13-inch x 9-inch x 2-inch baking pan with nonstick cooking spray. Press batter into bottom of pan.

- Cream together the cream cheese and powdered sugar. Add 2 eggs, 1 at a time, mixing well after each addition. Beat in 1 teaspoon vanilla. Spread the cream cheese mixture on top of the flour mixture.

- Bake at 350° for 55 minutes. Allow to cool completely before cutting into squares.

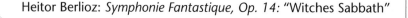

Heitor Berlioz: *Symphonie Fantastique, Op. 14:* "Witches Sabbath"

# FRESH PEACH CAKE

*Serves 12 to 16*

*Cake*

| | |
|---|---|
| 1 | cup butter |
| 2 | cups sugar |
| 3 | eggs |
| 3 | cups flour |
| 2 | teaspoons baking soda |
| ¾ | cup fresh peach juice |
| 2 | cups mashed peeled peaches |
| 2 | teaspoons cinnamon |
| | Cream Filling |
| | Whipped cream |

*Cream Filling*

| | |
|---|---|
| 2 | tablespoons flour |
| 1 | cup whipping cream |
| 1 | egg |
| 1 | cup sugar |
| ½ | cup butter |
| 1 | teaspoon vanilla |

- Cream butter and sugar. Add eggs 1 at a time, beating well after each addition. Stir together flour and soda; add to batter alternately with peach juice and peaches, beginning and ending with flour. Mix in cinnamon. Pour batter into 3 greased and floured round or square cake pans. Bake at 350° for about 30 minutes or until a toothpick inserted in center comes out clean. Cool on racks.

- To serve, place 1 cake layer on serving plate. Spread with half of the Cream Filling. Place a second layer on top of the filling. Spread with remaining half of filling. Top with third cake layer. Spread whipped cream over top and sides of cake.

- Whisk all ingredients together in medium saucepan. Cook until soft and creamy, whisking constantly. Allow to cool completely before assembling cake.

 "Cake Walking Babes From Home" as performed by Turk Murphy or Bob Scoby or Lou Watters

# HAZELNUT-CHOCOLATE MERINGUE TORTE

*Serves 12 to 16*

*Chocolate-Hazelnut Meringues*
- 2 cups hazelnuts
- 4 egg whites
- 1 cup powdered sugar
- 2 tablespoons cocoa
- 1 teaspoon vanilla

- Place hazelnuts in a shallow baking dish. Roast at 400° until nuts are colored a rich brown, shaking occasionally (watch carefully to avoid scorching). Allow nuts to cool slightly. Working with a small handful of nuts at a time, roll them between your palms to loosen and remove the skins. Chop nuts with knife or in processor until they resemble moist crumbs. Measure ½ cup and reserve for garnish. Set remaining crumbs aside.

- Using wire whisk or electric mixer, beat egg whites until soft peaks form. Add sugar gradually, continuing to beat until stiff peaks form. Beat in cocoa and vanilla. Stir in the hazelnuts (except reserved ½ cup).

- Line 2 or 3 large baking sheets with parchment paper. Using a 10-inch cake pan, trace 3 separate circles onto the paper. Mound ⅓ of egg white mixture into center of each circle; use the back of a spoon to spread the mixture out to fill the circle. Bake meringues at 225° for 2 hours. Turn oven off, but leave pans inside until assembly time.

*Rich Chocolate Mousse*
- 2½ cups chilled whipping cream
- ⅓ cup honey
- 12 ounces bittersweet chocolate, broken or chopped

- Heat ¾ cup whipping cream and honey in medium saucepan over low heat. Add chocolate; remove from heat and allow to stand 2 minutes. Whisk mixture until chocolate is melted and thoroughly combined, returning to low heat if necessary. Cool, stirring occasionally.

## HAZELNUT-CHOCOLATE MERINGUE TORTE *continued*

- Beat remaining 1¾ cups whipping cream until soft peaks form. Fold half of whipped cream into chocolate mixture to lighten it; fold remaining whipped cream in. Reserve 1 cup and set aside. If mousse must be held for a while, place in refrigerator. It will set firmly, so whip it a bit before trying to spread it on torte.

- In small mixing bowl, beat mousse with electric mixer until soft and fluffy. Combine instant coffee and boiling water; stir until dissolved. Allow to cool slightly. Beat into mousse.

- In large mixing bowl, beat whipping cream until soft peaks form. Beat in mousse and continue whipping until fairly firm peaks form (not stiff).

### Mocha Cream

| | |
|---|---|
| 1 | cup Rich Chocolate Mousse |
| 2 | tablespoons instant espresso or dark roast coffee |
| 2 | tablespoons boiling water |
| 2 | cups chilled whipping cream |

### Assembly

- Peel parchment from meringues. Place one meringue on a large flat platter. Spread with half the Rich Chocolate Mousse. Spread 1 cup of Mocha Cream over mousse. Top with second meringue and spread with remaining mousse; cover with 1 cup of Mocha Cream. Place third meringue on top. Use remaining Mocha Cream to cover top and sides of torte, filling in any gaps between layers. Cover top of torte with reserved ½ cup chopped or ground hazelnuts.

- To serve within 2 hours, cover torte and store in refrigerator. To delay serving, cover the torte completely with plastic wrap and freeze for 3 hours or up to 3 days. Remove from freezer 1 hour before serving and allow to stand at room temperature.

# EARL GREY CAKE

*Serves 12 to 16*

- 2 Earl Grey tea bags
- ⅔ cup boiling water
- 8 ounces bittersweet chocolate, chopped
- ⅔ cup orange marmalade
- 1 cup unsalted butter, room temperature
- 1 cup sugar
- 6 eggs
- ⅓ cup chopped walnuts
- 1 teaspoon vanilla
- 2 cups flour
- 1½ teaspoons baking powder
- ½ cup whipping cream
- 6 ounces bittersweet chocolate, finely chopped

- Place tea bags in heatproof cup or mug; add boiling water and steep for 5 minutes. Remove and discard tea bags. Allow tea to cool. Melt 8 ounces chocolate over double boiler, stirring until smooth. Cool chocolate to room temperature. Puree marmalade in processor or blender until smooth.

- In large bowl of electric mixer, cream butter and sugar until fluffy; add eggs 1 at a time, beating well after each addition. Stir in melted chocolate, marmalade, walnuts, and vanilla. Stir together flour and baking powder. Beat dry ingredients and tea alternately into mixture in 2 additions (do not overbeat).

- Pour batter into a buttered 10-inch angel food cake pan. Bake at 325° for 70 minutes or until toothpick inserted near center comes out with moist crumbs attached. Cool on rack 10 minutes. Cut around cake edges to loosen; turn onto rack to cool.

- Bring whipping cream to boil. Remove from heat; add 6 ounces finely chopped chocolate. Let stand for 2 minutes. Stir until smooth and cool completely. Place cake on platter. Drizzle glaze over top, allowing it to drip down sides.

 Franz Joseph Haydn: *Symphony in D*

# FLOURISHES: *Libations & Lagniappe*

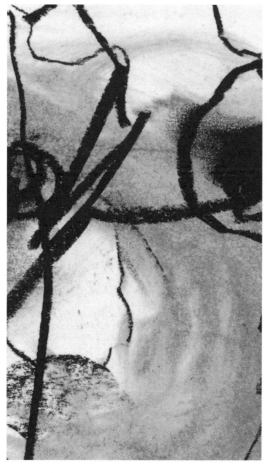

# A MENU FOR AUTUMN

### *Appetizer*
Croutons with Apple, Pecan Butter, and Brie

### *Soup*
Butternut-Double Ginger Soup

### *Main Plate*
Cornish Hens with Blackberry Sauce
Mélange of Bright Vegetables
White Corn with Crispy Sage

### *Dessert*
Irish Coffee Pie

 Ottorino Respighi: *The Fountains of Rome*

# DADDY'S FORTY PARTY PUNCH

*Makes 2 gallons*

- Combine boiling water with sugar, gelatin, and frozen juice concentrates. Stir well to dissolve. Add pineapple juice and extract. Freeze in 4 empty, rinsed half-gallon milk cartons or in zippered plastic freezer bags.

- To serve, remove frozen blocks of punch from cartons or bags and put in large punch bowl. Pour club soda over frozen punch and allow to sit until punch begins to thaw. Stir until sparkly slushy.

*Freezing in multiple containers or bags allows you to prepare half at a time, either for separate occasions or so that you can refill the bowl with fresh punch. Simply use 1 frozen block and pour 1 liter of club soda over.*

*A little rum added with the club soda does wonders for this punch.*

| | |
|---|---|
| 4 | cups boiling water |
| 6 | cups sugar |
| 3 | (3-ounce) packages orange gelatin |
| 1 | (3-ounce) package lemon gelatin |
| 2 | (6-ounce) cans frozen lemonade |
| 1 | (6-ounce) can frozen orange juice |
| 2 | (46-ounce) cans pineapple juice |
| 2 | tablespoons almond extract |
| 4 | liters club soda |

"Non-Alcoholic" as performed by Woody Herman

# RUSSIAN TEA

*Serves 40*

| | |
|---|---|
| 3 | cups water |
| 3 | cups sugar |
| 2 | cinnamon sticks |
| 12 | whole cloves |
| 2 | teaspoons grated dried orange peel |
| 1 | (46-ounce) can pineapple juice |
| 1 | cup lemon juice |
| 10 | tea bags |
| 8 | cups boiling water |

- Bring 3 cups water to boil. Stir in sugar and remove from heat. Continue stirring until sugar is fully dissolved. Put cinnamon sticks, cloves, and orange peel on a small square of cheesecloth. Draw up corners and tie into a pouch using thread or string. Put spice bag in syrup and return to boil. Boil for 1 minute.

- Remove spice bag and add pineapple juice and lemon juice; allow to simmer for a few minutes. Put 10 tea bags into 8 cups boiling water. Allow to steep for 5 minutes. Remove bags and add tea to simmering mixture. Pour into tea urn and serve hot.

 Pyotr Ilyich Tchaikovsky: *The Nutcracker:* "Russian Dance"

# PEPPERMINT COCOA MIX

*Serves 50*

- Mix all ingredients together. Store in an airtight canister or zippered plastic bag.

- To make Peppermint Cocoa, stir 2 heaping tablespoons mix into 8 ounces boiling water. Stir until dissolved.

*For a dressy presentation, top steaming mug of cocoa with whipped cream or marshmallows; add a peppermint stick stirrer.*

*This mix makes a wonderful gift. Seal a portion inside a small plastic bag and attach preparation instructions. Tuck into a mug and decorate with ribbons or slip into a gift bag. The full recipe can be given inside a gift canister; add a set of mugs for a memorable house gift.*

| | |
|---|---|
| 1 | (25-ounce) package powdered milk |
| 1 | (16-ounce) box powdered milk chocolate mix |
| 1 | (6-ounce) canister non-dairy coffee creamer |
| ¾ | cup powdered sugar |
| 1-2 | cups finely crushed peppermint sticks |

Johann Sebastian Bach: *Suite #2 in B minor for Flute & Strings*

# WHITE SANGRÍA

*Makes 2½ quarts*

- 2 oranges, sliced and seeded
- 1 lemon, sliced and seeded
- 1 lime, sliced and seeded
- ⅔ cup brandy
- ½ cup sugar
- 2 cinnamon sticks
- 2 (750-milliliter) bottles Chablis or other dry white wine, chilled
- 1 quart club soda, chilled

- Combine fruit slices, brandy, sugar, and cinnamon sticks in a large pitcher; stir well. Cover and chill at least 4 hours, stirring occasionally (sugar should eventually dissolve).

- Remove and discard cinnamon sticks. Add wine to the mixture, stirring well. Cover and chill at least 2 hours. Stir in club soda and serve over ice.

 "Bubbles in the Wine" as performed by Freddy Martin

# ROYAL FROZEN MIMOSAS

*Serves 8 to 12*

- Combine half the champagne, orange juice, Cointreau, and ice cubes in blender. Whirl until slushy. Repeat with remaining ingredients. Serve in champagne flutes or martini glasses garnished with orange slices.

1 (750-milliliter) bottle champagne
1 quart orange juice
2 jiggers Cointreau or other orange liqueur
3 cups ice cubes
1 fresh orange, sliced

 Georg Frideric Handel: *Solomon:* "The Arrival of the Queen of Sheba"

# PEACH SPRITZERS

*Makes 9 cups*

6 large peaches, peeled and halved
1 (750-milliliter) bottle champagne, chilled
1 (23-ounce) bottle sparkling mineral water

- Place peaches in container of blender or processor. Cover and process until smooth.

- Combine 3 cups peach puree, champagne, and mineral water in large pitcher. Stir well. Pour into chilled wine glasses and serve immediately.

 "Keen and Peachy" as performed by Shorty Roberts

# VODKA LEMONADE

*Serves 6*

- Mix sugar and lemon juice; stir until sugar dissolves. Add vodka and refrigerate for 30 minutes to 2 hours.

- Fill 6 tall glasses with crushed ice. Pour in lemonade and garnish with lemon slices or mint sprigs.

| | |
|---|---|
| ⅔ | cup sugar |
| 1 | cup lemon juice |
| 1½ | cups vodka, plain or lemon-flavored |
| 6 | lemon slices or mint sprigs |

Once, during Prohibition, I was forced to live for days on nothing but food and water.

*W.C. Fields*

 "Something Cool" as performed by June Christy

# TEQUILA SLUSH

*Makes 3 quarts*

4½ cups water
2 (6-ounce) cans frozen limeade, thawed
1 (6-ounce) can frozen orange juice, thawed
¾ cup lime juice
1 cup tequila
1 (28-ounce) bottle grapefruit soda

- Mix together water, thawed limeade, and thawed orange juice. Stir in lime juice and tequila. Add grapefruit soda. Pour mixture into a freezer container; freeze overnight or until firm.

- Remove from freezer and allow to stand 30 minutes. Stir until slushy. Serve in margarita glasses.

Padre Antonio Soler: *Fandango*

# PUNCH OF THE ISLANDS

*Makes 3½ quarts*

- Combine water and sugar in a small saucepan. Bring to a boil; stir until sugar dissolves and remove from heat. Set aside.

- In a blender, whirl thawed orange juice, thawed lemonade, pineapple juice, and mashed banana until smooth. Combine sugar syrup and juice mixture in large freezer container. Add rum and ginger ale, stirring well. Cover and freeze.

- To serve, let stand at room temperature for 30 minutes. Stir well and serve in punch cups or wine glasses.

3 cups water
1 cup sugar
1 (12-ounce) can frozen orange juice, thawed
1 (6-ounce) can frozen lemonade, thawed
½ cup pineapple juice
1½ cups mashed ripe banana, about 3 medium bananas
2 cups white rum
1 quart ginger ale

*This punch is tasty even without the "punch," so omit rum for a non-alcoholic beverage.*

Guiseppe Verdi: *La Traviata:* "Brindigi"

# FUNKY RUM PUNCH  *Serves 12 to 16*

| | |
|---|---|
| 2 | (12-ounce) cans mango nectar |
| 2 | (12-ounce) cans guava nectar |
| 2 | cups pineapple juice |
| 1½ | cups sweetened canned coconut cream |
| ¼ | cup lime juice |
| 2 | cups gold rum |
| 18 | cups ice cubes or crushed ice |
| | Fresh fruit for garnish |

- Combine all liquids in a pitcher; mix well. Whirl with ice in a blender until smooth, using 1 cup punch and 2 cups ice per batch.

- Serve in punch cups or margarita glasses garnished with festive fresh fruit.

 "My Bucket's Got A Hole in It" as performed by Louis Armstrong

# CHOCOLATE-RASPBERRY CREAM

*Serves 1*

- In a small, stemmed cordial or sherry glass, layer the ingredients by pouring each in separately over the back of a spoon. Begin with raspberry liqueur, then chocolate, and top with cream. If the layers are not clearly visible, simply stir the drink before serving.

1 tablespoon raspberry liqueur
1 tablespoon chocolate liqueur
1 tablespoon whipping cream

"Cocktails for Two" as performed by Spike Jones

# MOCHA MAGIC

*Serves 2*

| | |
|---|---|
| 3 | tablespoons Irish cream liqueur |
| 2 | tablespoons chocolate-flavored liqueur |
| 1 | tablespoon coffee-flavored liqueur |
| 2 | cups vanilla ice cream |

- Mix all liqueurs in a glass and stir well. Put 2 half-cup scoops of ice cream in each of two old-fashioned glasses. Pour liqueurs over ice cream; stir well. Sip through straw.

**Variations:** Double the amount of ice cream for a tall Mocha Cooler.

Music was invented to confirm human loneliness.

*Lawrence Durrell*

 "Coffee in the Morning, Kisses at Night" as performed by Eddie Duchin

# DOUBLE IRISH COFFEE

*Serves 1*

- Pour coffee into stemmed mug. Add sugar if desired and stir until dissolved. Pour in whiskey and liqueur; stir well. Top with a dollop of whipped cream dusted with cocoa.

6 ounces hot freshly brewed strong coffee
1 teaspoon sugar (optional)
2 tablespoons Irish whiskey
2 tablespoons Irish cream liqueur
Whipped cream

 "Hot Toddy" as performed by Ralph Flanagan

# COFFEE KEDM

*Serves 2*

| | |
|---|---|
| 1 | tablespoon hazelnut liqueur |
| 1 | tablespoon chocolate liqueur |
| 1 | tablespoon coffee liqueur |
| 2 | tablespoons Irish cream liqueur |
| 1 | tablespoon brandy (optional) |
| 1-1½ | cups freshly brewed dark roast coffee |
| | Whipped cream |

- Divide liqueurs into 2 large coffee cups or stemmed mugs. Top with hot coffee. Spoon or spritz plenty of whipped cream on top.

 "You're the Cream in My Coffee" as performed by Chris Connor

# CHOCOLATE TRUFFLE SAUCE

*Makes 2 cups*

- Bring cream and butter to simmer in medium saucepan and remove pan immediately from heat. Add chopped chocolate and vanilla extract; whisk until sauce is smooth. This sauce will keep in refrigerator for 2 weeks.

*Serve over ice cream, brownies, or cake. This sauce makes a delicious dip for fresh fruit and cubes of pound cake.*

½ cup plus 1 tablespoon whipping cream
¼ cup unsalted butter, cut into pieces
12 ounces semisweet chocolate, chopped
1 teaspoon vanilla

Thomaso Albinoni: *Adagio in G Minor*

# CHOCOLATE-CARAMEL SAUCE

*Makes 1½ cups*

| | |
|---|---|
| 1¼ | cups sugar |
| ⅓ | cup bourbon |
| ¾ | cup whipping cream |
| 3 | tablespoons unsalted butter, cut in pieces |
| 1½ | ounces bittersweet chocolate, chopped |

- Stir sugar and bourbon in heavy saucepan over low heat until sugar dissolves. Increase heat to medium-high; boil without stirring until mixture turns deep amber, brushing sides occasionally with a wet pastry brush. Remove from heat.

- Add cream to the saucepan; sugar mixture will boil up rapidly. Whisk until the caramel is smooth. Return to boil, whisking constantly. Remove from heat. Add butter and chocolate and stir until smooth. This sauce will keep for 1 week in the refrigerator (rewarm before serving).

*Serve over ice cream, brownie, or cake. Dip banana chunks into sauce or use as topping glaze for cheesecake.*

**Variations:** *For Buttery Caramel Sauce, omit the chocolate.*

 Johann Sebastian Bach: "Bist du bri mir"

# WHITE CHOCOLATE-ESPRESSO SAUCE

*Makes 1¼ cups*

- Bring cream just to boil in a medium saucepan. Add espresso beans. Remove pan from heat and allow beans to steep for 30 minutes. Strain the cream and discard the beans.

- Return cream to boil. Remove from heat and add chocolate. Allow to stand for 2 minutes; whisk until smooth.

*This sauce perfectly complements a rich, dark chocolate brownie.*

8 ounces whipping cream
¼ pound espresso or dark roast coffee beans
6 ounces white chocolate, chopped

 "Coffee Bean" as performed by Les Baxter

# BLENDER MAYONNAISE

*Makes 2 cups*

2 whole eggs
1 tablespoon dry mustard
2 teaspoons paprika
1 teaspoon salt
3 tablespoons lemon juice
2 cups oil

- Put eggs, mustard, paprika, salt, and lemon juice into blender. Whirl on low until mixed well. Pour oil in a very thin stream gradually into blender container with machine running on high. It will take several minutes to incorporate the oil; do not pour oil too quickly or mayonnaise will separate. This mayonnaise keeps for 1 week in refrigerator.

*Although the lemon juice does "cook" the eggs, you may wish to avoid this recipe if you are uncomfortable about consuming raw egg.*

Johann Strauss, Jr: *Wo die zitronen bluth'n, Op. 364* ("Where the Lemon Trees Blossom")

# BLENDER HOLLANDAISE

*Makes ⅔ cup*

- Melt butter in microwave or on stovetop until bubbling. Put lemon juice, cayenne, egg yolks, and salt in blender. Turn on high and blend for a few seconds. Slowly add the hot butter in a thin stream; don't pour too fast or sauce will separate.

  The lemon juice does "cook" the eggs, but if you are uncomfortable about consuming raw egg, avoid this recipe.

½ cup unsalted butter
2 tablespoons lemon juice
Dash of cayenne pepper
2 egg yolks
⅛ teaspoon salt

 Frederic Chopin: *Waltz in D Flat, Op. 64:* #1 ("The Minute Waltz")

# GREEN GODDESS DRESSING

*Makes 1⅓ cups*

½ cup mayonnaise
½ cup sour cream
⅓ cup chopped chives
1 green onion, chopped
1 clove garlic, peeled
1 tablespoon tarragon vinegar
1 teaspoon chopped fresh tarragon or ½ teaspoon dried
1 teaspoon sugar
1 teaspoon Worcestershire sauce
Salt and black pepper

- Blend or process all ingredients until smooth. Season with salt and pepper. This dressing will keep for 3 days.

 Basia: *The Sweetest Illusion:* "An Olive Tree"

# CHEDDAR CHEESE SALAD DRESSING

*Serves 8*

- Combine all ingredients in blender. Cover and whirl until smooth.

| | |
|---|---|
| ¾ | cup mayonnaise |
| ¾ | cup sour cream |
| ½ | cup buttermilk |
| 1 | cup shredded sharp cheese |
| 1 | teaspoon Worcestershire sauce |
| 2 | tablespoons red wine vinegar |
| ⅛ | teaspoon salt |
| ⅛ | teaspoon black pepper |
| 1-2 | cloves garlic, minced |
| 4 | green onions, chopped |

"That's All" as performed by Kenny Rankin

# CLASSIC VINAIGRETTE

*Makes 2 cups*

| | |
|---|---|
| 1 | tablespoon chopped garlic |
| ⅓ | cup wine vinegar |
| 1 | tablespoon Dijon mustard |
| 1 | teaspoon salt |
| 1 | teaspoon coarse black pepper |
| 1 | cup olive oil |

- In processor or blender, combine garlic, vinegar, mustard, salt, and pepper. Whirl until garlic is finely chopped. Add olive oil in a steady stream while machine is running. Store dressing in refrigerator for up to 1 week.

*Similar results can be achieved by whisking ingredients in a medium bowl.*

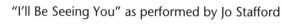
"I'll Be Seeing You" as performed by Jo Stafford

# FRENCH VINAIGRETTE

*Makes 5 cups*

- Put all ingredients except olive oil in food processor or blender. Process until everything is finely chopped.

- With the machine running, slowly add the olive oil until the dressing has a thick and creamy consistency. Store covered in refrigerator for up to 2 weeks.

| | |
|---|---|
| 6-7 | shallots, peeled and coarsely chopped |
| 6 | cloves garlic |
| 1½ | tablespoons salt |
| 3 | tablespoons pepper |
| 2 | tablespoons sugar |
| 1 | tablespoon Dijon mustard |
| 1 | tablespoon water |
| ¾ | cup tarragon vinegar |
| 4 | cups olive oil |

"Love and Paris Rain" as performed by The Yellowjackets

# SUN-DRIED TOMATO VINAIGRETTE

*Makes 1½ cups*

- ¼ cup drained, chopped, oil-packed sun-dried tomatoes
- ¼ cup fresh basil leaves, packed
- ¼ cup balsamic vinegar
- 1 cup olive oil
- Freshly ground black pepper

- In blender or processor, puree tomatoes, basil, and vinegar. Add olive oil in a steady stream while machine is running. Grind in some black pepper.

*Serve over mixed greens or drizzle over a roasted veggie sandwich. This vinaigrette dresses a grilled or poached chicken salad beautifully. On crunchy green beans or asparagus, steamed and chilled cauliflower, corn and lima bean salad, warm yellow squash or zucchini—the possibilities for using this dressing are limited only by your imagination.*

Al Jarreau, Jay Graydon, Clif Magness, Glen Ballard: *High Crime:* "Imagination"

# SAVORY SAUCE

*Makes ½ cup*

- Boil beef broth rapidly in a small saucepan until reduced to 1 tablespoon. While broth is reducing, combine oil and butter in another saucepan. Add rosemary and garlic. Sauté until garlic is soft and golden-brown, about 5 minutes. Stir in reduced beef broth and set saucepan aside until ready to use.

- Strain sauce through a fine sieve, removing the garlic and rosemary, before serving.

*Toss sauce with cooked spaghetti and sprinkle with grated Parmesan. Brush sauce on sliced French bread and broil or grill with steak or chops. Toss 1 tablespoon sauce with steamed green beans just before serving. Brush sauce on both sides of thick eggplant slices; grill or broil and serve on crusty rolls or hamburger buns. Serve sauce as dip for rare roast beef or lamb sandwiches. Add this sauce to mashed potatoes (a few cloves of roasted garlic wouldn't hurt either). Versatile is the word—just add this sauce whenever you need a burst of savory flavor.*

| | |
|---|---|
| 1 | cup beef broth |
| 2 | tablespoons olive oil |
| 6 | tablespoons unsalted butter |
| 4 | (3-inch) sprigs fresh rosemary |
| 4 | large cloves garlic, coarsely chopped |

There's no sauce in the world like hunger.

*Miguel de Cervantes*

 Al Jarreau, Jay Graydon, David Foster: *High Crime:* "After All"

# ROASTED PEPPER AND GARLIC SAUCE

*Makes 1 to 1½ cups*

3 bell peppers of different colors
1 large head of garlic
1 teaspoon olive oil
Whipping cream

- Place whole peppers on a foil-lined baking sheet which has been coated with non-stick spray. Slice top off garlic head and place beside peppers. Drizzle olive oil over garlic. Place baking sheet in 375° oven and roast vegetables. Turn peppers a few times so that they will roast on all sides. The garlic will probably brown before the peppers, so remove when ready. When peppers are roasted on all sides, remove them from the oven and place them in a paper bag for 10 minutes.

- Peel peppers and put into blender or processor. Squeeze roasted garlic onto the peppers. Whirl or pulse until smooth. Slowly add whipping cream until you reach a creamy sauce consistency. Store in refrigerator for up to a week.

*Toss this sauce with pasta, adding Parmesan cheese and more whipping cream as desired. Pour over cooked vegetables or use to top mashed potatoes or noodles. Drizzle over or swirl into cold or hot soups. Serve over poached or roasted chicken.*

 "Le Jazz Hot" as performed by Julie Andrews

# LIME-CILANTRO SOUR CREAM

*Makes 1½ cups*

- Mix all ingredients in a small bowl. Season with salt and pepper. Refrigerate for 1 hour.

  *Use this spunky sour cream to top any Mexican, Tex-Mex, or Southwestern food, or drop a dollop onto gazpacho, black bean soup, or seafood soup. Marinate chicken breasts in this mixture for up to 4 hours; shake off excess and grill or broil until done.*

- 1 cup sour cream
- 1 tablespoon lemon juice
- 1 tablespoon lime juice
- ½ cup chopped fresh cilantro
- Salt and black pepper

"Spirit of the West" as performed by The Yellowjackets

# GREEN TOMATO PASTA SAUCE

*Makes 6 cups*

| | | |
|---|---|---|
| 3 | pounds green tomatoes | |
| 2 | medium onions, chopped | |
| ⅓ | cup olive oil | |
| 2 | large cloves garlic, minced | |
| 1 | teaspoon salt | |
| ½ | teaspoon pepper | |
| ½ | cup Chardonnay | |
| 1 | tablespoon fresh thyme leaves or 1 teaspoon dried | |
| 1 | cup sour cream | |

- Seed tomatoes and coarsely chop. Puree in blender; set aside.

- Sauté onions in oil until translucent. Add garlic and sauté 1 minute longer. Add tomatoes, salt, pepper, and wine. Simmer 10 minutes, stirring occasionally. Watch sauce carefully to avoid scorching. Add thyme and simmer 1 minute more. Stir in sour cream and heat without allowing sauce to reach simmer. Serve over pasta. Store in refrigerator for up to 3 days.

 "I Love Paris" as performed by Les Negresses Vertes

# ROSEMARY JELLY

*Makes 3½ cups*

- Bring wine to a boil in large saucepan or Dutch oven. Add rosemary. Turn off heat and allow to steep until wine is cool. Strain liquid, removing rosemary.

- Bring wine to a boil. Add sugar and lemon juice; return to boil and add pectin. Bring to a rolling boil and boil hard for 1 minute. Strain off foam.

- Pour hot jelly into clean, hot 4-ounce jelly jars (about 7), filling to within ⅛-inch from top. Wipe jar rims with a damp cloth followed by a dry cloth. Put on lids, close tightly, and turn jars upside down. Leave upside down for 2 to 3 minutes and then turn right side up. Listen for the "ping" of the jars sealing as they cool. Always check for seal.

2 cups dry red wine
3-4 branches fresh rosemary
¼ cup lemon juice
4 cups sugar
1 package liquid pectin (do not use dry pectin)

*Serve jelly with biscuits or spoon over cream cheese and spread on crackers. Try serving with roasted meats such as beef, pork, or lamb. Add jelly to pan juices for a delicious sauce for roasted poultry.*

"Rosemary" as performed by Robert Morse

# THREE-PEPPER JELLY

*Makes 3 cups*

- ½ cup chopped red bell pepper
- ¼ cup chopped yellow bell pepper
- ¼ cup finely chopped jalapeño pepper
- 6½ cups sugar
- 1½ cups apple cider vinegar
- 1 box or bottle pectin

- Bring chopped peppers, sugar, and vinegar to a hard rolling boil. Boil for 10 minutes. Remove from heat and add pectin; mix well.

- Pour into hot, clean 4-ounce jars (about 6); top with sterilized lids and rings and screw rings closed loosely. After lids seal with a ping, tighten jar rings.

*Serve over cream cheese for spreading on crackers or alongside meats.*

**Variations:** *Substitute ¼ cup hot red peppers for ¼ cup red bell peppers for more fire in the jelly.*

"Summertime" as performed by Janis Joplin

# CREAMY LEMON FILLING

*Makes 1½ cups*

- Put whole eggs and yolks into top of double boiler. Whisk until mixed. Add butter, sugar, lemon juice, and lemon zest. Stir with wooden spoon and cook over gently boiling water until mixture reaches the consistency of mayonnaise.

- Allow to cool and store in covered jars in refrigerator. This filling will keep for several weeks. Serve in a pie shell or in individual tart shells, or spoon over fresh berries.

| | |
|---|---|
| 2 | whole eggs |
| 2 | egg yolks |
| ½ | cup unsalted butter |
| 1 | cup sugar |
| | Juice and zest from 2 lemons |

Sylvester Stewart: "(You Caught Me) Smilin'"

# CLASSIC PESTO

*Makes 1½ cups*

| | |
|---|---|
| 2 | cups fresh basil leaves |
| 3-6 | cloves garlic |
| ½ | cup pine nuts |
| ¾ | cup grated Parmesan cheese |
| ⅓-⅔ | cup olive oil |

- In processor or blender, combine basil and garlic; process until finely chopped. Add pine nuts and Parmesan cheese. Puree the mixture until nearly smooth. Add oil in a slow stream until mixture forms a moist paste.

- Spoon into an airtight container; drizzle 1 tablespoon of olive oil over the top to prevent discoloration. Store in refrigerator for up to 1 week or freezer for up to 4 months.

*For Classic Pesto Pasta, cook fresh linguine or spaghetti; toss hot pasta with 1 to 2 tablespoons Pesto per serving.*

**Variations:** *About the only constant ingredients in pesto are garlic and olive oil. Try substituting other fresh herbs for basil, including parsley, fennel, or cilantro. Pine nuts can be replaced by walnuts, almonds, or even pecans. Parmesan cheese may be omitted or other grated hard cheeses can be used. Consider adding roasted peppers, sun-dried tomatoes, ripe olives, or green olives.*
*For Olive Pesto add ½ cup Greek olives with the basil and garlic.*

 "You Belong to Me" as performed by Patti Page

# PESTO DELUXE

*Makes 3 cups*

- Mix butter, garlic, pepper, basil, and olive oil in blender or processor until smooth. Add remaining ingredients 1 at a time, blending thoroughly after each. Serve over hot pasta.

| | |
|---|---|
| ½ | cup butter |
| ½ | tablespoon chopped garlic |
| | Freshly ground black pepper |
| 3 | cups fresh basil leaves, packed |
| ¾ | cup olive oil |
| ⅓ | cup walnuts |
| ¼ | cup pine nuts |
| ¼ | cup whipping cream |
| 3 | tablespoons cream cheese |
| ¼ | pound grated Parmesan cheese |
| ¼ | pound grated Romano cheese |

 Michael Franks: *Dragonfly Summer:* "How I Remember You"

# CILANTRO PESTO

*Makes ¾ cup*

- 1 cup loosely packed fresh cilantro
- 2 cloves garlic
- 2 tablespoons pine nuts, lightly toasted
- 2 tablespoons olive oil
- 2 tablespoons lemon or lime juice
- 2 tablespoons grated Parmesan cheese
- Salt and freshly ground black pepper

- Place all ingredients in blender or processor. Whirl until smooth. Do not prepare more than 2 hours ahead, preferably less, as cilantro is fragile and quickly loses color and flavor.

*Perfect on grilled chicken quesadillas, nachos, or pasta.*

**Variations:** For Walnut-Cilantro Pesto, substitute ⅓ cup walnuts for pine nuts and omit Parmesan cheese.

 "Miles and Miles of Texas" as performed by Asleep at the Wheel

# IMPROVISATIONS

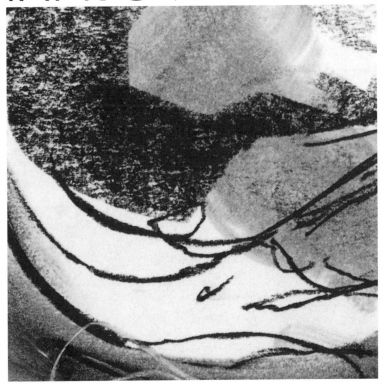

# A MENU FOR WINTER

Of course, the music is a great difficulty. You see, if one plays good music, people don't listen. If one plays bad music, people don't talk.

*Oscar Wilde*

*Appetizer*
Roquefort-Walnut Tartlets

*Salad*
Creamy Apple-Beet Salad

*Main Plate*
Roasted Beef Shanks and Shallots with Wine
Honeyed Carrots
Gorgonzola Grits

*Dessert*
Cappuccino Brownies with White Chocolate Espresso Sauce

 "Moonlight in Vermont" as performed by Sarah Vaughan

*Flexible*

# DESSERT IN A STEM

- For a simple but elegant dessert in a hurry, improvise using a set of stemmed wine, cocktail, or champagne glasses filled with fruits, liqueurs, and sauces such as these. Garnish with shreds of lemon, lime, or orange zest, cookie crumbs, or crystallized ginger.

*Ginger Pears:*
Drain the liquid from pear halves canned in their own juice into a small saucepan. Bring to simmer over medium heat; add chopped crystallized ginger. Cool slightly; pour over pear halves in stemmed glasses.

*Chamberries:*
Slice strawberries and soak in black raspberry liqueur for 15 to 60 minutes. Transfer to stemmed glasses; top with whipped cream and a whole berry.

*Lemonberries:*
Fill stemmed glasses with fresh raspberries or blueberries. Top with lemon curd.

*Brandied Peaches:*
Soak sliced fresh peaches in a syrup of equal parts honey and brandy. Serve in stemmed glasses.

*Green Melon:*
Put cubed honeydew melon into stemmed glasses. Top with drained canned lychee fruit and melon-flavored or orange-flavored liqueur.

*Ginger Cream Melon:*
Put cubed canteloupe into stemmed glasses. Top with cream that has been whipped with ginger-flavored liqueur.

*Coinberries:*
Heat ⅔ cup whole berry cranberry sauce, 3 tablespoons orange-flavored liqueur, and 1 teaspoon grated orange zest in small saucepan over medium. Bring to simmer; remove from heat and cool to room temperature. Layer sauce with vanilla ice cream in stemmed glasses.

*Spirited Vanilla:*
Scoop vanilla ice cream into stemmed glasses. Top with liqueur flavored with chocolate, raspberry, mint, coffee, hazelnut, almond, or banana.

*Spirited Caffeine:*
Scoop chocolate or coffee ice cream into stemmed glasses. Top with liqueur flavored with chocolate, coffee, mint, or hazelnut, or with Irish cream liqueur.

# SCONES

*Makes 12*

**Basic Recipe**

| | |
|---|---|
| 3 | cups flour (use whole wheat, unbleached white, or a combination) |
| ⅓ | cup sugar |
| 2½ | teaspoons baking powder |
| 1 | teaspoon salt |
| ½ | teaspoon baking soda |
| ¾ | cup unsalted butter, chilled, cut into ½-inch pieces |
| 1 | cup chilled buttermilk |

- Preheat oven to 400°. Line a rectangular baking sheet with parchment paper.

- Sift dry ingredients together. Add butter and rub with fingertips until mixture resembles coarse meal. (Mix in any additional flavoring ingredients at this point.) Add buttermilk and stir with a fork until all flour begins to cling to dough.

- Turn out onto lightly floured surface. Knead a few turns until all of the dough holds together. Divide dough in half. Pat each half out to a circle about 1 inch thick (about 5 to 6 inches in diameter). Cut each round into 6 wedges.

- Place wedges about 2 inches apart on baking sheet. Bake until the tops are golden, about 15 to 20 minutes. Let stand on baking sheet to cool. Serve warm or at room temperature. For a typical English presentation, serve with strawberry jam and Thick & Tangy Cream.

**Thick & Tangy Cream**

| | |
|---|---|
| ½ | cup sour cream |
| 1 | tablespoon powdered sugar |

- Mix sour cream and sugar until smooth.

## SCONES *continued*

*Improvisations*
- Add these flavorings after the butter is rubbed and before the buttermilk is added. These variations are only the beginning. Using the proportions as a guide, choose other dried fruits, nuts, seeds, and herbs to create your own signature scones.

*Cranberry-Orange:*
1   tablespoon orange zest
¾   cup dried cranberries
½   cup finely chopped pecans

*Lemon-Blueberry:*
1   tablespoon lemon zest
¾   cup dried blueberries

*Raisin-Walnut:*
¾   cup golden raisins
½   cup finely chopped walnuts

*Currant:*
¾   cup currants

*Cherry-Almond:*
¾   cup dried cherries
½   cup sliced almonds

*Lemon-Sage:*
2   tablespoons lemon zest
2   tablespoons sliced fresh sage

*Lemon-Poppyseed:*
1   tablespoon lemon zest
¼   cup poppyseeds

*Rosemary-Walnut:*
2   tablespoons chopped fresh rosemary
½   cup chopped walnuts

*Sun-Dried Tomato-Pine Nut:*
¼   cup chopped dried tomatoes (not oil-packed)
½   cup pine nuts

Nothing seems to please a fly so much as to be taken for a currant, and if it can be baked in a cake and palmed off on the unwary, it dies happy.

*Mark Twain*

# TARTLETS SWEET AND SAVORY

*Makes 24 (all of these recipes can be multiplied as needed)*

### Tartlet Shells
1   (9-inch) refrigerated pie crust (½ of 15-ounce package)
1   24-cup 1⅝-inch mini muffin tin

- Unfold pie crust and lay flat on lightly floured surface. Using a 2-inch round biscuit cutter, cut 1 dough circle from the crust and set it aside. Cut another circle as close as possible to the first. Continue until 24 dough circles have been cut (there will be a moderate amount of dough left over for another use).

- Using a mini-muffin pan with 24 cups that are 1 5/8 inches in diameter, place each dough circle on top of a muffin cup. Gently press dough down into the cup (dough will not reach top of cup sides). Prick bottoms of pastry shells with a fork.

- Bake at 400° for 6 to 8 minutes or until golden brown for tartlets which will have a cold filling or until pale gold for tartlets which will be baked again after they are filled. Turn shells out onto a clean towel and then transfer to a rack to cool (or use fork to lift pastry shells out of cups and onto a rack). Cool completely.

- For a chilled presentation, place shells on serving dish and fill shortly before serving. For a baked presentation, return pastry shells to muffin tins. Fill shells with mixture and bake at 400° for 6 to 8 minutes or until filling is set. Use fork to transfer filled shells to rack. Serve hot or at room temperature.

# TARTLETS SWEET AND SAVORY *continued*

## COLD FILLINGS

### Smoked Oyster Tartlets

*Makes 24*

- Blend sour cream and mustard. Drain oysters and use paper towels to blot as much oil as possible.

- Put 1 teaspoon of sour cream mixture into each tartlet shell. Top with 2 to 3 smoked oysters, depending on size. Chill until served.

- Garnish as desired.

| | |
|---|---|
| 24 | baked tartlet shells |
| ½ | cup sour cream |
| 1 | tablespoon Dijon mustard |
| 1 | can smoked oysters |
| | Dill fronds or lemon shreds for garnish (optional) |

### Ham Cream Tartlets

*Makes 48*

- Blend sour cream and cream cheese until smooth. Stir in mustard and orange zest. Add ham and mix thoroughly.

- Spoon mixture into tartlet shells. Sprinkle with chives. Chill until served.

| | |
|---|---|
| 48 | baked tartlet shells |
| ⅓ | cup sour cream |
| 3 | ounces cream cheese, room temperature |
| ¼ | teaspoon dry mustard |
| 1 | tablespoon grated orange zest |
| ½ | cup minced ham |
| 2 | tablespoons sliced chives |

### Chocolate-Peanut Butter Tartlets

*Makes 72*

- Cream peanut butter and cream cheese in mixer until fluffy. Add sugar and beat well.

- Drop 1 teaspoon peanut butter mixture into each tartlet shell; smooth with back of teaspoon. Top with ½ teaspoon Chocolate Truffle Sauce.

- Store covered in single layer in refrigerator until serving. Before serving, remove from refrigerator and let stand for 15 minutes.

| | |
|---|---|
| 72 | baked tartlet shells |
| 1 | cup chunky peanut butter |
| ½ | cup cream cheese |
| 2 | tablespoons powdered sugar |
| ¾ | cup Chocolate Truffle Sauce, see page 309 |

*continued on next page*

# TARTLETS SWEET AND SAVORY continued

### Jewel Tartlets
*Makes 24*

- 24 baked tartlet shells
- ½ cup sour cream
- 1 tablespoon powdered sugar
- Assorted jams and jellies

- Blend sour cream and powdered sugar. Fill each tartlet shell with 1 teaspoon sour cream mixture.

- Top cream mixture with ½ teaspoon jam or jelly. Vary the flavors and colors for an attractive presentation. This is a good opportunity to use some less common preserves, such as guava jelly, fig preserves, or red currant jelly.

### Lemon-Berry Tea Tartlets
*Makes 24*

- 24 baked tartlet shells
- ½ cup Creamy Lemon Filling, see page 325, or purchased lemon curd
- Whole strawberries, raspberries, or blueberries

- Place 1 teaspoon of lemon curd in each tartlet shell. Top with 1 whole strawberry or 2 to 3 whole raspberries or blueberries.

## BAKED FILLINGS

### Roquefort-Walnut Tartlets
*Makes 48*

- 48 lightly baked tartlet shells
- ½ cup crumbled Roquefort or other bleu cheese
- 1 egg
- 1 egg yolk
- ½ cup whipping cream
- ½ cup chopped walnuts

- Blend cheese and eggs by hand or in processor until a paste forms. Gradually stir in whipping cream (mixture will be thin).

- Return tartlet shells to muffin tin. Spoon 1 teaspoon of creamy mixture into each tartlet shell. Sprinkle with walnuts.

- Bake at 375° for 6 to 8 minutes or until filling is set. Use fork to transfer tartlets from muffin tin to rack. Serve warm or at room temperature.

*continued on next page*

# TARTLETS SWEET AND SAVORY *continued*

### Makes 48

- Use a fork to mix the chicken and green chiles. Add Jack cheese and cumin; mix thoroughly.

- Blend egg and cream together. Add to chicken mixture and stir to the consistency of a chunky paste.

- Return tartlet shells to muffin tin. Fill each with 1 teaspoon chicken mixture. Top with cheddar cheese.

- Bake at 375° for 6 to 8 minutes or until cheddar cheese is melted and bubbly. Use fork to transfer tartlets to rack. Serve warm or at room temperature.

## Green Chile Chicken Tartlets

| | |
|---|---|
| 48 | lightly baked tartlet shells |
| ⅓ cup | shredded, cooked chicken or canned chicken |
| 2 tablespoons | chopped green chiles, mild or hot |
| ¼ cup | shredded Monterey Jack cheese |
| 1 tablespoon | cumin seed, lightly toasted |
| 1 | egg, beaten |
| ¼ cup | whipping cream |
| ¼ cup | shredded cheddar cheese |

### Makes 48

- Sauté diced bacon in a small skillet over medium high heat until browned and crisp. Remove from skillet with a slotted spoon and drain on paper towel. Sauté onion in the bacon drippings until very soft. Remove with slotted spoon and blot with paper towel.

- Using wire whisk, beat eggs until light. Whisk in whipping cream until eggs and cream are thoroughly blended. Stir in cheese.

- Return tartlet shells to muffin tin. Place ½ teaspoon of onion in bottom of each shell. Spoon 1 teaspoon of creamy mixture over the onion. Top each tartlet with a sprinkle of bacon.

- Bake at 375° for 6 to 8 minutes or until set. Serve warm or at room temperature.

## Quichelets

| | |
|---|---|
| 48 | lightly baked tartlet shells |
| 4 | strips bacon, finely diced |
| 1 | small onion, quartered lengthwise and thinly sliced |
| 2 | eggs |
| ½ cup | whipping cream |
| ½ cup | shredded Swiss cheese |

*continued on next page*

# TARTLETS SWEET AND SAVORY *continued*

### Strawberry-Almond Tartlets

*Makes 48*

| | |
|---|---|
| 48 | lightly baked tartlet shells |
| ⅓ | cup unsalted butter |
| ⅔ | cup sugar |
| ⅛ | teaspoon salt |
| 2 | eggs |
| 1 | tablespoon flour |
| 1 | teaspoon almond extract |
| ½ | cup strawberry preserves |
| | Sliced almonds |

- Cream butter with sugar and salt. Blend in eggs one at a time. Stir in flour and almond extract.

- Return tartlet shells to muffin tin. Put ½ teaspoon preserves in the bottom of each shell. Top with 1 teaspoon of butter-sugar mixture. Place 2 slices of almond on each tartlet.

- Bake at 375° for 6 to 8 minutes or until topping is lightly browned. Use fork to transfer tartlets to rack. Serve warm, at room temperature, or chilled.

There are hundreds of delicious fillings that can go into these shells. Here are a few more suggestions. Now improvise.

**Cold fillings:** tuna, chicken, or salmon salad, creamy fruit salad, wild rice & pine nut salad, pie filling topped with whipped cream, cream cheese topped with pâté

**Baked fillings:** hot crab dip, cheesecake fillings, marinara sauce topped with mozzarella cheese

# FRUIT SORBET

*Makes 1 pint*

- Combine fruit puree or juice, sugar (using more for sour or bitter fruits, less for sweet fruits), lemon juice (only with puree, not with juice), and vodka in large bowl. Stir until sugar is dissolved.

- Pour mixture into a container, seal or cover, and refrigerate until the liquid reaches a temperature of no more than 40°.

- Pour mixture into container of an ice cream machine; churn according to directions until frozen. Scoop sorbet into airtight container. Seal and freeze for several hours before serving; store in freezer for up to 3 days.

*If you don't have an ice cream maker, freeze chilled mixture in a glass baking dish for 2 hours. Remove from freezer and break sorbet apart. Put pieces into blender and puree until smooth. Pour back into pan and refreeze. Repeat blending process and freeze once more. Scoop into airtight container and store in freezer.*

**Sorbet Recipe**

- 2 cups fruit puree or juice
- ¾-1¼ cups sugar
- 2 tablespoons lemon juice (only use with fruit puree, not juice)
- 1 tablespoon vodka (prevents ice crystals from forming)

## FRUIT PUREES

**Blueberry:**
puree 2½ cups berries, ½ cup cold water

**Grapefruit:**
stir together 2 teaspoons grapefruit zest, 1½ cups freshly squeezed juice, ½ cup cold water

*continued on next page*

## FRUIT SORBET *continued*

**Lemon or Lime:**
stir together 2 teaspoons lemon or lime zest, ½ cup juice, 1½ cups cold water

**Mango:**
peel and pit 3 mangoes; puree with ½ cup cold water

**Peach:**
peel and pit 6 medium peaches; puree with ½ cup cold water

**Mixed Berry:**
puree 3 cups berries with ½ cup cold water; strain to eliminate seeds

No opera plot can be sensible, for in sensible situations people do not sing.

*WH Auden*

# FIVE MINUTES AND A CUP OF MAYONNAISE

### Oriental Mayonnaise
- 1 cup mayonnaise
- 1 teaspoon ground ginger
- 1 tablespoon dark sesame oil
- 1 tablespoon soy sauce
- Sliced green onions or toasted sesame seeds for garnish

*Makes 1¼ cups*
- In a medium bowl, whisk together the mayonnaise, ginger, sesame oil, and soy sauce. Chill for 2 hours (can be made one day ahead). Garnish with green onions or toasted sesame seeds.

- Serve as a dip with blanched asparagus, snow peas, and green beans, or with red pepper strips and carrot slices or sticks.

### Lime-Cayenne Mayonnaise
- 1 cup mayonnaise
- 1 lime
- ¼ teaspoon cayenne pepper

*Makes 1 cup*
- Spoon mayonnaise into a medium bowl. Using a zester, remove all of the green zest from the lime. Cut lime in half and squeeze juice. Add zest and juice to bowl along with cayenne pepper. Stir or whisk until well blended.

- Serve as dip with boiled shrimp, crab claws, banana sticks, or plantain slices; use as sauce over red snapper or tuna or as dressing for shrimp salad.

### Rosemary-Horseradish Mayonnaise
- 1 cup mayonnaise
- ¼ cup prepared horseradish
- 1 tablespoon chopped fresh rosemary or 1 teaspoon dried

*Makes 1¼ cups*
- Whisk all ingredients together until well blended.

- Use as a spread on roast beef or turkey sandwiches, as a dipping sauce for prime rib, or as a topping for scalloped potatoes.

*continued on next page*

# FIVE MINUTES AND A CUP OF MAYONNAISE *continued*

### Lemon-Sage Mayonnaise

*Makes 1⅓ cups*

- 1 cup mayonnaise
- ¼ cup thinly sliced fresh sage leaves (1½ teaspoons dried)
- 1 tablespoon lemon juice
- 1 tablespoon grated lemon zest
- 1½ teaspoons minced garlic
- ½ teaspoon cracked blacked pepper

- Whisk all ingredients in small bowl until well blended. Will keep in refrigerator for up to 2 days.

- Serve on sandwiches of roast pork or turkey, or use as dip with ½-inch cubes of turkey or smoked turkey or sausage balls.

### Rosemary-Tapenade Aïoli

*Makes 1¼ cups*

- 4 garlic cloves, peeled
- 1½ tablespoons chopped fresh rosemary
- 1 cup mayonnaise
- 4 tablespoons Classic Tapenade, see page 24
- 3 tablespoons olive oil
- 3 teaspoons balsamic vinegar
- Salt and black pepper to taste

- Chop garlic and rosemary finely in processor or with knife.

- Add remaining ingredients and mix thoroughly. Season with salt and pepper.

- Serve with grilled or roasted lamb, beef, or chicken, or spread on toasted baguette slices and run under broiler until bubbly.

### Curry Mayonnaise

*Makes 1 cup*

- 1 cup mayonnaise
- 1 teaspoon ground cumin
- 1 teaspoon turmeric
- 1 teaspoon ground clove
- 1 teaspoon ground coriander
- ¼ teaspoon ground Egyptian or other very hot chile

- Combine all ingredients. Chill for two hours to develop flavors (can be made 1 day ahead).

- Serve as a dip for cooked chicken cubes, raw veggies, sliced apple, or sliced banana. This mayonnaise is also delicious on grilled chicken or as a dressing for fruit salad or chicken and fruit salad.

*Substitute 2 tablespoons curry powder and ¼ teaspoon cayenne pepper for all spices.*

*continued on next page*

# FIVE MINUTES AND A CUP OF MAYONNAISE *continued*

*Makes 1⅓ cups*
- Combine all ingredients. Chill for two hours.
- Serve as dip for boiled shrimp or crab claws, or serve over grilled fish, shrimp, or chicken. This aïoli makes a tasty dressing for potato salad (use unpeeled red potatoes).

*Makes 1⅓ cups*
- Using a fork, mash the cheese with part of the mayonnaise to form a smooth paste. Stir in the remaining mayonnaise and the rosemary. Chill for two hours. Serve as a dip for celery, croutons, or crackers, or as a spread on roast beef, steak, or lamb sandwiches. Spread on baguette slices and run under the broiler until bubbly. Try a dollop on a grilled or pan-fried beef steak.

*Makes 2⅓ cups*
- Combine all ingredients. Chill overnight.
- Serve as dip for raw vegetables, chips, or crackers, or use as dressing for shrimp salad or tuna salad.

*Makes 3 cups*
- Mix all ingredients and pour into a shallow 1-quart baking pan.
- Bake at 350° until golden and bubbly, about 45 minutes.
- Serve with toasted baguette slices, toast points, or crackers.

### Lemon-Basil Aïoli
- 1 cup mayonnaise
- 2 cloves garlic, pressed
- 3 tablespoons chopped basil or lemon basil
- Juice and grated zest of 1 large lemon

### Rosemary-Roquefort Mayonnaise
- 1 cup mayonnaise
- ¼ cup crumbled Roquefort cheese
- 1 tablespoon chopped fresh rosemary

### Dill Dip
- 1 cup mayonnaise
- 1 cup sour cream
- 1 tablespoon fresh dill
- 1 tablespoon minced onion
- 1 tablespoon chopped parsley
- 2 tablespoons mixed fresh herbs such as thyme, oregano, basil, rosemary, chives

### Hot Artichoke Dip
- 1 cup mayonnaise
- 1 cup Parmesan cheese or Swiss cheese, shredded
- 1 can artichoke hearts, drained and quartered

# BISTRO-STYLE MASHED POTATOES

*Serves 4 to 8*

*Parmesan Mashed Potatoes*
- 2 pounds russet potatoes, peeled and cut into 1½-inch chunks
- ½ cup chicken stock or canned low-salt broth (or more), heated
- 4 tablespoons olive oil
- ½ cup freshly grated Parmesan cheese
- 2 tablespoons lightly toasted pine nuts
- 2 tablespoons sliced basil
- Salt and black pepper

- Boil potatoes until tender. Drain and return to pan. Shake pan over medium heat for 1 minute. Using electric mixer, beat potatoes with stock and oil. Season with salt and pepper. Stir in Parmesan. Put potatoes into serving dish; sprinkle with pine nuts and basil.

*Tangy Mashed Potatoes*
- 2 pounds red potatoes
- ¼ cup milk
- 2 tablespoons butter
- ¼ cup sour cream
- ½ cup sliced green onions
- Salt and black pepper

- Boil whole unpeeled potatoes until tender when pierced with a fork. Drain and return to pan. Mash potatoes with a potato masher, adding milk, butter, and sour cream as you work. Season to taste with salt and pepper. Stir in green onions.

*Cabbage Mash*
- 2 pounds russet potatoes, peeled and cut into 1½-inch chunks
- 2 cups chopped cabbage
- ½ cup milk
- 2 tablespoons butter
- Salt and black pepper
- Toasted caraway seeds (optional)

- Boil potatoes until tender. While potatoes are cooking, bring 2 cups water to boil in a medium saucepan. Add the cabbage and cook until just tender, 3 to 5 minutes. Drain. Set aside. Drain cooked potatoes and return to saucepan. Shake pan over medium heat until any remaining liquid evaporates. Using electric mixer, beat potatoes with milk and butter. Season with salt and pepper. Stir in cabbage. Sprinkle with toasted caraway seeds if desired.

# BISTRO-STYLE MASHED POTATOES *continued*

- Place garlic heads on sheet of foil. Drizzle with olive oil and wrap tightly in foil. Roast at 400° for about 45 minutes. Remove from oven and allow to cool.

- Peel onions and slice thinly, about 1/8-inch thick. Melt butter with 3 tablespoons olive oil in a large skillet over medium heat. Add onion slices and cook for about 5 minutes, stirring frequently, until onions begin to soften and separate into rings. Lower heat and cook until onions are "melting" and golden, about 45 minutes.

- Boil potatoes until tender. Drain and return to pan, shaking over medium heat to dry potatoes slightly. Mix in half & half; mash potatoes with hand masher. Season with salt and pepper. Squeeze roasted garlic into potatoes and stir in onions.

- Cook potatoes in boiling water until very tender. Drain and transfer to mixing bowl. Add milk and butter. Beat with electric mixer until smooth. Stir in olives; season with salt and pepper. Transfer to serving bowl. Sprinkle with parsley; drizzle olive oil on top.

### Mashed Potatoes with Caramelized Onions and Roasted Garlic

| | |
|---|---|
| 2 | large heads garlic |
| | Olive oil |
| 2 | large yellow onions |
| 3 | tablespoons butter |
| 3 | tablespoons olive oil |
| 3 | pounds russet potatoes, peeled and cut into 1½-inch chunks |
| ¼ | cup half & half |
| | Salt and black pepper |

### Mashed Potatoes with Greek Olives

| | |
|---|---|
| 3 | pounds russet potatoes, peeled and cut into 1-inch cubes |
| ⅔ | cup milk |
| 5 | tablespoons butter |
| ⅔ | cup chopped Greek olives |
| | Salt and black pepper |
| 2 | tablespoons chopped fresh parsley |
| 2 | tablespoons olive oil |

# GLOBETROTTER POTATO SALADS

*Serves 6 to 8*

### Italian Potato Salad

| | |
|---|---|
| 2 | pounds red potatoes |
| 4 | tablespoons olive oil |
| 3 | tablespoons lemon juice |
| 1 | tablespoon grated lemon zest |
| 1½ | tablespoons capers |
| 1 | tablespoon chopped fresh rosemary |
| 1 | teaspoon minced garlic |
| ⅓ | cup sliced green onions |
| | Salt and black pepper |

- Boil unpeeled potatoes until just tender; drain. When slightly cooled, slice ¼-inch thick. Mix olive oil, lemon juice, lemon zest, capers, rosemary, and garlic; season with salt and pepper. Place half the potatoes in a serving bowl. Top with half the green onions and half the dressing. Repeat layers. Garnish with fresh rosemary.

### French Potato Salad

| | |
|---|---|
| 2 | pounds red potatoes |
| ¼ | cup red wine vinegar |
| 2 | tablespoons Dijon mustard |
| ⅓ | cup olive oil |
| 2 | tablespoons fresh parsley |
| 1 | tablespoon minced shallots |
| 2 | tablespoons white wine |
| | Salt and black pepper |

- Boil unpeeled potatoes until just tender; drain. When slightly cooled, slice ¼-inch thick. Mix vinegar, mustard, olive oil, parsley, shallots, and white wine. Toss with potatoes; season with salt and pepper.

# GLOBETROTTER POTATO SALADS *continued*

- Peel potatoes and cut into 1½-inch cubes. Boil until tender; drain. Mix together the olive oil, lemon juice, and oregano. Place potatoes, olives, and onions in a large serving bowl. Add the dressing and mix thoroughly, breaking potatoes up a bit (they should resemble coarsely mashed potatoes).

*Greek Potato Salad*
3    pounds russet potatoes
½    cup olive oil
3    tablespoons lemon juice
3    tablespoons fresh oregano or 2 teaspoons dried
½    cup pitted and chopped Greek olives
½    large red onion, slivered
Salt and black pepper

- Boil unpeeled potatoes until just tender; drain. When slightly cooled, slice ¼-inch thick. Toss gently with Lemon-Basil Aïoli; sprinkle cracked pepper over top.

*Provençal Potato Salad*
2    pounds red potatoes
Lemon-Basil Aïoli, see page 343
Cracked black pepper

- Peel potatoes and cut into 1-inch cubes. Boil until just tender, adding peas during last 2 minutes of cooking. Drain. Mix Curry Mayonnaise into peas and potatoes.

*Indian Potato Salad*
2    pounds russet potatoes
1    cup frozen peas
Curry Mayonnaise

- Boil potatoes until tender; drain. When slightly cool, slice ¼-inch thick. Mix olives, capers, and orange zest. Place half of potatoes in large serving bowl. Top with half the onion slices and half the olive mixture. Drizzle with 2 tablespoons oil and 1 tablespoon lemon juice. Repeat layers.

*Spanish Potato Salad*
2    pounds red potatoes
¼    cup stuffed green olives, sliced
1    tablespoon capers
1    tablespoon shredded orange zest
1    small red onion, thinly sliced
4    tablespoons olive oil
2    tablespoons lemon juice

*continued on next page*

## GLOBETROTTER POTATO SALADS *continued*

### Thai Potato Salad

| | |
|---|---|
| 3 | pounds russet potatoes |
| 1 | serrano chile |
| ¼ | cup sliced fresh lemongrass |
| ¼ | cup chopped fresh cilantro |
| 2 | tablespoons vinegar |
| ¼ | cup peanut oil |
| | Chopped peanuts (optional) |

- Peel potatoes and cut into 1½-inch cubes. Boil until tender; drain. Remove stem and seeds from chile and slice thinly. Put potatoes, chile, lemongrass, and cilantro in a serving bowl. Toss with vinegar. Toss again with oil. Sprinkle peanuts on top, if desired.

### Mexican Potato Salad

| | |
|---|---|
| 3 | pounds russet potatoes |
| 1 | tablespoon minced jalapeño pepper |
| ½ | cup chopped onion |
| ½ | cup chopped fresh cilantro |
| ½ | cup chopped tomato |
| ¼ | cup vegetable oil |
| 2 | tablespoons lime juice |
| 1 | tablespoon toasted cumin seeds |
| | Salt and black pepper |

- Peel potatoes and cut into 1-inch cubes. Boil until tender; drain. Toss all ingredients together. Season with salt and pepper.

# HAND PIES

*Makes 8 pies*

- Roll or pat each biscuit out on lightly floured surface to a round of about 5 inches in diameter. Brush egg glaze along the edge of half the circle. Place 2 tablespoons filling on the half where edge has been glazed; spread slightly, staying within the line of glaze. Fold empty half over filled half, pressing air out and sealing edges. Crimp edges with a fork. Place the filled pies on an ungreased baking sheet. Prick each pie with the tines of a fork in 2 places. Brush tops with remaining glaze. Bake pies at 375° until golden brown, about 10 minutes.

- Cook sausage and onion in a saucepan or skillet until meat is no longer pink. Use paper towel to blot excess fat. Add cumin, allspice, cloves, and red pepper flakes; sauté for 1 minute to release spice flavors. Add sweet potato and continue to sauté for 2 minutes. Add stock, cover, and cook until sweet potato is tender, about 10 minutes. Season to taste with salt and pepper. Allow to cool; add pecans just before filling pies. Bake as directed.

**Crust**

| | |
|---|---|
| 1 | (8-count) can of oversized refrigerated biscuits |
| | Flour |
| 3 | egg yolks, beaten |

**Southern Spice Hand Pies**

| | |
|---|---|
| ½ | pound bulk pork sausage |
| ¼ | cup chopped onion |
| ½ | teaspoon ground cumin |
| ½ | teaspoon ground allspice |
| ¼ | teaspoon ground cloves |
| ¼ | teaspoon crushed red pepper flakes |
| 1 | small sweet potato, peeled and finely diced |
| ⅓ | cup beef stock or canned broth (preferably unsalted) |
| ¼ | cup chopped pecans, lightly toasted |
| | Salt and black pepper |

*continued on next page*

## HAND PIES *continued*

### Middle Eastern Hand Pies
- 3 tablespoons olive oil
- ½ pound ground round
- 1 small onion, finely chopped
- ⅓ cup pine nuts
- 1 teaspoon cinnamon
- ½ teaspoon salt
- ½ teaspoon black pepper
- ¼ cup beef stock or canned broth (preferably unsalted)

• Heat oil in skillet. Cook beef, onion, and pine nuts until the onion softens and the meat is no longer pink. Add cinnamon, salt, pepper, and broth. Simmer uncovered until liquid is nearly gone, about 10 minutes. Allow to cool. Fill and bake pies as directed.

### Southwestern Hand Pies
- 3 tablespoons olive oil
- ½ pound ground round
- 1 small onion, finely chopped
- ½ cup finely chopped red bell pepper
- 1 jalapeño pepper, seeded and minced
- 1 large clove garlic, minced
- ¼ cup finely chopped tomato
- ¼ cup chopped cilantro
- 1 teaspoon cumin
- Salt and black pepper
- 1 cup shredded Monterey Jack cheese

• Heat olive oil in a skillet. Cook the ground round for 2 minutes, breaking up meat with spoon. Add onions, both peppers, and garlic; continue to cook until vegetables are soft. Add tomato and cook an additional 2 minutes, stirring frequently. Add cilantro and season with salt and plenty of black pepper. Stir well. Add cheese; remove from heat and stir until melted. Allow to cool. Fill and bake as directed.

### Blueberry-Cheese Hand Pies
- 1 cup ricotta cheese
- 1-2 tablespoons powdered sugar
- Grated zest from 1 lemon
- 1 cup fresh or frozen blueberries

• Blend ricotta and sugar; stir in lemon zest. Mix in blueberries and stir well. Fill and bake pies as directed.

### Cherry-Almond Hand Pies
- ⅔ cup dried cherries
- ⅔ cup ricotta cheese
- 1 tablespoon almond-flavored liqueur
- ¼ cup sliced almonds

• Put cherries in a 2-cup glass measure. Pour boiling water over them and allow to stand for 15 minutes. Drain cherries thoroughly.

• Blend ricotta and liqueur. Stir in cherries. Fill and bake pies as directed, sprinkling the top of each with sliced almonds.

# INDEX

## A

A to Z Bread .................................. 239
Angel Biscuits ............................... 241
Appetizers *(also see Dips & Spreads)*
   Artichoke Bruschetta ................. 41
   Bleu Balls ...................................... 18
   Bleu Cheesecake with
      Rosemary Walnuts ................. 63
   Brie Pinwheel ............................... 62
   Caesar Bruschetta ....................... 41
   Caponata Bruschetta ................. 41
   Caviar Squares ............................ 44
   Caviartichokes ............................ 45
   Chicken-Dove Roll with
      Cilantro-Cumin Sauce
      and Roasted Peppers .............. 52
   Cocktail Sandwiches ................... 33
   Creamy Mushroom-Herb Pasta ... 33
   Croutons with Apple,
      Pecan Butter, and Brie ............ 42
   Goat Balls .................................... 46
   Greek Meatballs .......................... 50
   Greek Salad Skewers .................. 48
   Lemon Olives ............................... 14
   Lemon-Rosemary Wafers ........... 19
   Marinated Mushrooms ............... 16
   Mediterranean Stuffed Bread ..... 58
   Mexican Cheesecake .................. 64
   Orange Olives ............................. 15
   Paprika Triangles ........................ 28
   Pesto Cheesecake ....................... 66
   Pesto Rounds .............................. 40
   Pizza with Bleu Cheese
      and Mushrooms ...................... 59
   Roasted Red Peppers
      with Fresh Mozzarella ............. 49
   Rosemary Walnuts ...................... 13
   Spicy Cheddar Snaps .................. 17

   Three-Cheese Spinach Bread ..... 43
   Tomatoes Stuffed with
      Goat Cheese and Chives .......... 47
   Tomato-Feta Bruschetta ............ 39
Artichokes
   Artichoke Bruschetta .................. 41
   Artichoke Soufflé ........................ 98
   Caviartichokes ............................ 45
   Chicken-Artichoke Fettuccine ..... 121
   Extraordinary Chicken ............... 156
   Hot Artichoke Dip ...................... 343
Asian Sesame-Soy Vinaigrette ..... 113
Asian Shrimp Balls ....................... 142
Asparagus
   Fresh Asparagus and
      Egg Casserole ......................... 99
   Linguine Salad with
      Marinated Tomatoes .............. 205
   Mélange of Bright Vegetables ..... 208
   Oven-Grilled Veggies ................ 206
   Roasted Asparagus .................... 210
Authentic Greek Salad ................. 196
Avocado Tapenade ........................ 25

## B

Baby Banana Cakes ...................... 237
Baby Greens with Feta
   and Orange Vinaigrette .......... 195
Baby Greens with Pear,
   Bleu Cheese, and Walnuts ....... 194
Baked Crab Dip .............................. 37
Baked Potato Soup ........................ 80
Baker's Choice Bread ................... 248
Banana Omelette ........................... 95
Banana-Caramel Pie .................... 279
Basil-Cheese Strata ....................... 55
Basil-Eggplant Soup ...................... 75
Bay-Roasted Potatoes .................. 230

351

Beef
- Filet Mignon with Red Wine-Shallot Sauce .............. 172
- Greek Meatballs ........................ 50
- Middle Eastern Hand Pies ........ 350
- Oxtail Soup ............................... 90
- Paprika Stew ............................ 170
- Rib-Eye with Rosemary-Wine Sauce ................. 172
- Roast Beef and Brie Sandwich ....................... 105
- Roasted Beef Shanks and Shallots with Wine ......... 173
- Southwestern Hand Pies ........... 350
- Southwestern Spoonbread ....... 246
- Spiced Beef Tenderloin .............. 174
- Stifado ..................................... 171
- Tipsy Stew ............................... 169

Beet Salad .................................... 212
Bistro-Style Mashed Potatoes ....... 344
Bittersweet Chocolate-Orange Fondue with Fresh Fruits .......... 273
Black Bean Tostadas .................... 131
Black-Eyed Pea Salad ................... 189
Blackberry Pinwheel Cobbler ....... 274
Blender Hollandaise .................... 313
Blender Mayonnaise .................... 312
Bleu Balls ..................................... 18
Bleu Cheese Biscuits .................... 242
Bleu Cheesecake with Rosemary Walnuts ............ 63
Bleu-Green Beans ........................ 210

Blueberries
- Blueberry-Cheese Hand Pies .... 350
- Blueberry-Lemon Muffin Tops ..... 234
- Lemon-Berry Tea Tartlets ......... 336
- Lemon-Blueberry Scones ......... 333
- Lemonberries ........................... 331

Blush Vinaigrette ......................... 193
Brandied Peaches ........................ 331

Breads
- A to Z Bread .............................. 239
- Angel Biscuits ........................... 241
- Baby Banana Cakes .................. 237
- Baker's Choice Bread ................ 248
- Bleu Cheese Biscuits ................. 242
- Blueberry-Lemon Muffin Tops ..... 234
- Bread of the Islands ................. 238
- Cheddar-Onion Biscuits ............ 242
- Cherry-Almond Scones ............. 333
- Classic Buttermilk Biscuits ....... 242
- Cranberry-Orange Scones ........ 333
- Currant Scones ........................ 333
- Fresh Herb Biscuits .................. 242
- Harvest Muffins ....................... 236
- Hot Water Cornbread ............... 244
- Icebox Rolls .............................. 247
- Iron Skillet Cornbread .............. 243
- Lemon Biscuits ........................ 242
- Lemon-Blueberry Scones ......... 333
- Lemon-Poppyseed Scones ....... 333
- Lemon-Sage Scones ................. 333
- Morning Glory Muffins ............. 235
- Pear-Ginger Muffin Tops .......... 234
- Rosemary-Walnut Scones ........ 333
- Seed Biscuits ........................... 242
- Scones ..................................... 332
- Southwestern Spoonbread ....... 246
- Spicy Corn Bites ...................... 245
- Sun-Dried Tomato-Pine Nut Scones ............................ 333
- Sweet Potato-Pecan Muffin Tops ................. 234
- Sweet Potato-Sage Biscuits ....... 242
- Tomato Bread .......................... 240

Brie Omelette ............................... 96
Brie Pinwheel ............................... 62
Broccoli Crunch ........................... 187

Brunch Dishes
- Artichoke Soufflé ...................... 98
- Banana Omelette ..................... 95
- Black Bean Tostadas ................ 131
- Brie Omelette ........................... 96
- Chicken-Artichoke Fettuccine ..... 121
- Creamy Mushroom-Herb Pasta ..... 33
- Curried Chicken and Dried Cherry Salad ................ 107

Fresh Asparagus and
   Egg Casserole ............................ 99
Frittata ............................................ 97
Greek Pasta ................................ 116
Green Chile Pie ........................... 129
Grilled Tuna Quesadillas ........... 125
Ham Cakes ................................. 123
Hominy Soufflé ............................ 94
Huevos Jose ................................ 132
Huevos Rancheros ..................... 133
Linguine with
   Bacon and Peas ...................... 118
Lower East Side Pepper
   & Egg Sandwich ..................... 134
Madras Rice and
   Chicken Salad ......................... 110
Marinated Shrimp Salad ........... 124
Onion Tart .................................. 106
Pasta Gremolata ........................ 114
Pasta with Bacon,
   Fried Pecans, and Corn ........... 119
Pasta with Burnt Butter
   and Cheese ............................ 111
Pasta with Garlic
   and Hot Peppers .................... 115
Pasta with Ham, Bleu Cheese,
   and Walnuts ........................... 122
Pasta with Pesto Chicken
   and Red Peppers ................... 120
Quichelets .................................. 337
Ratatouille Pizza ......................... 103
Roast Beef and Brie Sandwich ... 105
Salmon Baked Alaska ................ 126
Salsa Quiche .............................. 128
Sassy Shrimp Risotto ................. 127
Savory Grits ................................. 93
Spinach, Cheese,
   and Tomato Pie ..................... 100
Tamale Veggie Pie ..................... 130
Tomato-Cheese Tart .................. 102
Tomatoes and Fresh
   Mozzarella with Caponata
   and Peperonata ..................... 108
Brussels Sprouts with
   Chives and Lemon Zest .......... 213
Bulghur Salad ............................ 198

Buttercream Filling ..................... 264
Butternut and Double
   Ginger Soup ............................. 72
Buttery Caramel Sauce .............. 310

## C

Cabbage Mash ........................... 344
Cabbage Salad ........................... 183
Caesar Bruschetta ....................... 41
Cajun Shrimp Balls .................... 142
Cakes
   Chocolate-Amaretto
     Cheesecake ......................... 283
   Cold Oven Pound Cake .......... 285
   Cream Cheese Pound Cake .... 286
   Earl Grey Cake ....................... 292
   Extravagant Pound Cake ........ 284
   Fresh Peach Cake .................. 289
   Golden Sin ............................. 288
   Hazelnut-Chocolate
     Meringue Torte ..................... 290
   Rum Cake .............................. 287
Calypso Soup .............................. 84
Caponata ................................... 108
Caponata Bruschetta ................... 41
Cappuccino Brownies ................ 270
Carrot-Green Onion Salad ........ 182
Carrot-Turnip Salad ................... 182
Carrots with Leeks ..................... 215
Casseroles
   Artichoke Soufflé ..................... 98
   Chicken-Black
     Bean Casserole .................... 152
   Creamy Potatoes
     with Fresh Herbs .................. 231
   Extraordinary Chicken ............ 156
   Fresh Asparagus
     and Egg Casserole ................ 99
   Frittata .................................... 97
   Gorgonzola Grits ................... 228
   Hominy Soufflé ....................... 94
   Huevos Rancheros ................. 133

Jalapeño Potatoes ................. 232
Potatoes with Cheese,
  Garlic, and Pesto ................. 233
Roma-Zucchini Wheel ............ 225
Squash Pecan ........................ 222
Tamale Veggie Pie ................. 130
Turnip Soufflé ....................... 227
Catfish Parmesan .................. 139
Cauliflower Salad .................. 186
Cauliflower-Cheddar Chowder ..... 81
Cauliflower-Potato Salad
  with Marinated Red Onions .... 201
Caviar Squares ...................... 44
Caviartichokes ....................... 45
Chamberries .......................... 331
Chard Soup, Cream of ............ 79

Cheese
  Artichoke Soufflé ................. 98
  Baby Greens with Feta
    and Orange Vinaigrette ..... 195
  Basil-Cheese Strata .............. 55
  Bleu Balls ............................ 18
  Bleu Cheese Biscuits ............ 242
  Bleu Cheesecake
    with Rosemary Walnuts ..... 63
  Blueberry-Cheese Hand Pies .... 350
  Brie Omelette ...................... 96
  Brie Pinwheel ...................... 62
  Cauliflower-Cheddar Chowder .... 81
  Cheddar Cheese
    Salad Dressing .................. 315
  Cheddar-Onion Biscuits ......... 242
  Chihuahua Cheese Spread ..... 34
  Crawfish Saganaki ............... 38
  Croutons with Apple,
    Pecan Butter, and Brie ....... 42
  Extraordinary Chicken .......... 156
  Fiesta Dip ........................... 31
  Frittata .............................. 97
  Goat Balls .......................... 46
  Goat Cheese Pesto Platter .... 57
  Gorgonzola Grits ................. 228
  Green Chile Pie ................... 129

Grilled Veggie
  Focaccia Sandwich .............. 104
Hot Artichoke Dip .................. 343
Jalapeño Potatoes ................. 232
Mediterranean Stuffed Bread ..... 58
Mesclun with
  Warm Goat Cheese .............. 191
Mexican Cheesecake .............. 64
Mexican Red Chicken ............. 149
Parmesan Mashed Potatoes ..... 344
Parmesan Pie Crust ............... 100
Pasta with Ham,
  Bleu Cheese, and Walnuts .... 122
Pesto Cheesecake .................. 66
Pesto Deluxe ........................ 327
Pizza with Bleu Cheese
  and Mushrooms .................. 59
Potatoes with Cheese,
  Garlic, and Pesto ................. 233
Radio Shrimp ....................... 60
Ratatouille Pizza ................... 103
Roast Beef and Brie Sandwich ..... 105
Roasted Red Peppers
  with Fresh Mozzarella .......... 49
Roquefort-Walnut Tartlets ...... 336
Rosemary-Roquefort
  Mayonnaise ....................... 343
Salsa Quiche ........................ 128
Savory Grits ........................ 93
Smoky Cheese Pâté ............... 54
Southwestern Spoonbread ...... 246
Spicy Broccoli Soup ............... 76
Spicy Cheddar Snaps ............. 17
Spicy Corn Bites ................... 245
Spinach, Cheese, and
  Tomato Pie ........................ 100
Stuffed Brie ......................... 61
Three-Cheese Spinach Bread .... 43
Tomato-Cheese Tart .............. 102
Tomatoes and Fresh Mozzarella with
  Caponata and Peperonata ..... 108
Tomatoes Stuffed with
  Goat Cheese and Chives ...... 47
Tri-Color Torta .................... 56

| | | | |
|---|---|---|---|
| Warm Bleu Cheese Spread with Pecans | 35 | White Chocolate-Espresso Sauce | 311 |

Warm Bleu Cheese Spread
  with Pecans .............................. 35
Cherry Pie with Crunchy
  Oatmeal Crust .......................... 276
Cherry-Almond Hand Pies .......... 350
Cherry-Almond Kisses ................. 263
Cherry-Almond Scones ................ 333
Chewy Oatmeal Brownies ........... 265

Chicken (see Poultry)
Chihuahua Cheese Spread ............ 34
Chilled Cucumber Soup ................ 69

Chocolate
  Bittersweet Chocolate-Orange
    Fondue with Fresh Fruits ....... 273
  Cappuccino Brownies ............... 270
  Chocolate Truffles .................... 260
  Chocolate Truffle Sauce ........... 309
  Chocolate-Amaretto
    Cheesecake ............................ 283
  Chocolate-Caramel Sauce ........ 310
  Chocolate-Mint Meringues ...... 263
  Chocolate-Peanut
    Butter Tartlets ....................... 335
  Chocolate-Raspberry Cream .... 305
  Cream Cheese Brownies
    with Strawberry Glaze ........... 268
  Earl Grey Cake ......................... 292
  Forgotten Cookies .................... 263
  Hazelnut-Chocolate
    Meringue Torte ...................... 290
  Heavenly Chocolate
    Ice Cream ............................... 256
  Martha Washington Candy ..... 260
  Mocha Cream .......................... 291
  Peanut Butter-Chocolate
    Fast Fudge .............................. 258
  Pecan Fudge Pie ....................... 280
  Peppermint Cocoa Mix ............ 297
  Poached Pears with
    Mascarpone and Chocolate ..... 272
  Raspberry-Chocolate Bars ........ 267
  Rich Chocolate Mousse ............ 290
  Strawberry Yogurt Pie ............... 257
  Whipped Cream Godiva .......... 269

White Chocolate-Espresso
  Sauce ....................................... 311
Cilantro Pesto ............................. 328
Cilantro-Cumin Sauce .................. 53
Classic Bruschetta ........................ 39
Classic Buttermilk Biscuits .......... 242
Classic Pesto .............................. 326
Classic Tapenade ......................... 24
Classic Vinaigrette ..................... 316
Cocktail Sandwiches .................... 33
Coffee KEDM ............................. 308
Coinberries ................................ 331
Cold Oven Pound Cake .............. 285

Condiments, Sauces & Dressings
  Asian Sesame-Soy Vinaigrette ..... 113
  Blender Hollandaise ................ 313
  Blender Mayonnaise ................ 312
  Cheddar Cheese
    Salad Dressing ....................... 315
  Chocolate Truffle Sauce ........... 309
  Chocolate-Caramel Sauce ........ 310
  Cilantro Pesto .......................... 328
  Cilantro-Cumin Sauce ............... 53
  Classic Pesto ........................... 326
  Classic Vinaigrette .................. 316
  Creamy Lemon Filling ............. 325
  Curry Mayonnaise ................... 342
  Dill Dip .................................... 343
  French Vinaigrette ................... 317
  Green Chile Butter .................. 216
  Green Goddess Dressing .......... 314
  Green Tomato Pasta Sauce ...... 322
  Lemon-Basil Aïoli .................... 343
  Lemon-Sage Mayonnaise ......... 342
  Lime-Cayenne Mayonnaise ..... 341
  Lime-Cilantro Sour Cream ....... 321
  Olive Pesto .............................. 326
  Oriental Mayonnaise ............... 341
  Pesto Deluxe ........................... 327
  Roasted Pepper and
    Garlic Sauce .......................... 320
  Rosemary-Horseradish
    Mayonnaise ........................... 341
  Rosemary Jelly ........................ 323

INDEX 355

Rosemary-Roquefort
  Mayonnaise .......................... 343
Rosemary-Tapenade Aïoli ........ 342
Savory Sauce ............................ 319
Spicy Peanut Dressing .............. 113
Sun-Dried Tomato Vinaigrette .... 318
Three-Pepper Jelly ..................... 324
Tomato Gravy ........................... 143
Walnut-Cilantro Pesto ............... 328
White Chocolate-
  Espresso Sauce ........................ 311
Yogurt Nehru ............................ 153
Confetti Pasta Salad ................... 204

Cookies & Bars
  Cappuccino Brownies .............. 270
  Cherry-Almond Kisses .............. 263
  Chewy Oatmeal Brownies ........ 265
  Chocolate-Mint Meringues ...... 263
  Cream Cheese Brownies
    with Strawberry Glaze ........... 268
  Crème Wafer Cookies .............. 264
  Forgotten Cookies ................... 263
  Honey-Spice Bars ..................... 266
  Peanut Butter Miracles ............. 262
  Raspberry-Chocolate Bars ........ 267

Corn
  Corn, Black Bean, and
    Hearts of Palm Salad ............. 190
  Fiesta Dip .................................. 31
  Fresh Corn and Chicken Soup ... 83
  Pasta with Bacon,
    Fried Pecans, and Corn .......... 119
  Roasted Corn with
    Green Chile Butter ................. 216
  Southwestern Spoonbread ....... 246
  Spicy Corn Bites ....................... 245
  Succotash Salad ....................... 188
  Tamale Veggie Pie .................... 130
  White Corn Soup
    with Sautéed Scallops ............. 85
  White Corn with Crispy Sage ... 217
Cornbread Salad ....................... 197
Cornish Hen
  with Blackberry Sauce ............. 157

Cornish Hens with
  Rosemary-Mustard Sauce ........ 158
Crab au Gratin ............................. 82
Cranberry-Orange Scones ........... 333
Crawfish Étouffée ........................ 143
Crawfish Saganaki ........................ 38
Crawfish Stuffed Cajun Peppers ..... 144
Cream Cheese Brownies
  with Strawberry Glaze ............ 268
Cream Cheese Pound Cake ........ 286
Cream Filling ............................... 289
Cream of Chard Soup .................. 79
Creamy Apple-Beet Salad ........... 181
Creamy Lemon Filling ................. 325
Creamy Mushroom-Herb Pasta ..... 33
Creamy Potatoes
  with Fresh Herbs ..................... 231
Creamy Spinach ......................... 220
Crème Wafer Cookies ................. 264
Crispy Slaw with
  Soy Vinaigrette ........................ 185
Croutons with Apple,
  Pecan Butter, and Brie .............. 42
Crunchy Oatmeal Crust .............. 276
Crust .......................................... 349

Cucumbers
  Chilled Cucumber Soup ............. 69
  Garden Gazpacho ...................... 68
  Gazpacho Con Gusto ................. 67
  Greek Salad Skewers .................. 48
  Tzatziki ...................................... 22
  Yogurt Nehru ........................... 153
Currant Scones .......................... 333
Curried Chicken and
  Dried Cherry Salad .................. 107
Curry Mayonnaise ..................... 342

D

Daddy's Forty Party Punch ........ 295
Desserts *(also see Cakes, Cookies & Bars,
  Pies & Tarts)*
  Candies
    Chocolate Truffles ................. 260

Martha Washington Candy ... 260
Mexican Pralines ................... 259
Mountain of Divinity ............ 261
Peanut Butter-Chocolate
  Fast Fudge ........................ 258

*Frozen Desserts*
Fresh Peach Ice Cream ......... 255
Fruit Sorbet............................ 339
Heavenly Chocolate
  Ice Cream ........................... 256
Lemon-Espresso Granita ........ 251
Orange-Campari Granita ..... 251
Peach Sorbet ........................ 253
Pear-Pernod Granita............. 251
Spirited Caffeine ................... 331
Spirited Vanilla ..................... 331
Strawberry Sorbet ................. 252
White Wine Sherbet............... 254

*Icings & Frostings*
Buttercream Filling ................ 264
Cream Filling ........................ 289
Meringue-Nut Topping .......... 267
Rum Glaze ............................ 287
Strawberry Glaze .................. 269
Whipped Cream Godiva ....... 269

*Miscellaneous Desserts*
Bittersweet Chocolate-Orange
  Fondue with Fresh Fruits ..... 273
Blackberry Pinwheel Cobbler 274
Brandied Peaches ................. 331
Chamberries ......................... 331
Coinberries ........................... 331
Ginger Cream Melon ............. 331
Ginger Pears ......................... 331
Green Melon ......................... 331
Lemonberries ........................ 331
Mocha Cream ...................... 291
Pavlova ................................ 275
Poached Pears with
  Mascarpone and Chocolate ... 272
Poached Spiced Pears ........... 272
Rich Chocolate Mousse ......... 290
Warm Pear and Cherry
  Conserve with Triple Ginger ..... 271

*Sauces*
Buttery Caramel Sauce .......... 310
Chocolate Truffle Sauce ......... 309
Chocolate-Caramel Sauce ..... 310
Creamy Lemon Filling ........... 325
White Chocolate-
  Espresso Sauce ................... 311
Deviled Shrimp ........................... 141

Dips & Spreads
Avocado Tapenade ..................... 25
Baked Crab Dip .......................... 37
Basil-Cheese Strata ..................... 55
Chihuahua Cheese Spread ........ 34
Cilantro-Cumin Sauce ............... 53
Classic Tapenade ....................... 24
Dill Dip ..................................... 343
Eggplant Dip ............................. 29
Fiesta Dip ................................... 31
Fresh Spinach Dip ...................... 30
Fromage Provençal .................... 51
Garden Salsa .............................. 21
Green Fire .................................. 20
Goat Cheese Pesto Platter .......... 57
Guacamole ................................. 65
Herbed Cheese .......................... 33
Hot Artichoke Dip ................... 343
Hummus ..................................... 23
Mango Salsa ............................ 123
Mushroom-Olive Spread ............ 32
Peanut-Cilantro Pesto ................ 26
Roasted Garlic Hummus ............ 23
Roasted Red Pepper
  and Almond Pesto ................... 27
Roasted Red Pepper Hummus .... 23
Salsa Diablo ............................... 65
Smoky Cheese Pâté .................... 54
Smooth Salsa ........................... 125
Tzatziki ....................................... 22
Warm Bleu Cheese Spread
  with Pecans ............................. 35
Wild Duck Pâté .......................... 36

Drinks
Chocolate-Raspberry Cream .... 305

Coffee KEDM ............................ 308
Daddy's Forty Party Punch ....... 295
Double Irish Coffee .................. 307
Funky Rum Punch .................... 304
Mocha Magic ............................ 306
Peach Spritzers ........................ 300
Peppermint Cocoa Mix ............ 297
Punch of the Islands ................ 303
Royal Frozen Mimosas ............. 299
Russian Tea .............................. 296
Tequila Slush ............................ 302
Vodka Lemonade ..................... 301
White Sangría ........................... 298
Duck Breasts with Wine
  and Marmalade Sauce ............ 159
Duck Gumbo .............................. 87

# E

Earl Grey Cake ........................... 292
Eggplant
  Basil-Eggplant Soup .................. 75
  Caponata ................................ 108
  Chicken Wings with Green
    Tomatoes and Couscous ........ 150
  Eggplant Dip ............................ 29
  Garden Fresh Ratatouille ......... 219
  Greek Island Vegetables ........... 209
  Oven-Grilled Veggies ............... 206
Eggs
  Artichoke Soufflé ...................... 98
  Banana Omelette ...................... 95
  Brie Omelette ........................... 96
  Fresh Asparagus
    and Egg Casserole ................. 99
  Frittata .................................... 97
  Green Chile Pie ....................... 129
  Hominy Soufflé ......................... 94
  Huevos Jose ............................ 132
  Huevos Rancheros .................. 133
  Lower East Side Pepper
    & Egg Sandwich ................... 134
  Salsa Quiche .......................... 128

Extraordinary Chicken ............... 156
Extravagant Pound Cake ........... 284

# F

Fiesta Dip .................................... 31
Filet Mignon with Red
  Wine-Shallot Sauce ................. 172
Fish
  Catfish Parmesan .................... 139
  Grilled Tuna Quesadillas ......... 125
  Salmon Baked Alaska ............. 126
  Sole with Brown Butter Sauce ... 138
  Swordfish with
    Tomato-Parsley Sauce ........... 137
  Trout with Lemon
    and Brown Butter ................. 138
Forgotten Cookies ..................... 263
French Potato Salad ................. 346
French Vinaigrette .................... 317
Fresh Asparagus
  and Egg Casserole .................. 99
Fresh Beets and Greens ............ 212
Fresh Corn and Chicken Soup ....... 83
Fresh Herb Biscuits ................... 242
Fresh Peach Cake ..................... 289
Fresh Peach Ice Cream ............. 255
Fresh Spinach Dip ...................... 30
Frittata ...................................... 97
Fromage Provençal ..................... 51
Fruit Sorbet .............................. 339
Funky Rum Punch ..................... 304

# G

Game
  Chicken-Dove Roll with
    Cilantro-Cumin Sauce
    and Roasted Peppers ............. 52
  Duck Breasts with Wine
    and Marmalade Sauce .......... 159
  Duck Gumbo ............................ 84
  Wild Duck Pâté ........................ 36

Garden Fresh Ratatouille ............ 219
Garden Gazpacho ........................ 68
Garden Salsa ................................. 21
Garlic Chicken ............................ 147
Gazpacho Con Gusto ................... 67
Ginger Carrots ........................... 214
Ginger Cream Melon .................. 331
Ginger Pears .............................. 331
Glazed Turnips ........................... 226
Globetrotter Potato Salads .......... 346
Goat Balls .................................... 46
Goat Cheese Pesto Platter ............ 57
Golden Sin ................................. 288
Gorgonzola Grits ....................... 228
Grand Finale Pie ........................ 278
Greek Island Vegetables ............. 209
Greek Meatballs ........................... 50
Greek Pasta ............................... 116
Greek Potato Salad .................... 347
Greek Salad Skewers .................... 48
Green Beans with
  Garlic and Pine Nuts ............... 218
Green Chile Butter ..................... 216
Green Chile Chicken Tartlets ....... 337
Green Chile Pie .......................... 129
Green Fire ................................... 20
Green Goddess Dressing ............. 314
Green Melon .............................. 331
Green Tomato Pasta Sauce ......... 322
Grilled Lamb Chops ................... 177
Grilled Lamb Chops Greek-Style ..... 177
Grilled Pork Skewers .................. 161
Grilled Tuna Quesadillas ............ 125
Grilled Veggie
  Focaccia Sandwich .................. 104
Guacamole .................................. 65

# H

Ham Cakes ................................ 123
Ham Cream Tartlets ................... 335
Ham Steak with
  Ginger-Pear Conserve ............. 271
Hand Pies .................................. 349

Harvest Muffins ......................... 236
Hazelnut-Chocolate
  Meringue Torte ....................... 290
Hearts of Palm Salad, Corn,
  Black Bean, and ...................... 190
Hearty Tortellini Soup ................. 88
Heavenly Chocolate Ice Cream ... 256
Herbed Cheese ............................ 33
Hominy Soufflé ........................... 94
Honey-Mustard Dressing ............ 193
Honey-Spice Bars ...................... 266
Honeyed Carrots ....................... 214
Hot Artichoke Dip ..................... 343
Hot Water Cornbread ................ 244
Huevos Jose .............................. 132
Huevos Rancheros .................... 133
Hummus ..................................... 23

# I

Icebox Rolls .............................. 247
Indian Potato Salad ................... 347
Irish Coffee Pie .......................... 281
Iron Skillet Cornbread ............... 243
Italian Potato Salad ................... 346
Italian Stuffed Peppers .............. 160

# J

Jalapeño Potatoes ..................... 232
Jewel Tartlets ............................ 336

# L

Lamb
  Grilled Lamb Chops ................ 177
  Grilled Lamb Chops
    Greek-Style .......................... 177
  Lamb with Lentils ................... 175
  Rack of Lamb with
    Hazelnut-Walnut Crust ......... 178
  Rosemary-Scented Lamb
    with Penne ........................... 176
Lemon Biscuits .......................... 242

INDEX 359

Lemon Olives ................................. 14
Lemon-Basil Aïoli ........................ 343
Lemon-Berry Tea Tartlets ............ 336
Lemon-Blueberry Scones ............. 333
Lemon-Dijon Chicken ................. 148
Lemon-Espresso Granita .............. 251
Lemon-Poppyseed ....................... 333
Lemon-Poppyseed Scones ........... 333
Lemon-Rosemary Wafers ............. 19
Lemon-Sage Mayonnaise ........... 342
Lemon-Sage Scones ..................... 333
Lemonberries .............................. 331
Lime Chicken with
   Green Chile Butter ................... 216
Lime Vinaigrette ......................... 190
Lime-Cayenne Mayonnaise ........ 341
Lime-Cilantro Sour Cream .......... 321
Linguine Salad with
   Marinated Tomatoes ................ 205
Linguine with Bacon and Peas .... 118
Louisiana Swamp Pie .................. 277
Lower East Side Pepper
   & Egg Sandwich ...................... 134

## M

Madras Rice and Chicken Salad ..... 110
Mango Salsa ................................ 123
Marinated Mushrooms ................. 16
Marinated Shrimp Salad ............. 124
Marinated Tomatoes ................... 205
Martha Washington Candy ........ 260
Mashed Potatoes with
   Caramelized Onions
   and Roasted Garlic .................. 345
Mashed Potatoes
   with Greek Olives .................... 345
Mediterranean Rice Salad ........... 199
Mediterranean Stuffed Bread ........ 58
Mélange of Bright Vegetables ...... 208
Meringue-Nut Topping ............... 267
Mesclun with
   Warm Goat Cheese .................. 191
Mexican Cheesecake ..................... 64
Mexican Potato Salad ................. 348

Mexican Pralines ......................... 259
Mexican Red Chicken ................. 149
Middle Eastern Hand Pies ........... 350
Mocha Cream .............................. 291
Mocha Magic .............................. 306
Morning Glory Muffins ............... 235
Mountain of Divinity .................. 261
Mushroom-Olive Spread .............. 32

## O

Olives
   Authentic Greek Salad ............ 196
   Avocado Tapenade ..................... 25
   Caponata ................................. 108
   Chicken-Artichoke Fettuccine ..... 121
   Classic Tapenade ....................... 24
   Greek Potato Salad .................. 347
   Greek Salad Skewers .................. 48
   Lemon Olives ............................. 14
   Mashed Potatoes with
      Greek Olives ......................... 345
   Mushroom-Olive Spread ........... 32
   Olive Pesto .............................. 326
   Ratatouille Pizza ..................... 103
   Spanish Potato Salad ............... 347
   Tamale Veggie Pie .................... 130
Onion Tart .................................. 106
Orange Olives ............................... 15
Orange Vinaigrette ..................... 195
Orange-Campari Granita ............ 251
Oriental Mayonnaise .................. 341
Orzo Salad ................................. 200
Ouzo Soup ................................... 71
Oven-Grilled Veggies .................. 206
Oxtail Soup .................................. 90

## P

Paprika Stew .............................. 170
Paprika Triangles ......................... 28
Parmesan Mashed Potatoes ........ 344
Parmesan Pie Crust .................... 100

Parmesan Potatoes ............... 230

Pasta
   Chicken-Artichoke Fettuccine ..... 121
   Confetti Pasta Salad ............... 204
   Creamy Mushroom-Herb Pasta ... 33
   Greek Pasta ............... 116
   Hearty Tortellini Soup ............... 88
   Linguine Salad with
      Marinated Tomatoes ............ 205
   Linguine with
      Bacon and Peas ............... 118
   Orzo Salad ............... 200
   Pasta Gremolata ............... 114
   Pasta with Bacon,
      Fried Pecans, and Corn ......... 119
   Pasta with Burnt Butter
      and Cheese ............... 111
   Pasta with Garlic
      and Hot Peppers ............... 115
   Pasta with Ham,
      Bleu Cheese, and Walnuts ..... 122
   Pasta with Pesto Chicken
      and Red Peppers ............... 120
   Pesto Pasta Salad ............... 203
   Thai Peanut Chicken
      and Noodle Salad ............... 112
   Tortellini Soup
      with Baby Spinach ............... 89
   Tortellini with
      Greens and Walnuts ............... 117
Pavlova ............... 275

Peaches
   Brandied Peaches ............... 331
   Fresh Peach Cake ............... 289
   Fresh Peach Ice Cream ............... 255
   Peach Sorbet ............... 253
   Peach Spritzers ............... 300
Peanut Butter Miracles ............... 262
Peanut Butter-Chocolate
   Fast Fudge ............... 258
Peanut-Cilantro Chicken ............... 26
Peanut-Cilantro Pesto ............... 26
Pear-Ginger Muffin Tops ............... 234
Pear-Pernod Granita ............... 251

Pecan Fudge Pie ............... 280
Peperonata ............... 109
Peppermint Cocoa Mix ............... 297
Pesto Cheesecake ............... 66
Pesto Deluxe ............... 327
Pesto Green Beans ............... 218
Pesto Pasta Salad ............... 203
Pesto Rounds ............... 40

Pies & Tarts
   Banana-Caramel Pie ............... 279
   Blueberry-Cheese Hand Pies .... 350
   Cherry Pie with Crunchy
      Oatmeal Crust ............... 276
   Cherry-Almond Hand Pies ....... 350
   Chocolate-Peanut
      Butter Tartlets ............... 335
   Crunchy Oatmeal Crust ........... 276
   Crust ............... 349
   Grand Finale Pie ............... 278
   Hand Pies ............... 349
   Irish Coffee Pie ............... 281
   Jewel Tartlets ............... 336
   Lemon-Berry Tea Tartlets ......... 336
   Louisiana Swamp Pie ............... 277
   Pecan Fudge Pie ............... 280
   Roquefort-Walnut Tartlets ........ 336
   Strawberry Yogurt Pie ............... 257
   Strawberry-Almond Tartlets ..... 338
   Tartlet Shells ............... 334
   Three-Citrus Tart with
      Mangoes and Papayas ......... 282
Pizza with Bleu Cheese
   and Mushrooms ............... 59
Poached Spiced Pears ............... 272
Poached Pears with
   Mascarpone and Chocolate ..... 272

Pork
   Calypso Soup ............... 89
   Chicken and Sausage Gumbo .... 86
   Grilled Pork Skewers ............... 161
   Ham Cakes ............... 123
   Ham Cream Tartlets ............... 335
   Ham Steak with
      Ginger-Pear Conserve ........... 271

Hearty Tortellini Soup ............... 88
Italian Stuffed Peppers ............. 160
Linguine with Bacon
 and Peas ................................ 118
Pasta with Bacon,
 Fried Pecans, and Corn .......... 119
Pasta with Ham, Bleu Cheese,
 and Walnuts ......................... 122
Pork Loin with
 Creamy Leek Sauce ............... 165
Pork Medallions with
 Cognac-Mustard Cream ........ 166
Pork Tenderloin with
 Brandy Cream Sauce ............. 164
Pork Tenderloin with Figs ......... 163
Roasted Pork Loin with
 Lemon and Fresh Herbs ......... 162
Southern Spice Hand Pies ........ 349
Warm Sausage
 and Potato Salad .................. 202

Potatoes
 Baked Potato Soup ..................... 80
 Bay-Roasted Potatoes ............... 230
 Bistro-Style Mashed Potatoes ...... 344
 Cabbage Mash ......................... 344
 Cauliflower-Potato Salad
  with Marinated Red Onions ..... 201
 Creamy Potatoes
  with Fresh Herbs ................... 231
 French Potato Salad ................. 346
 Frittata ..................................... 97
 Globetrotter Potato Salads ........ 346
 Greek Island Vegetables ............ 209
 Greek Potato Salad ................... 347
 Indian Potato Salad .................. 347
 Italian Potato Salad .................. 346
 Jalapeño Potatoes .................... 232
 Mashed Potatoes
  with Greek Olives .................. 345
 Mexican Potato Salad .............. 348
 Parmesan Mashed Potatoes ..... 344
 Parmesan Potatoes .................. 230
 Potatoes with Cheese,
  Garlic, and Pesto ................... 233
 Provençal Potato Salad ............ 347
 Roasted Red Potatoes .............. 230
 Spanish Potato Salad ............... 347
 Spicy Broccoli Soup .................... 76
 Tangy Mashed Potatoes ........... 344
 Thai Potato Salad .................... 348
 Warm Sausage
  and Potato Salad .................. 202

Poultry
 Chicken and Sausage Gumbo ... 86
 Chicken Indira ......................... 153
 Chicken Wings with Green
  Tomatoes and Couscous ........ 150
 Chicken with
  Tarragon Cream .................... 155
 Chicken-Artichoke
  Fettuccine ............................. 121
 Chicken-Black Bean
  Casserole .............................. 152
 Chicken-Dove Roll
  with Cilantro-Cumin
  Sauce and Roasted Peppers ..... 52
 Cornish Hen with
  Blackberry Sauce ................... 157
 Cornish Hens with
  Rosemary-Mustard Sauce ...... 158
 Curried Chicken
  and Dried Cherry Salad ......... 107
 Extraordinary Chicken ............. 156
 Fresh Corn and Chicken Soup ... 83
 Garlic Chicken ......................... 147
 Green Chile Chicken Tartlets ... 337
 Lemon-Dijon Chicken .............. 148
 Lime Chicken with
  Green Chile Butter ................ 216
 Madras Rice and
  Chicken Salad ....................... 110
 Mexican Red Chicken .............. 149
 Pasta with Pesto Chicken
  and Red Peppers ................... 120
 Peanut-Cilantro Chicken ........... 26
 Satellite Chicken ..................... 154
 Scaloppine Marsala ................. 167
 Skillet Chicken Provençal ........ 146
 Soy Sauce Chicken .................. 145

Thai Peanut Chicken
  and Noodle Salad .................. 112
Provençal Potato Salad ............... 347
Punch of the Islands ..................... 303

## Q

Quichelets ..................................... 337

## R

Rack of Lamb with
  Hazelnut-Walnut Crust ............ 178
Radio Shrimp ................................. 60
Raisin-Walnut Scones .................. 333
Raspberry-Chocolate Bars ........... 267
Ratatouille Pizza .......................... 103
Rib-Eye with
  Rosemary-Wine Sauce .............. 172

Rice & Risotto
  Chicken-Black
    Bean Casserole ...................... 152
  Madras Rice and
    Chicken Salad ........................ 110
  Mediterranean Rice Salad ........ 199
  Sassy Shrimp Risotto ................ 127
  Soy Sauce Chicken ................... 145
  Spa Salad ................................. 198
  Sweet Onion Risotto ................ 229
Rich Chocolate Mousse ............... 290
Roast Beef and Brie Sandwich ..... 105
Roasted Asparagus ...................... 210
Roasted Beef Shanks
  and Shallots with Wine ............ 173
Roasted Corn with
  Green Chile Butter ................... 216
Roasted Garlic Hummus ............... 23
Roasted Pepper
  and Garlic Sauce ...................... 320
Roasted Pork Loin with
  Lemon and Fresh Herbs ........... 162
Roasted Red Pepper
  and Almond Pesto ..................... 27

Roasted Red Pepper
  and White Wine Soup ................ 77
Roasted Red Pepper Hummus ....... 23
Roasted Red Peppers
  with Fresh Mozzarella ................ 49
Roasted Red Potatoes ................... 230
Roasted Tomatoes and Garlic ...... 224
Roma-Zucchini Wheel ................. 225
Roquefort-Walnut Tartlets ........... 336
Rosemary-Horseradish
  Mayonnaise ............................. 341
Rosemary Jelly ............................. 323
Rosemary Walnuts ......................... 13
Rosemary-Roquefort
  Mayonnaise ............................. 343
Rosemary-Scented Lamb
  with Penne .............................. 176
Rosemary-Tapenade Aïoli ........... 342
Rosemary-Walnut Scones ............ 333
Royal Frozen Mimosas ................ 299
Rum Cake .................................... 287
Rum Glaze ................................... 287
Russian Tea ................................. 296

## S

Salad Dressings
  Asian Sesame-Soy Vinaigrette ..... 113
  Blush Vinaigrette ..................... 193
  Cheddar Cheese
    Salad Dressing ...................... 315
  Classic Vinaigrette ................... 316
  French Vinaigrette ................... 317
  Green Goddess Dressing .......... 314
  Honey-Mustard Dressing ......... 193
  Lime Vinaigrette ...................... 190
  Orange Vinaigrette .................. 195
  Soy Vinaigrette ........................ 185
  Spicy Peanut Dressing .............. 113
  Sun-Dried Tomato Vinaigrette ..... 318

Salads
  Authentic Greek Salad ............. 196
  Baby Greens with Feta
    and Orange Vinaigrette ........ 195

INDEX 363

Baby Greens with Pear,
   Bleu Cheese, and Walnuts ..... 194
Beet Salad ................................. 212
Black-Eyed Pea Salad ............... 189
Broccoli Crunch ........................ 187
Bulghur Salad ........................... 198
Cabbage Salad .......................... 183
Carrot-Green Onion Salad ....... 182
Carrot-Turnip Salad ................. 182
Cauliflower Salad ..................... 186
Cauliflower-Potato Salad
   with Marinated Red Onions ..... 201
Confetti Pasta Salad ................. 204
Corn, Black Bean, and
   Hearts of Palm Salad ............ 190
Cornbread Salad ....................... 197
Creamy Apple-Beet Salad ........ 181
Crispy Slaw with
   Soy Vinaigrette ...................... 185
French Potato Salad ................. 346
Globetrotter Potato Salads ....... 346
Greek Potato Salad ................... 347
Indian Potato Salad ................. 347
Italian Potato Salad ................. 346
Linguine Salad with
   Marinated Tomatoes ............. 205
Marinated Shrimp Salad .......... 124
Marinated Tomatoes ................ 205
Mediterranean Rice Salad ........ 199
Mesclun with
   Warm Goat Cheese ................ 191
Mexican Potato Salad .............. 348
Orzo Salad ................................ 200
Pesto Pasta Salad ..................... 203
Provençal Potato Salad ............ 347
Shredded Salad ........................ 184
Spa Salad .................................. 198
Spanish Potato Salad ............... 347
Spring Greens with
   Clementines and Red Onion ..... 192
Succotash Salad ....................... 188
Thai Potato Salad .................... 348
Warm Sausage
   and Potato Salad .................. 202

Salmon Baked Alaska ................ 126
Salsa Diablo ................................. 65
Salsa Quiche ............................... 128
Sandwiches
   Grilled Veggie Focaccia
      Sandwich ............................. 104
   Lower East Side Pepper
      & Egg Sandwich .................. 134
   Roast Beef and Brie Sandwich ..... 105
Satellite Chicken ....................... 154
Savory Grits ................................ 93
Savory Sauce ............................. 319
Scaloppine Marsala .................. 167
Scones ....................................... 332
Seafood
   Asian Shrimp Balls ................. 142
   Baked Crab Dip ........................ 37
   Cajun Shrimp Balls ................. 142
   Crab au Gratin ......................... 82
   Crawfish Étouffée ................... 143
   Crawfish Saganaki ................... 38
   Crawfish Stuffed
      Cajun Peppers ..................... 144
   Deviled Shrimp ...................... 141
   Marinated Shrimp Salad .......... 124
   Radio Shrimp ........................... 60
   Sassy Shrimp Risotto ............. 127
   Seafood Gumbo ........................ 84
   Sherried Crab Soup .................. 82
   Shrimp Eggdrop Soup .............. 74
   Shrimp Louisiana ................... 140
   Smoked Oyster Tartlets ........... 335
   Thai Shrimp Broth ................... 73
   White Corn Soup
      with Sautéed Scallops ............. 85
Seed Biscuits ............................. 242
Shredded Salad ........................ 184
Skillet Chicken Provençal ........ 146
Smoky Cheese Pâté .................... 54
Smooth Salsa ............................ 125
Sole with Brown Butter Sauce ..... 138

**Soups**
- Baked Potato Soup ................... 80
- Basil-Eggplant Soup .................. 75
- Butternut and Double
  Ginger Soup .......................... 72
- Calypso Soup ............................ 89
- Cauliflower-Cheddar Chowder .... 81
- Chicken and Sausage Gumbo .... 86
- Chilled Cucumber Soup ............. 69
- Crab au Gratin ........................... 82
- Cream of Chard Soup ................ 79
- Duck Gumbo .............................. 84
- Fresh Corn and Chicken Soup .... 83
- Garden Gazpacho ...................... 68
- Gazpacho Con Gusto ................. 67
- Hearty Tortellini Soup ................ 88
- Ouzo Soup .................................. 71
- Oxtail Soup ................................ 90
- Paprika Stew ............................ 170
- Roasted Red Pepper
  and White Wine Soup ............. 77
- Seafood Gumbo ........................... 84
- Sherried Crab Soup .................... 82
- Shrimp Eggdrop Soup ................ 74
- Spicy Broccoli Soup ................... 76
- Spring Pea Soup ......................... 70
- Summer Squash Soup .......... 79, 85
- Thai Shrimp Broth ..................... 73
- Tipsy Stew ................................ 169
- Tortellini Soup with
  Baby Spinach .......................... 89
- White Corn Soup
  with Sautéed Scallops ............. 85
- Wild Mushroom Bisque ............. 78

Southern Spice Hand Pies ........... 349
Southwestern Hand Pies ............. 350
Southwestern Spoonbread ........... 246
Soy Sauce Chicken ....................... 145
Soy Vinaigrette ............................. 185
Spa Salad ....................................... 198
Spanish Potato Salad .................... 347
Spiced Beef Tenderloin ................. 174
Spicy Cheddar Snaps ...................... 17
Spicy Corn Bites ............................ 245

Spicy Peanut Dressing ................. 113

**Spinach**
- Creamy Spinach ...................... 220
- Fresh Spinach Dip ..................... 30
- Greek Pasta ............................. 116
- Spinach, Cheese,
  and Tomato Pie ..................... 100
- Three-Cheese Spinach Bread ..... 43
- Tortellini Soup with
  Baby Spinach .......................... 89
- Tortellini with
  Greens and Walnuts ............. 117

Spirited Caffeine .......................... 331
Spirited Vanilla ............................. 331
Spring Greens with
  Clementines and Red Onion .... 192
Spring Pea Soup ............................. 70

**Squash**
- A to Z Bread ............................ 239
- Butternut and Double
  Ginger Soup .......................... 72
- Garden Fresh Ratatouille ......... 219
- Greek Island Vegetables ........... 209
- Mélange of Bright Vegetables ... 208
- Oven-Grilled Veggies ................ 206
- Roma-Zucchini Wheel ............. 225
- Squash Acadien ....................... 221
- Squash Pecan .......................... 222
- Summer Squash Soup .......... 79, 85

Stifado ........................................... 171
Strawberry Glaze .......................... 269
Strawberry Sorbet ......................... 252
Strawberry Yogurt Pie .................. 257
Strawberry-Almond Tartlets ........ 338
Stuffed Brie .................................... 61
Succotash Salad ............................ 188
Summer Squash Soup ............. 79, 85
Sun-Dried Tomato Vinaigrette .... 318
Sun-Dried Tomato-
  Pine Nut Scones ....................... 333
Sweet Onion Risotto .................... 229
Sweet Potato-Pecan Muffin Tops ..... 234
Sweet Potato-Sage Biscuits .......... 242

Swordfish with
  Tomato-Parsley Sauce ............ 137

# T

Tamale Veggie Pie ....................... 130
Tangy Mashed Potatoes ............... 344
Tartlet Shells .................................. 334
Tartlets Sweet and Savory ........... 334
Tequila Slush ............................... 302
Thai Peanut Chicken
  and Noodle Salad .................... 112
Thai Potato Salad ........................ 348
Thai Shrimp Broth ......................... 73
Three-Cheese Spinach Bread ......... 43
Three-Citrus Tart with
  Mangoes and Papayas ............. 282
Three-Pepper Jelly ........................ 324
Tipsy Stew .................................... 169
Tomato Bread ............................... 240
Tomato Gravy ............................... 143
Tomato-Cheese Tart ..................... 102
Tomato-Feta Bruschetta ................ 39
Tomatoes and Fresh
  Mozzarella with Caponata
  and Peperonata ....................... 108
Tomatoes Stuffed with
  Goat Cheese and Chives ............ 47
Tortellini Soup
  with Baby Spinach ..................... 89
Tortellini with
  Greens and Walnuts ................. 117
Tri-Color Torta ............................... 56
Trout with Lemon
  and Brown Butter .................... 138
Turnip Soufflé ............................... 227
Tuscan Beans with Greens ........... 211
Tzatziki .......................................... 22

# V

Veal
  Scaloppine Marsala ................. 167
Veal with Green
  Peppercorn Sauce ................... 168
Vodka Lemonade ......................... 301

# W

Walnut-Cilantro Pesto ................. 328
Warm Bleu Cheese
  Spread with Pecans ................... 35
Warm Cherry Tomatoes
  with Pine Nuts ......................... 223
Warm Pear and Cherry
  Conserve with Triple Ginger .... 271
Warm Sausage
  and Potato Salad ..................... 202
Whipped Cream Godiva .............. 269
White Chocolate-Espresso Sauce ..... 311
White Corn Soup
  with Sautéed Scallops ................ 85
White Corn with Crispy Sage ...... 217
White Sangría .............................. 298
White Wine Sherbet .................... 254
Wild Duck Pâté .............................. 36
Wild Mushroom Bisque ................. 78

# Y

Yogurt Nehru ............................... 153

# ORDER FORM

**Mail to:**   Friends of KEDM
225 Stubbs Hall
University of Louisiana ~ Monroe
Monroe, LA 71209

**Quantity:** \_\_\_\_\_ x $19.95 = _____

**Taxes:** Louisiana residents add 4% sales tax   _____

**Shipping:** $3.50 per address   _____

**Total Due:** _____

**Name:** _____

**Address:** _____

**City:** _____ **State:** _____ **Zip:** _____

**Telephone:** _____

**E-Mail:** _____

Write additional addresses for gift books on reverse of this coupon; attach an additional sheet if necessary.

- - - - - - - - - - - - - - - - - - - - - - - - - - - - - -

# ORDER FORM

**Mail to:**   Friends of KEDM
225 Stubbs Hall
University of Louisiana ~ Monroe
Monroe, LA 71209

**Quantity:** \_\_\_\_\_ x $19.95 = _____

**Taxes:** Louisiana residents add 4% sales tax   _____

**Shipping:** $3.50 per address   _____

**Total Due:** _____

**Name:** _____

**Address:** _____

**City:** _____ **State:** _____ **Zip:** _____

**Telephone:** _____

**E-Mail:** _____

Write additional addresses for gift books on reverse of this coupon; attach an additional sheet if necessary.

# GIFT COPIES

**Recipient's Name:** _____
**Address:** _____
**City:** _____ **State:** _____ **Zip:** _____
**Quantity:** _____
**Note on Card:** _____


**Recipient's Name:** _____
**Address:** _____
**City:** _____ **State:** _____ **Zip:** _____
**Quantity:** _____
**Note on Card:** _____


**Recipient's Name:** _____
**Address:** _____
**City:** _____ **State:** _____ **Zip:** _____
**Quantity:** _____
**Note on Card:** _____

------------------------------------------------------------

# GIFT COPIES

**Recipient's Name:** _____
**Address:** _____
**City:** _____ **State:** _____ **Zip:** _____
**Quantity:** _____
**Note on Card:** _____


**Recipient's Name:** _____
**Address:** _____
**City:** _____ **State:** _____ **Zip:** _____
**Quantity:** _____
**Note on Card:** _____


**Recipient's Name:** _____
**Address:** _____
**City:** _____ **State:** _____ **Zip:** _____
**Quantity:** _____
**Note on Card:** _____